# WHAT IS SAVING FAITH?

# BOOKS BY GORDON H. CLARK

1. Revised as *What Do Presbyterian Believe?* (1965)
2. Combined as *William James and John Dewey* (1995)
3. Combined as *I & II Peter* (1980) and revised as *New Heavens, New Earth* (1993)
4. Part One appeared as *An Introduction to Christian Philosophy* (1993)
5. Combined as *Predestination* (1987)
6. Combined as *What Is Saving Faith?* (2004)
7. Chapter 5 of *Religion, Reason and Revelation*

# WHAT IS SAVING FAITH?

GORDON H. CLARK

The Trinity Foundation

# Contents

## THE JOHANNINE LOGOS

# Faith and Saving Faith

# FOREWORD

L ONG BEFORE the Neo-orthodox theologians thought of saying that faith is an encounter with a divine Person rather than assent to a proposition, preachers who ought to have known better taught that faith is trust in a person, not belief in a creed. This writer, when a teenager, was told that some people would miss Heaven by twelve inches – the distance between the head and the heart – because they believed the Gospel with their heads but not with their hearts. Today it is easier for a camel to pass through the eye of a needle than it is to find a minister – a conservative minister – who does not believe and teach that one must have a "personal relationship" with Christ in order to be saved. But what that "personal relationship" consists of is either not made explicit or, when made explicit, contradicts what the Bible teaches about saving faith. The result is that both Christians and non-Christians are either needlessly confused or totally misled. Perhaps the world is not responding to the churches' message because the message is garbled. Neither the churches nor the world knows exactly what to do to have eternal life.

Statements such as these about the head and the heart and trusting a person, not believing a creed, are not only false; they have also created the conditions for the emergence of all sorts of religious subjectivism, from Modernism to the Charismatic movement and beyond. No one will miss Heaven by twelve inches, for there is no distance between the head and the heart: "As a man thinks in his heart, so is he." The head/heart dichotomy is a figment of modern secular psychology, not a doctrine of divine revelation. St. Sigmund, not St. John, controls the pulpit in nearly all churches.

Further, "trust in a person" is a meaningless phrase unless it means assenting to certain propositions about a person, propositions such as "I believe in God the Father Almighty…and in Jesus Christ his only Son, our Lord, who was conceived by the Holy Ghost, born of the Virgin Mary, suffered under Pontius Pilate, was crucified, dead, and buried; the third day he rose again from the dead; he ascended into Heaven, and sits on the right hand of God the Father Almighty; from

*St. Sigmund, not St. John, controls the pulpit in nearly all churches.*

thence he shall come to judge the living and the dead." Trust in Christ, unless it includes belief of these propositions – as well as the Gospel of justification by faith – is totally without value. "Christ" means these propositions – and a lot more, to be sure, but at least these. No one who trusts in the Christs of Karl Barth, Paul Tillich, C. S. Lewis, or N. T. Wright will be saved.

As for having a "personal relationship" with Christ, if the phrase means something more than assenting to true propositions about Jesus, what is that something more? Feeling warm inside? Coffee has the same effect. Surely "personal relationship" does not mean what we mean when we say that we know someone personally: Perhaps we have shaken his hand, visited his home or he ours, or eaten with him. John had a "personal relationship" with Christ in that sense, as did all the disciples, including Judas Iscariot. But millions of Christians have not, and Jesus called them blessed: They have not seen and yet have believed. The difference between Judas Iscariot and the other disciples is not that they had a "personal relationship" with Jesus and he did not, but that they believed, that is, assented to, certain propositions about Jesus, while Judas did not believe those propositions. Belief of the Gospel, nothing more and nothing less, is what separates the saved from the damned. Those who maintain that there is something more than belief needed for justification, are, quite literally, beyond belief.[1]

Since we first published *Faith and Saving Faith* twenty years ago in 1983 (the book was largely ignored by the clergy and the churches), there has been a widespread defection from the Gospel of Jesus Christ in Reformed churches – both Baptist and Presbyterian – a defection specifically from the doctrine of justification by faith alone. That defection is accelerating.

Several factors have contributed to the growing rejection of the Gospel in the churches, and one of those factors is confusion about the nature of faith. That confusion is common to those who oppose the doctrine of justification by faith alone, and to some of those who defend it. Faith, rather than being recognized as belief of a statement, that is, intelligent assent to an understood proposition – and saving faith being belief of the truth, that is, intelligent assent to Biblical propositions – rather than faith being understood in Scriptural terms, faith is seen as something more than belief – as "commitment to a person," "trust of a person," "encounter with a person," "surrender to a person," or a "personal relationship." This common viewpoint is not in accord with Scripture, for it makes a fatal dichotomy between persons and propositions, and regards faith as trust in or commitment to a person, rather than belief of a proposition.

Those who deny justification by faith alone may say that saving faith includes, or is identical to, obedience and good works. They define that vague "something more than belief" as something "objective": baptism, obedience, and good works. The deniers of justification by faith alone begin by agreeing with those who confusedly defend justification by faith alone: Faith is not "mere assent." Faith is more

*No one who trusts in the Christs of Karl Barth, Paul Tillich, C. S. Lewis, or N. T. Wright will be saved.*

1. There is one context in which the phrase "personal relationship" might have some Biblical meaning: if it is used to deny that an ecclesiastical, organizational, or sacramental relationship is saving.

than belief, they say. Thus those who deny justification by faith alone, and many of those who wish to defend it, are united in this opinion – which Dr. Clark shows by painstaking exegesis of Scripture to have no support in Scripture – that faith is not intelligent assent to an understood proposition, not "mere" belief, but something more.

Deniers of justification by faith alone may say that faith is not mere assent, for it is obedience as well. They make the vague "something more than assent" definite by their assertion that saving faith includes works. This allows them – watch their sleight-of-hand carefully – to assert that justification by faith alone is true, as the *Westminster Confession* teaches, because they have redefined *faith* to include works. So when they assert that "justification is by faith alone," they mean, "justification is by works, too."

Many of those who wish to defend justification by faith alone are embarrassed because of their agreement with the deniers of justification that faith is not mere belief, not intelligent assent to an understood proposition. And they should be embarrassed, for their faulty understanding of faith has opened the door to the current widespread denial of justification by faith alone.

*Faith and Saving Faith* is not primarily about the doctrine of justification by faith alone, but its exegesis and analysis are fundamental to that doctrine. To understand the doctrine of justification by faith alone, one must understand the doctrine of faith, as well as the doctrine of justification. Err on either doctrine, and one errs on the doctrine of justification by faith alone. So one might misunderstand justification as a process, or progressive, or two-staged, or based on infused righteousness, or conditioned on one's obedience, rather than as an irrevocable legal act of God. And one might misunderstand faith as a complex psychological feat, which, if it is not performed satisfactorily by the sinner, and confirmed by meticulous introspection, cannot justify. One can make faith into a work such as "complete commitment," "unconditional surrender," "life-changing encounter," and "total trust." Many people, including many teachers in conservative churches and schools, are offended by the simplicity of the Gospel, and add to the statements of Scripture. They thus destroy the assurance of Christians by making them wonder if they have "surrendered" enough, "trusted" enough, or been "committed" enough to be saved.

This creates a spiritual climate of doubt in which those who deny justification by faith alone can flourish. To those who have been needlessly worried by this un-Scriptural doctrine of faith as a complex psychological feat, the deniers of justification by faith alone say: Look, we offer you assurance of salvation: Look to your baptism, look to your works, which are visible and objective and photographable. Who can tell if you have performed some complicated psychological feat or not? But everyone can tell whether you have been baptized, or if you are doing good works. So rest your assurance on those visible, photographable, "objective" things.

*To understand the doctrine of justification by faith alone, one must understand the doctrine of faith, as well as the doctrine of justification.*

Both the defenders and deniers of justification by faith alone need to learn the lessons about faith that Scripture teaches. One of them is this:

> The strength or kind of faith required is nowhere stated [in Scripture]. The Holy Spirit has said nothing as to quantity or quality on which so many dwell and over which they stumble, remaining all their days in darkness and uncertainty. It is simply in *believing* – feeble as our faith may be – that we are invested with this righteousness [of Christ]. For faith is not work, nor merit, nor effort, but the cessation from all these and the acceptance in place of them of what another has done – done completely and forever. The simplest, feeblest faith suffices: It is not the excellence of our act of faith that does anything for us, but the excellence of him who suffered for sin – the just for the unjust – that he might bring us to God.... Many a feeble hand – perhaps many a palsied one – was laid on the head of the burnt offering (*Leviticus* 1:4), but the feebleness of that palsied touch did not alter the character of the sacrifice or make it less available in all its fullness for him who brought it.... The weakest touch sufficed to establish the connection between it and him. [2]

*The common Protestant view of saving faith as something more than belief of the Gospel has fueled and will continue to fuel denials of justification by faith alone.*

Unintentionally and unwittingly, the defenders of justification by faith alone, by their un-Scriptural doctrine of faith (which makes faith a complex psychological act rather than simple assent to the truth), have created and sustained the theological climate in which those who deny justification by faith alone can flourish. The defenders of justification by faith alone have asserted that it is not enough to believe the Gospel, for even the demons believe the Gospel,[3] and the demons are lost. Belief is not enough, they say. In order to be saved, one must do more than believe; one must commit, surrender, trust, encounter, relate, or emote.

The deniers of justification by faith alone agree: It is not enough to believe the Gospel in order to be saved. But rather than urging people to perform some further psychological task in addition to belief, they tell them to do good works in order to be saved. Their works (or their baptism) will complete what is lacking in belief alone. In this way, both the defenders and the deniers of justification by faith alone have lost sight of what in fact saves: The perfect, imputed righteousness of Christ, completely outside the sinner, and received by the simple instrument of belief alone.

The current controversy over justification has broken out in conservative churches because Christians recognize that the Bible denies justification by works, whether works are regarded as a ground, condition, or an instrument of justification. But what most Christians have not yet recognized is that the common Protestant view of saving faith as something more than belief of the Gospel has fueled and will continue to fuel denials of justification by faith alone so long as it prevails. Until faith is understood as mere belief – the Bible makes no distinction between the two words – the justification controversy will continue, and those defending justification by faith alone will continue to

2. Horatius Bonar, *The Everlasting Righteousness*, 40-41.

3. Of course, there is no Scriptural evidence for this at all.

be embarrassed by their agreement with the deniers of justification, that belief of the Gospel is not enough for salvation.

In the pages that follow, Dr. Clark defends the view that faith is assent to a proposition, and that saving faith is assent to propositions found in the Bible. Saving faith is neither an indescribable encounter with a divine Person, nor heart knowledge as opposed to head knowledge. According to the author of *Hebrews*, those who come to God must believe at least two propositions: That he is God, and that he is a rewarder of them that diligently seek him. Mindless encounters and non-intellectual relationships are not saving faith. Truth is propositional, and one is saved and sanctified only through believing true statements. Faith comes by hearing, and hearing comes by the Word of God.

The anti-intellectual cast of virtually all modern thought, from the university chair to the barroom stool, controls the pulpits as well. It is this pious anti-intellectualism that emphasizes encounter rather than information, emotion instead of understanding, "personal relationship" rather than knowledge. But Christians, Paul wrote, have the mind of Christ. Our relationship to him is intellectual. And since Christ is his mind and we are ours, no relationship could be more intimate than that. That is precisely why the Scriptures use the analogy of marriage to illustrate the intellectual relationship between Christians and Christ – and marriage is an inadequate illustration, for the penetration of minds is far more profound and intimate than marriage.

This recognition of the primacy of the intellect, the primacy of truth, is totally missing from contemporary theology. One of the twentieth-century's greatest theologians and writers, J. Gresham Machen, wrote a book titled *What Is Faith?* fifty years ago. His words are as appropriate today as they were then:

> This anti-intellectual tendency in the modern world is no trifling thing; it has its roots deep in the entire philosophical development of modern times. Modern philosophy…has had as its dominant note, certainly as its present day result, a depreciation of the reason and a skeptical answer to Pilate's question, "What is truth?" This attack upon the intellect has been conducted by men of marked intellectual powers; but an attack it has been all the same. And at last the logical results of it, even in the sphere of practice, are beginning to appear. A marked characteristic of the present day is a lamentable intellectual decline, which has appeared in all fields of human endeavor except those that deal with purely material things. The intellect has been browbeaten so long in theory that one cannot be surprised if it is now ceasing to function in practice….
>
> As over against this anti-intellectual tendency in the modern world, it will be one chief purpose of the present little book to defend the primacy of the intellect, and in particular to try to break down the false and disastrous opposition which has been set up between knowledge and faith.

*Saving faith is neither an indescribable encounter with a divine Person, nor heart knowledge as opposed to head knowledge.*

That, too, is a chief purpose of this little book. The following pages argue that it is rational to believe what God says; it is irrational to disbelieve God. No argument is more urgently needed than that.

John W. Robbins

*It is rational to believe what God says; it is irrational to disbelieve God.*

# PREFACE

THE MOTIVATION for this study of the nature of faith is the edification of Christians: "Let all things be done for edification" (*1 Corinthians* 14:26). More specifically, this book is addressed to conservative-minded, orthodox, evangelical, Bible-believing Protestants.

Naturally the author would be happy to have some secularists read it too. Most of them are so uninformed as to the theology of the Protestant Reformation that their remarks on religion just about qualify as bigotry. The presidential campaign of 1980, on one side, virtually tried to reduce Bible-believing Christians to the status of second-class citizens, or worse.

But the people to whom this material is addressed merit some castigation too. Many of them think that secularists have nothing worthwhile to offer. One should by all means preach the Gospel to them with the hope that in their darkness they may see a great light; but the idea that antichristian philosophers can actually help Christians to understand the Bible is anathema.

However, contemporary evangelicalism has deteriorated so greatly from the theological achievements of the sixteenth and seventeenth centuries that one might suppose it has reverted to the Romish views of an "implicit" faith of unknown content.

Therefore, whatever small literary skill this author may have developed during his teaching career has here been defaced both by some extremely elementary Scriptural exegesis and also by constant reminders that Christians should pay a certain amount of attention to secular scholars. The secular material itself not only impinges on New Testament teaching, but is really very interesting, at least to a theologian; and to every patient reader it will prove edifying.

*The motivation for this study of the nature of faith is the edification of Christians.*

# 1. Introduction

The thief on the cross said, "Lord, remember me"; and Jesus replied, "Today you shall be with me in paradise." After a life of crime, one of the three worst criminals in the nation – Barabbas had been released – this thief received assurance of Heaven.

He could hardly have known much about Jesus. He certainly had no notion of saving faith, let alone of the Trinity, the atonement, or the Second Advent. Yet, on the authority of Jesus, we know that he was saved. Is it necessary then to have saving faith, or faith of any kind? Must we know what saving faith is? Does one have to read the Bible and listen to evangelistic sermons? What is the relation between faith and knowledge? Surely entrance into Heaven does not require a degree from a theological seminary. The thief was saved in ignorance.

However, let us not exaggerate. Very probably, indeed certainly, the thief knew more than most people think he did. For one thing, he knew the charge on which Christ had been condemned. Even if he had been so illiterate that he could not have read the inscription on Christ's cross, he could not help hearing the screams of the crowd as they ridiculed Christ's claim to be King, Savior, and God. He also knew the charge on which he himself had been condemned. He had lived a life of serious crime, and now he acknowledged that his condemnation and execution were just. In reply to the other thief's participation in ridiculing Jesus, he said, "Do you not even fear God, since you are under the same sentence of condemnation? And we indeed justly, for we are receiving what we deserve for our deeds." Not only did he fear God and admit his guilt, but he added, "This man has done nothing wrong." How did he know that Jesus had done nothing wrong? Being such an enterprising criminal and cognizant of the daily news from the cities and villages, he must have heard rumors about this itinerant preacher. As Christ preached to the multitudes, the thief might have been picking their pockets and also picking up some few ideas of what Christ was saying. We must therefore not underestimate the extent of the thief's knowledge; but we can be pretty sure that he had no theological theory about the nature of saving faith.

Even knowing so little, the thief compares favorably with some Americans today. They do not know they are guilty, nor do they fear

*Even knowing so little, the thief compares favorably with some Americans today. They do not know they are guilty, nor do they fear God.*

God. Some do not even believe there is a God. Then there is one thing the thief knew which hardly any American knows. He knew he would die within a few hours. Our contemporaries, comfortably ensconced before their televisions, do not have such somber expectations. When we stop to think, we see that the thief knew more than we first suspected. But all in all; he still did not know very much.

If now he got to Heaven without much knowledge, why should we bother to examine the psychology of saving faith or trouble ourselves with theological investigations? If knowledge is indeed required, a very little will suffice. If we do not know what it means to believe, still we believe and are saved.

However, that one piece of knowledge which the thief had and which we do not have prevents us from taking him as a norm for our action. He knew he would be dead before nightfall. We do not. He had no opportunity of living a Christian life. We do. To suppose that ignorance is sufficient for a Christian life is to be ignorant of what a Christian life requires.

Remember that Christ said, "Make disciples of all the nations… teaching them to observe all that I commanded you." The thief on the cross, and anyone else who is on his death-bed, is excused from obeying this commandment. But the rest of us are not. We are obliged to teach, and before we can teach, we must learn – learn all, or all we can, of what Christ himself taught and what he taught through his disciples. Remember also that *all* Scripture has been breathed out by God and that it is *all* profitable for teaching. But we cannot teach the Christian message without first learning it. This small book endeavors to explain what the New Testament teaches about faith.

## 2. Generic Faith: Brand Blanshard

This small book, as was just said, aims to expound what the New Testament, and the Bible as a whole, says about saving faith. But saving faith is a species of faith in general. Faith is not limited to Christian faith. Jewish faith, Islamic faith, and even secular faiths are faith. Not only Christian theologians, but secular philosophers also have been interested in and have written about faith. Some small acquaintance with their views will prove profitable, even if only by sharp contrast, in understanding Christian faith. The devout Christian reader expects, and will not be disappointed, to find a great deal of Biblical material in this study. In fact, the Bible is the main source and only authority. Nevertheless, a few pages on one or two secular views make a good preliminary section.

First, let us consider Brand Blanshard's *The Nature of Thought*,[1] because in it we also find the views of two other secular thinkers. His first remarks are rather discouraging: "What is ordinarily meant when we say we *believe* something? One may reply that it is the acceptance or conviction or adoption or affirmation or mental assertion of some proposition; but these are all synonyms, not definitions. The fact is that

*To suppose that ignorance is sufficient for a Christian life is to be ignorant of what a Christian life requires.*

1. Brand Blanshard, *The Nature of Thought*. 1939, Volume I, 112.

belief, central as it is in the life of thought, and perhaps because it is so essential, is indefinable and probably indescribable."[2]

A most patient and persistent attempt to explain belief, according to Blanshard, was that of the Wurzburg School. One of them reduced belief to an indescribable *Bewusstseinslagen* (contents of consciousness or awareness), neither determinate ideas nor volitions. Another used the phrase "a content imagelessly present as knowledge." A third spoke of an intellectual attitude which "may be just a glow or halo of indescribable consciousness." Others said similar things.

For the benefit of the Christian reader who knows little about the history of psychology and is anxious to arrive at a Biblical view of the matter, it may be suggested that the second view – "a content imagelessly present as knowledge" – may be of some help, but that the others are of little value for anything.

Not all psychologists were as disappointing as the Wurzburgers. Bertrand Russell was somewhat more definite. Russell was of course a vigorous enemy of Christianity; furthermore, he changed his opinions rather often; nevertheless, his view of belief is a background against which a Christian must work. "The content of a belief," says Russell, "may consist of words only, or of images only, or of a mixture of the two, or of either or both together with one or more sensations.... In this [latter] case your belief consists of a sensation and an image suitably related."[3]

On this section, not given here in full, Blanshard remarks, "Now a rough count discloses in this passage some fifteen distinguishable propositions about such judgements of perception, of which one seems to me true, one doubtful, and thirteen false." Obviously, therefore, secular philosophers disagree considerably as to the nature of belief. Though none of them is interested in defending Christianity, Christians might nonetheless find some worthwhile suggestions as to the nature of faith. The material certainly offers us a wide choice.

This welter of conflicting opinions, continues Blanshard,

> tends to support the view of [William] James that belief is "perfectly distinct, but perfectly indescribable in words," that "it feels like itself – and that is about as much as we can say." However this is not quite all we can say. We can say that belief is *not* sensation, that it is *not* the use of words or images, though these may accompany it, and that it is *not* the same as desire or feeling.... James, to be sure, thinks it *is* a feeling, and speaks of those states of intoxication "in which a man's very soul will sweat with conviction, and he be all the while unable to tell what he is convinced of at all."[4]

Unfortunately, at least in the present writer's opinion, many Christians, motivated by an irrational pragmatism or by an even more extremely irrational mysticism, consider belief to be an emotion or feeling. To be sure, some beliefs stir the emotions, but the very sober belief that a man has five fingers on each hand is as much a belief as some shattering bad news. Nor can believing good news, namely the Good News, be a mere emotion.

*Many Christians, motivated by an irrational pragmatism or by an even more extremely irrational mysticism, consider belief to be an emotion or feeling.*

2. Blanshard, I, 113.
3. Blanshard, I, 113.
4. Blanshard, I, 114-115.

Blanshard appropriately notes that two Roman Catholic philosophers, René Descartes and John Henry Cardinal Newman, in different ways, made belief an act of will. He himself holds that this is too specific and definite – a strange criticism – but then he adds that belief is "virtually identical with mind on its intellectual side." As corroboration he quotes John Stuart Mill: "Its distinctive character is such, Mill said, that 'when we arrive at it, we seem to have reached, as it were, the central point of our intellectual nature,' which all other mental functions presuppose." In defense of this proposition he adduces the following instance.

> How important belief is for perception may be made clear by considering (1) that if in perceiving an orange our thought were confined to what we see, we should remain penned in a coloured patch and never arrive at an orange at all, and (2) that to say, as some writers do, that we should even see a coloured patch is, strictly, wrong. One can no doubt see a colour, but at the level at which one apprehends a coloured patch, rudimentary judgement is present. To talk of "sensing patches of colour," except by way of metonymy, is to talk loosely; no patch could possibly be sensed.[5]

College students, bank tellers, and many Christian apologists exhibit surprised disbelief that one cannot sense a patch of color. What can possibly be more evident than that we see color? But Blanshard, independently arriving at a conclusion that Augustine long ago expressed, insists that adults, if not babies, can have no sensation of blue minus all intellectual interpretation. Here the serious reader should begin to consider what a sensation might be, and how, if there be such a thing, it can fit into a theory of learning.

Although Blanshard was not a Christian, he was not particularly motivated by antichristian bias in these passages.[6] Therefore, it is just possible that some of his observations could be incorporated into a Christian philosophy. At any rate, there are good orthodox Christian apologetes today who, in my opinion, teach nonsense because they are unacquainted with professional studies of sensation, mind, and belief. Even their relatively faithful Biblical account of saving faith is defective because they do not understand faith *simpliciter*. The Biblical account of saving faith presupposes a view of human nature, not merely as sinful, but as natural. The assertion that men believe falsehoods, being deceived by Satan, does not excuse the apologete from searching out the Biblical view of sensation, perception, intellection, volition, and belief.

## 3. Generic and Secular Belief: H. H. Price

In 1960 Professor H. H. Price delivered one of the Gifford Lecture series at the University of Aberdeen. These lectures, considerably expanded, were published by George Allen & Unwin in 1969, under the title *Belief*. Some thoughts from its 488 pages will serve as another example of how secular scholars treat the general subject of belief.

5. Blanshard, I, 116.

6. It is otherwise in his 620-page *Reason and Belief* (George Allen & Unwin, 1974). Here he uncritically reproduces the "mistakes" of Moses in the Robert G. Ingersoll manner, the critical theories of Julius Wellhausen on Jewish history, without even mentioning these two names, and in general the destructive higher criticism. His exegesis is unconsidered and takes no account of conservative views. Two examples are the number of angels at the tomb Easter morning and the alleged impossibility that God can be both one substance and three Persons. In addition to these "contradictions," which any Christian garage mechanic can handle, there is another one less well-known. In *2 Samuel* 6:23, we read that Michal, the first wife of David, had no children to the day of her death; but in *2 Samuel* 21:8 she is said to have borne five sons. Blanshard, to the detriment of his scholarly reputation, suppresses the evidence that some manuscripts of the latter verse read *Merab*, not Michal. Even the liberal *Revised Standard Version* prints *Merab*.

Obviously no summary of the entire work is possible here.

The opening pages describe two contrasting methodologies between which, Price seems to say, every student of the problem must choose. The traditional method and the only method used until recently assumes that

> believing is a special sort of mental occurrence (sometimes described as a "mental act"…[which] need not necessarily be introspected by the person in whom it occurs; but it always could be….
>
> The modern way of treating belief is quite different. Believing something is now generally regarded not as an occurrence…but as a disposition…. [T]his is equivalent to a series of conditional statements describing what he would be likely to say or do or feel if such and such circumstances were to arise. For example, he would assert the proposition (aloud, or privately to himself) if he heard someone else denying it…. He would use it, when relevant, as a premiss in his inferences…. [H]e would act as if it were true. If [it] were falsified he would feel surprised, and would feel no surprise if it were verified….The occurrent believings or "acts of believing" which the traditional theorists discussed are on this view mythical entities….[7]

*Philosophically the initial act of believing is the more important.*

Although Professor Price here pictures these two views as mutually exclusive, and although the adherents of the contemporary method do so also, for they refer to the traditional view as mythical, Price nonetheless hints that the traditional view can accommodate the later view even if the latter cannot accommodate the former. This non-reciprocal relationship is of some importance, as will be seen some pages further on. At the moment, Price's hint can be expanded by saying that although believing something for many years may not be an instantaneous act, there must have been some such act when a person passes from ignorance, inattention, or even disbelief to a conscious acceptance of the proposition in question. The traditional analysis does not or need not deny that I believe two and two are four even when my mind is occupied with a chess problem or when I am asleep. The contemporary view sometimes makes use of prejudicial expressions. On page 189 Price says, "As Professor Ryle has pointed out, it sounds very odd indeed to say 'at half past three I was engaged in believing that Oxford would win the boat race.'" Price himself recognized the inappropriateness of Ryle's illustration and replies, "It does make sense to say that I assented to a proposition *p* at half past three today." Does this then not permit us to say that philosophically the initial act of believing is the more important? Christians, who read, "Believe on the Lord Jesus Christ, and you shall be saved," cannot minimize this initial act, no matter how useful it is to remember, on a later relevant occasion, that stuffed green peppers resulted in indigestion.

Perhaps these remarks relative to the first pages of Price's second lecture have pushed us a little too far forward. But the religious implication will return us to a noteworthy page in the first lecture. There Price makes an observation which this monograph also wishes to emphasize. Suppose someone says,

7. H. H. Price, *Belief.* George Allen & Unwin, 1969, 19-20.

What difference does it really make which of these two analyses of belief – if either – is the really correct one? Who cares whether "Jones believes that *p*" is or is not a purely dispositional statement about Mr. Jones?... My reply, however, is that in philosophy the longest way round is often the shortest way home.... If belief in a religious world-view is what interests us most, we shall be in a better position for considering this subject if we first pay some attention to the nature of belief in general....[8]

Price mentions one specific example of the coincidence of the secular and the religious problem: It is "the distinction between believing 'in' and believing 'that.'"[9] We may both believe *that* the President has wisely vetoed a bill, and, or, we may believe *in* the President. Pilate seems to have believed *that* Jesus was innocent, but he did not believe *in* Jesus. There must be some distinction between these two beliefs, whether their object is the President or Jesus. What is this distinction? If we mistake the difference, the result to ourselves will be more serious in the latter case than in the former. The present monograph will, later on, pay particular and detailed attention to what the New Testament teaches on this point.

Another element in secular philosophy which reappears in religious discussions, or rather, an element discussed in religion for centuries before Bertrand Russell and others latched on to it, is the alleged distinction between "knowledge by acquaintance" and "knowledge by description." Price, loquaciously enough to justify the omission of several phrases, writes as follows:

> [V]arious sorts of dependent clauses...follow the verb "to know." But sometimes it is not followed by any dependent clause at all. Instead, it governs an accusative – a noun or a noun-phrase. We speak of knowing Mr. Robinson Smith...or Kensington Gardens....This is very different from "knowledge that."[10]

The importance of this distinction, or, more accurately, the importance of deciding whether or not there is such a distinction, is considerable, and the devout non-philosophical Christian can hardly suspect at this point how important it is for understanding John's *Gospel*.
Price continues:

> "Knowledge that" may be called a "propositional attitude." But the knowledge we are now discussing is not a propositional attitude at all. It is sometimes called knowledge by acquaintance. One cannot have it unless one has actually encountered [by sensory perception?] the person or thing which is known.... Perhaps we cannot know anything by acquaintance without coming to know at least some facts or truths about it. But certainly we can know truths or facts about something without being acquainted with it.... Students of Roman history may know many facts about Julius Caesar, but they are not in a position to know *him*.[11]

The Christian must now ask himself, Can one know Jesus Christ with the knowledge of acquaintance, that is to say, by sensory percep-

*Pilate seems to have believed that Jesus was innocent, but he did not believe in Jesus. There must be some distinction between these two beliefs, whether their object is the President or Jesus. What is this distinction?*

8. Price, 23-24.
9. Price, 38.
10. Price, 50.
11. Price, 51.

tion? Or is our knowledge of Christ merely unimportant knowledge about him? Is "knowledge about" unimportant? Is there any knowledge that is not "knowledge about"?

Price, to support the contention that there are two distinct types of knowledge, adduces the use, in some languages, of two different words for *know: cognoscere* and *scire, connaître* and *savoir, kennen* and *wissen*. Price allows that English has now deleted this distinction. Price does not appeal to the Greek verbs *gignosko* versus *oida*. The use of these two verbs is much too confusing for Price's purpose. *Liddell and Scott* reports *gignosko* (same root as the Latin *cognoscere*) as "come to know, perceive, and in past tenses *know* with the accusative; as distinct from *oida* know by reflection, *gignosko* = know by observation." But then the lexicon adds a most interesting instance from Aristotle's *Posterior Analytics*: "It is difficult to know (*gnonai*) if one knows (*oiden*) or not; for it is difficult to know (*gnonai*) whether or not we know (*ismen*) by means of the first principles in each case" (76a26-27). *Ismen* is the first person indicative plural of *oida*. It is a second perfect of *eidon*, to see, related to the Latin *video*. Under *eido* Liddell and Scott gives "see, perceive,...before the eyes,...experience,...see mentally, perceive... examine, investigate,...consider.... *oida* I see with the mind's eye, *i.e.*, I know.... The aorist and perfect are usually supplied by *gignosko*...be acquainted with,...one acquainted with the fact...with knowing mind...*ouk oid'ei* I know not whether...."

Now try to explain Aristotle's meaning while observing Price's alleged distinction. Should we say, "It is difficult to know by reflection whether we perceive by the eyes"? Or, if *oida* means to know by reflection and *gignosko* means to know by observation, as the lexicon said (see above), should we translate Aristotle as "It is difficult to know by observation whether we know by reflection"? Hardly. Aristotle seems to use the two verbs synonymously. If indeed Latin, German, and French make a systematic distinction, why cannot we say that the Greeks were more philosophic than the Latins and the later English discovered that the earlier Anglo-Saxon was confused? In recent days several philosophic authors have tried to base their theories on linguistic usage. The present writer does not approve. Price's statement that "[I]n the examples mentioned earlier (knowing a person, or a country, or an object such as an oak tree) it was plausible to say that knowledge by acquaintance is not a propositional attitude at all"[12] is a statement which, plausible as it may seem to some people, seems to at least one person to be definitely false.

To examine all the details that Professor Price adduces, nearly every one of which is intensely interesting, at least to a philosopher, would discourage some less professional readers. However, even the less professional should be warned that Price's reliance on the occurrence of sense data (*e.g.*, 57ff.) is rejected by the Neo-Hegelian Blanshard as well as by the great Christian theologian Augustine. John Locke insisted on sense data; and Immanuel Kant, in a very different setting, spoke of *Das Gegebenes*, but the beginning student in philosophy must

*Is "knowledge about" unimportant? Is there any knowledge that is not "knowledge about"?*

12. Price, 52.

be warned that such is not a point of universal agreement. The subject is really quite complicated.

There is also another immediacy, often emphasized by contemporary conservative Christian apologetes. It is self-knowledge. Price says, "[S]urely each of us must know himself in some degree…. We certainly do possess it."[13] I acknowledge that Price adds some qualifications. But at the moment I merely want to cast doubt on the possibility of knowing one's self by quoting, "The heart is deceitful above all things and desperately wicked: Who can know it?" The following verse suggests that only God knows a man. If now knowledge by acquaintance is an unintelligible phrase, equally unacceptable is Price's and Russell's description of knowledge by description. In both cases the object of knowledge is misconstrued. Further elucidation here of the object of knowledge would too much tax the reader's patience. The main point is to realize how complicated the subject matter actually is.

*"The heart is deceitful above all things and desperately wicked: Who can know it?"*

Price's book is detailed, complicated, and very interesting. At times it is disappointing. At one point, discussing Locke's theory of degrees of assent, he says, "[T]hese doctrines of Locke…may strike us as just obvious common sense."[14] This phraseology does not bind Price to agreement with Locke, but they suggest that he does, for on the next page he adds, "[D]o we not all agree with Locke that a lower degree of assent may be justified when a higher degree would not be?" The answer to this rhetorical question is, No, we do not all agree, and Locke's view is not obvious "common sense." Price continues on the following page, "Locke's two doctrines, then – that assent has degrees [here I am not interested in the second]…may easily seem platitudinous."[15] Granted that he immediately continues by discussing Cardinal Newman's contrary argument, he yet seems to accept Locke too easily. Indeed, he says, "I shall try to show that Locke is more nearly right than Newman…." Later on (page 204) he again mentions Locke's theory that assent has degrees; and throughout the book he seems to delight in describing minute differences in consciousness; yet on page 207 Price admits that "You cannot partially decide for *p*, or half choose it." And after some interesting description of our reactions to implausible news, he allows that "assent may be voluntary in the long run, at least sometimes, even though in the short run it is quite beyond our voluntary control."[16]

Continuing this discussion of Newman many pages later, Price notes a fundamental blunder that nearly all empiricists fall into. Pages 324–330 describe the unusually vivid imagery by which Newman carried on his thinking: not only visual imagery, but the other four types as well. Then Newman, like Hume,[17] assumed that all people had similar imagery. Francis Galton, thirteen years after Newman's *Grammar of Assent*, in his *Inquiries into Human Faculty*, recorded empirical disproof of this assumption. Since the present writer is intimately acquainted with one who has no such imagery at all, he considers all empiricism to be vitiated *ab initio*. This applies to Price as well as to Newman and Hume. Of course some things Price and Newman say are inconsis-

13 Price, 62.
14. Price, 131.
15. Price, 133.
16. Price, 223.
17. See my *Thales to Dewey* [1957] 1989, 382–384; 2000, 299-301

tently true, or may be true by some adaptation, as when, for example, Price in a footnote on page 333 says "Newman seems to admit [that]... real assent 'is in itself an intellectual act.'"[18]

If some devout readers find these matters a little too far removed from religious importance, Price's next to last chapter can hardly fail to suggest that Christians can profit by such discussions. The title is, *Belief 'in' and Belief 'that.'*

On pages 426 and following, Price notes that in religious circles *belief in* is of more interest than *belief that*. The latter is a more secular concept; and the devout insist that there is a great difference between them. Philosophers, on the other hand, usually think not, and attempt to reduce *in* to *that*. However, as Price notes, even secularists use *belief-in*. A blind man believes-in his dog. Englishmen used to believe-in the British Empire. Some parents believe-in a liberal arts education for their children. Women's lib believes-in killing babies. Can these beliefs-in be reduced to beliefs-that? For example, belief *in* the Loch Ness monster simply means someone believes *that* there is such a creature. The Tories of the nineteenth century did not believe in Gladstone; that is, they did not believe *that* he was a good prime minister. But since a person who believes *in* God in the sense that there is a God may himself be irreligious, belief-in may seem to contain an irreducible factor.

Price thus concludes that *belief-in* has two senses, one reducible and the other not;[19] but his argument is weak. He makes a distinction between factual beliefs and evaluative beliefs, yet he has a hard time finding an evaluation that cannot be expressed factually. Does not belief-in militarism, or in pacifism, reduce to belief-that factually it is profitable in one way or another? Price's opponents argue that the *object* of such a belief is an evaluation, and we believe that the evaluation is correct. The difference between various beliefs lies in the objects or propositions believed, not in the nature of belief.

When Price begins to argue against the reduction of *belief-in* to *belief-that*, his line of thought becomes confused. Some of it is too trivial. For example, "believing in one's doctor certainly cannot be reduced to believing that he is a morally good man," or that "he is good at water-colour painting." He must be "good at curing diseases."[20] Precisely: This triviality is a systematic confusion, for belief in my physician is obviously belief that he is a good doctor. Making much of the distinction between a factual belief and an evaluative belief, he repudiates the reduction on the ground that the one is not the other. This device, clearly, substitutes one proposition for another; the object of belief is changed, but changing the object of the belief does not indicate any theoretical difference between factual and evaluative beliefs. To believe-in a certain value, virtue for example, is to believe-that virtue is a value. The logic, the analysis, the nature of "All a is b" remains identical no matter what values are assigned to the two variables.

By such a confused procedure, Price finally concludes

*The difference between various beliefs lies in the objects or propositions believed, not in the nature of belief.*

18. Read that literary gem, *The Passion for the Theoretical* (334-336). Price does not himself have the same enthusiasm he depicts in the mathematician and logician, but others do. May one add among these others the ideal theologian. By the time Price takes Newman to page 345, Newman seems to be an outright idolator. This is a constant danger in Romanism.

19. Price, 435.

20. Price, 442.

Trusting is not a merely cognitive attitude.... [T]he proposed reduction leaves out the "warmth" which is a characteristic feature of evaluative belief-in.... If it is disagreeable to be compelled to talk about "the heart," the fact remains that most of us have one, as well as a head.[21]

Later on the Biblical view of such a distinction between the heart and the head must be stated. Here, as this secular section comes to an end, one need note only that after pages and pages describing various beliefs, Price gives no explanation of his words *warmth, head*, or *heart*. The defect is major. He has solved his problem with meaningless words.

A technical point relative to this gap in Price's argument comes at the top of the same page: "Trusting is not a merely cognitive attitude." One need not reject this statement as false. Rather it is misapplied. No belief is a merely cognitive attitude. After spending so many pages on Newman's *Grammar of Assent*, Price should have considered the possibility that every belief is a volitional attitude, or volitional act. As such it has no bearing on the reducibility or irreducibility of *belief-in* to *belief-that*.

It should now be clear that secular analyses of belief are applicable to the same problem in Christian theology. Some Scriptural material is as descriptive as Price's many pages; some is more analytical. The problem is identical, and we should not refuse to learn even from those with whom we are in basic disagreement.

There is one further lesson we may learn. Professor Price is so very honest that he does all he can to find some value in every view he discusses. The result is that every view becomes equally or almost equally questionable. If we, like him, were left to our own natural resources, we could have little confidence in any view. Though Price states some preferences, the whole gives an impression of skepticism. The more we study his arguments, the more this impression is reinforced. But we Christians do not claim to rely on our natural resources. We claim to have received a supernatural revelation. If we patiently study this revelation and carefully avoid illogicalities, we shall reach the truth, or at least some of it.

*We Christians do not claim to rely on our natural resources. We claim to have received a supernatural revelation.*

## 4. Roman Catholic Views

In the preceding section the material from Price included some of his remarks on Cardinal Newman. More needs to be said about Roman Catholic views. Perhaps we should refer to the Roman Catholic view in the singular, for the several writers are in substantial agreement. Hence we shall go back to Newman's source, Thomas Aquinas, and forward to the recent M. C. D'Arcy, S. J.

Since the early Christians, before A.D. 325, had not settled upon the doctrine of the Trinity, it is not surprising that they had no clear view of faith. Tertullian spoke about believing on authority rather than by personal investigation and knowledge. After Athanasius, Augustine had more to say. Faith for him was voluntary assent to the truth. This is

21. Price, 452.

more to the point than Tertullian's very good, but quite inadequate, passages.

As one of the greatest thinkers in the history of philosophy and theology, Thomas Aquinas demands notice. Here a reference to a previous medieval theologian, Hugo St. Victor, will conveniently introduce the discussion. Hugo proposed a definition of faith that was widely accepted both before and after the Protestant Reformation: "Faith is a kind of certainty concerning absent realities that is superior to opinion and inferior to knowledge." This sort of division is reminiscent of the fine distinctions described by H. H. Price, which can be useful only if each is distinctly defined. Thomas, however, strikes deeper. He objects that a mean must always be homogeneous to its two extremes. Since both science and opinion have propositions as their objects, the objects of faith (which is intermediate between them) must likewise be propositions. Then Thomas, always willing to present an opponent's view, acknowledges that contrary to what he has just said, the Apostles' Creed asserts "I believe in God the Father Almighty," and this is different from the proposition, "God is Almighty." Therefore, echoing Hugo St. Victor, faith concerns a reality, not a proposition. Further, in Heaven faith gives way to vision, as *1 Corinthians* 13:12 says; and this is a vision of God himself, not a proposition; therefore, similarly, the object of faith is a person, not a proposition.

After stating opposing views Thomas does not always come down on one side as against the other. He sometimes effects a combination. Here, noting the divergency, he gives this conclusion in the *Summa Theologiae*:

> The way the known exists in the knower corresponds to the way the knower knows.... For this reason the human mind knows in a composite way things that are themselves simple.... From the perspective of the one believing, the object of faith is something composite in the form of a proposition.... In Heaven...that vision will not take the form of a proposition, but of a simple intuition. [22]

This quotation presents two-and-a-half puzzles. First is the triviality, tautology, or vagary that the way the known exists in the knower corresponds to the way the knower knows. This does not describe what these ways are, and therefore leaves in doubt whether or not the way the knower knows is the way the object itself exists. The second and third, or second-and-a-half puzzle, concerns the distinction between knowing in this life and knowing in Heaven. If God is so simple as not to be a proposition, so simple as not to be a subject with predicates, how can he turn into a subject and predicate when he enters a human mind? Or otherwise, if our propositional knowledge of God be true, what becomes of this truth in Heaven? Does it become false? Thomas says that God becomes a vision or simple intuition. *Vision*, however, as when Scripture says that we shall see him face to face, is clearly metaphorical, for God is not a visible body. And as for *intuition*, some philosophers have asserted the occurrence of intellectual intui-

*If our propositional knowledge of God be true, what becomes of this truth in Heaven?*

22. Thomas Aquinas, *Summa Theologiae.* Blackfriars edition, Volume 31, 11ff.

tions, especially axiomatic propositions. It is hard to credit the idea that truth can be non-propositional. The single word *cat* is neither true nor false. The proposition, "this cat is black," may be true; but how can a subject minus a predicate be true all alone by itself? Yet God is the truth, and his mind, his omniscience, is the totality of all truths.

Another of Thomas' points is even more clearly implausible. He insists that we cannot believe anything that is false. To quote:

> Nothing can be the completion of any potentiality…except in virtue of the formal objective of that power. For example, color cannot be the completion of sight except through light.…Nothing therefore can come under faith except in its status within God's truth, where nothing false has any place.…We can only conclude that nothing false can be the object of faith.

Such was not Augustine's view, and on the face of it Thomas' statement is just plain false. And if so, Thomas has believed a false proposition, which he said no one can do. People believe many false propositions. Augustine used as an example the belief of a boy that a certain man and woman were his parents, whereas he had actually been adopted soon after his birth.

This is so obvious that we must suppose Aquinas to have meant something else. If he had saving faith in mind, instead of faith in general, his statement would be true. Saving faith must be belief in something God has said, not something Herodotus or Celsus had said. Therefore the object of faith must be true and cannot be false. No one can be saved by believing a falsehood. But with this quite understandable meaning, the meaning of *faith* disappears. It reduces to a tautology, namely, faith can have no false statement as an object because we refuse the name *faith* to any belief that has a false statement as its object; and thus Thomas here gives no information as the nature of belief and its place in one's consciousness. Of course, this is not all Thomas said.

Some pages further on Thomas gives a fuller explanation:

> The verb *to think* can be used in three senses. The first is the widest sense – any act of intellectual knowing.…The second is a narrower sense, where *thinking* designates a thinking of the mind that is accompanied by a certain searching prior to reaching complete understanding in the certitude of seeing.…The third sense is an act of the cogitative power [and has no part in this discussion.].…In its first and broadest sense, "to think with assent" does not bring out the precise meaning.…If, however, *to think* is understood in its proper sense, the text does express the meaning distinctive of the act of belief. Among the acts of the intellect, some include a firm assent without pondering – thus when someone thinks about what he knows scientifically.…Other mental acts are…inconclusive…suspicion…opinion. The act of believing, however, is firmly attached to one alternative, and in this respect the believer is in the same state of mind as one who has science or understanding. [23]

*It is hard to credit the idea that truth can be non-propositional. The single word* cat *is neither true nor false.*

23. Page 61. The notes in the Blackfriars edition list other passages that go into further details.

Since this is not a treatise on Thomistic philosophy and cannot therefore analyze the innumerable details, a rather summary conclusion, minus the niceties and requisite modifications, may be permitted. The last of the quoted sentences, identifying the believing state of mind with the scientific state of mind, more or less justifies the conclusion that faith, for Thomas, is assent to an understood proposition. And to that extent we agree.

Somewhere in a discussion on faith, the Romish view of "implicit" faith should be considered. When an Italian or Irish peasant asserts that he believes whatever the Church teaches, though, of course, his knowledge of what the Church teaches embraces no more than one percent of the Tridentine confession, he is said to have implicit faith. Even an educated Catholic, a professor of philosophy in a secular university, did not know the essential element that makes baptism valid. But all such people profess belief in *whatever* the Church teaches. Protestantism has always rejected this proposition as absurd.

*No one can believe what he does not know or understand.*

It should be clear that no one can believe what he does not know or understand. Suppose a person who knows no French is told, "Dans ce roman c'est M. DuPrès qui est le meurtrier": Can he believe it? If he could, it would greatly ease the work of foreign missionaries: They could preach to the Chinese or Bantus in English without having to spend years learning the native language. But in reality no one can believe what he does not understand, even if it is expressed in his own mother tongue.

Certainly the Scriptures do not countenance faith in what is unintelligible. Speaking in foreign tongues, though God understands, does not edify because in the congregation no one understands. The message must be translated into the known language. It is better to speak five intelligible words than ten thousand in an unknown tongue. If the people do not understand, how can they say Amen? The sacred writers constantly emphasize doctrine, knowledge, wisdom, and edification. This argument, though given here in a negative form as an objection to an opposing view, must be taken as a positive element in the constructive conclusion that will eventually follow. Allow the addition of another verse. *Matthew* 28:20 says, "Teaching them to observe all things whatsoever I command you." Nothing is to be left untaught. A person cannot "observe" a doctrine or obey a command unless he knows it. Faith is strictly limited to knowledge.

Romanism's implicit faith contrasts with Calvin's discussion in the *Institutes*. Ridiculing their doctrine he says,

> Is it faith – to understand nothing?… Faith consists not in ignorance, but in knowledge…. By this knowledge [of Christ's propitiation], I say, not by the submission of our understanding, we obtain an entrance into the kingdom of Heaven…. the apostle [in *Romans* 10:10]… intimates that it is not enough to believe implicitly without understanding, or even inquiring; but he requires an explicit knowledge of God and of Christ.[24]

24. John Calvin, *Institutes of the Christian Religion*. III, ii, 2-3.

At this point it is a question whether it is better to continue with Calvin's refutation of implicit faith, and so extend the section on Romanism, or to postpone such material and use it positively in the exposition of Calvin. We shall do the latter and turn here to another Roman Catholic author.

M. C. D'Arcy, S. J., published a book of the title *The Nature of Belief.*[25] After a preliminary chapter, aptly described by one of its subheads, *Spiritual Crisis in the West*, chapter II discusses the possibility of truth.

In view of the irrationalism of contemporary society D'Arcy's first task, therefore, is "to restore confidence in the intellect."[26] He describes the various emotional tensions of the present age that interfere with the populace's ability to think clearly. To correct the present nihilism one must "first…show that the mind is not material." To do this D'Arcy depends largely on the argument that material bodies can be quantitatively measured, and that which cannot be quantified or dissected into parts is spirit or thought.

*People are certain of all sorts of things.*

The reader must not suppose that the present writer agrees with everything that D'Arcy says. In contrasting the mind's grasping a thought and the hand's grasping a coin, D'Arcy says, "The coin is or is not in my hand – that is a fact and not a truth."[27] Obviously it is a truth. Did he not print the proposition on the page? Another point of disagreement is D'Arcy's use of imagery, in which he resembles Cardinal Newman and Thomas, though he does not seem so extreme as they.

When one author constantly criticizes other authors, the reader may be repelled by the negativism. Let it be repeated that contrasting views bring both sides into sharper focus. And not only so, the writer criticized may set forth some very acceptable material. In these pages D'Arcy makes some excellent points on the distinction between soul and body to the discomfiture of behaviorists. However behaviorism is not the present subject.[28]

After chapter II has defended *The Possibility of Truth*, chapter III directly attacks the problem of *Belief.* He begins by distinguishing belief from knowledge. His argument is very plausible.

> Belief…carries us beyond the obvious in experience and the self-evident in propositions.…There is very little that we can know with the certainty of absolute proof.…
>
> All that falls short of demonstrable certainty has been included under the word "belief."[29]

Nevertheless

> we must be careful not to underrate this belief and reckon it necessarily uncertain.…
>
> This form [of belief] goes also by the name of faith, and on analysis seems to mean a state of mind…which plays the role of absolute certainty.[30]

The notion of certainty – a notion many other religious writers adopt – requires some scrutiny. People are certain of all sorts of things.

25. Martin C. D'Arcy, *The Nature of Belief.* [1931] 1971.

26. D'Arcy, 39.

27. D'Arcy, 41.

28. See Clark, *Behaviorism and Christianity.*

29. D'Arcy, 70–72.

30. D'Arcy, 52.

Roman Catholics of earlier centuries were certain about the *Donation of Constantine*; and Neo-Platonic mysticism infiltrated the church because all the churchmen were certain that Paul's Athenian convert, Dionysius the Areopagite, was the author of the *Divine Names.* His mysticism or negative theology still afflicts, in a variety of modified forms, a number of professing Christians even though they have never heard of the pagan Proclus whom Dionysius plagiarized. In lesser matters some people have been certain that a witch's brew could cure warts, and in government affairs the Communists are certain that they shall rule the world. It would seem, therefore, that certainty has little to do with truth. If so, its insertion in theology and apologetics only renders uncertain the nature and value of faith.

*Certainty has little to do with truth.*

As was said above, D'Arcy moderates some of Newman's extreme positions. It is not essential here to decide rigorously to what extent this is so, for the aim at the moment is more or less confined to presenting various views, even if negatively, as helpful suggestive material. We note therefore that D'Arcy quotes Newman as follows:

> [T]here are three conditions of certitude: that it follows on investigation and proof, that it is accompanied by a specific sense of intellectual satisfaction and relief, and that it is irreversible. If the assent is made without rational grounds, it is a rash judgment, a fancy, or a prejudice; if without the sense of finality, it is scarcely more than an inference; if without permanence, it is a mere conviction.[31]

Newman's conditions here certainly rule out the certainty that a witch's brew will cure warts. But do they leave anything untouched? Does "a specific sense of intellectual satisfaction" guarantee that a belief is based on truly rational grounds? Are not irrational grounds sometimes accepted as rational? If the assent is "without permanence," it is "a mere conviction." In that case, how can one distinguish between *certitude* and *conviction*? What justifies the assertion that "I shall never change my mind as long as I live"? Who knows what he will believe ten years from now? Newman gets rid of warts rather well, but he also removes certainty at the same time.

Although D'Arcy realizes that Newman used some vague and doubtful terms — such as *instinct, sense, illative sense,* and *probable* — he himself, in trying to avoid Newman's infelicities and to present a better version of the general theory, introduces terminology equally vague. He asserts in opposition to Newman that "notions can be absolutely valid, that first principles are not assumptions or instincts, and that therefore conclusions can be unconditional."[32] Suggesting timidly that *assent* is not distinct from *conclusion*, he allows that many arguments or conclusions "in which we can find no flaw leave us quite cold, while others touch us to the quick. " No doubt this is so, for no one is enthusiastically interested in every possible subject of debate. But if one understands an argument on an uninteresting subject, is not his assent, refrigerated as it may be, as much an assent as his passionate belief that Rubens is better than Rembrandt or that the New York Yankees are

31. D'Arcy, 132.
32. D'Arcy, 151-152.

*30*

superior to the Philadelphia Phillies? Applying his principle to belief in God D'Arcy continues, "Many listen to arguments for the existence of God, and, if unprejudiced, assent, but remain indifferent until some day, please God, they realize the value of God and the call to act on what they know to be true."[33] Here is a major flaw in D'Arcy's argument. He speaks as if we assent to God and are later moved to act on that assent. But this is a mistaken analysis, for in the situation described there are two assents, not just one. First, the man believes that God exists. This may mean that he believes there is some sort of Power in the universe superior to man. It might even mean there is Power that can be utilized, avoided, or ignored. Belief in God covers a multitude of sins. With three or four billion human beings inhabiting the Earth, belief in God usually does not mean belief in the Triune God. In fact "belief in God" hardly means anything. Then later, please the God and Father of our Lord Jesus Christ, the man believes something quite different. The nature of assent in the two cases is the same, but the propositions assented to are altogether different. One can never believe $x$; one must believe that $x$ is $y$.

*Belief in God covers a multitude of sins.*

Beyond this D'Arcy uses some terms as vague as Newman's: "comparative apprehension," "degrees of closeness and obscurity" (based on what I believe to be a misinterpretation of Descartes), "self-evidence," "direct apprehension of reality," "intuition," "dogmatic" as opposed to some other type of assent. In these pages there is much that is interesting and much that is suggestive – at least it suggests many problems – but an acceptable view of assent or belief seems to be absent.

If the unphilosophical reader finds a recital of D'Arcy's details somewhat boring, the present writer sympathizes with him. In chapters VI and X there are epistemological and metaphysical analyses, in great detail, but which seem, to one who disagrees with the underlying assumptions, seriously mistaken. What D'Arcy takes as self-evident, another looks on as impossible. Let us therefore skip over to the final chapter on *Divine Faith*, even if we have missed much of the preparatory material.

He briefly sums up this preliminary epistemological material (with which I thoroughly disagree) in a paragraph of rather pleasing literary merit:

> [W]e are constantly engaged on interpreting natural objects, friends, the world of politics and art and history, and that we carry this habit of mind to greater problems, to an interpretation in fact of the whole of reality. Only here we find that the task is too much for us.... We are encouraged to find, nevertheless, that knowledge is a trustworthy guide, [which allows us to see a] direction and pattern in the universe. To return to an old example, the interpretation of the work of a master in music or painting comes out right and unmistakable when we have assimilated his mind and made it our own by affectionate understanding.[34]

Why cannot we very well understand the mind and art of Felicien Rops with disgust and enmity instead of with affection?

33. D'Arcy, 152.
34. D'Arcy, 295-296.

Is it not, then, possible that there may be an interpretation of the whole of experience, strange and foolish to those who enjoy their prejudices, but to the ones [once?] initiated, the wisdom and power of God?...

[T]he credentials are there for all to examine, proofs are offered.... Faith is not vision...it is rather the beginning of a new life....[35]

On the next page he defines *faith* as

the act as that whereby we believe without doubting whatever God has revealed.... Faith is belief on the authority of God revealing. The motive of faith is the truthfulness of God who speaks. Faith is an act of submission of the intellect to God...and at the same time it is a laying hold of some truth which He has revealed.[36]

Divest this of the epistemological basis on which D'Arcy supports it and the statement is very good, with one exception. D'Arcy here makes a distinction between an act of submission to God and something else that happens "at the same time," namely, "a laying hold of" or belief in and acceptance of some true propositions. What is the distinction? Why are not these two the same thing?

Perhaps on the next two or three pages D'Arcy inadvertently tends to identify them, thus evincing some confusion; but of this the advanced student must judge for himself by reading the book. One of his sentences is, "Faith, therefore, is seen so far to consist in the believing of truths on the authority of God."[37]

Yet there is confusion or vagueness, for he continues on the next page to say, "The life of a fox-terrier is higher than that of a foxglove, and the life of a man is in turn above that of a dog. Let us suppose that a dog were for several hours of the day allowed to live the life of a human; it would then be exerting powers which were above the capacity of its nature." So it is with supernatural faith.

Other authors have pictured man as a bird, for whose instruction God must descend and chirp. The chirping is not divine language – birds cannot understand language – it is human language which God must use for his birds; but unfortunately the divine message cannot be put into bird language, and God finds it impossible to get his ideas across. This illustration of the inadequacy of human language is more extreme than D'Arcy's view, but both, in my opinion, misunderstand that man is the image of God (*1 Corinthians* 11:7). Since man is God's image, man's language is God's language, and we think God's thoughts after him – not some different analogical thoughts, but God's thoughts themselves. However, though we reject the Thomistic doctrine of analogical knowledge, Thomas' statement that "Faith is an act of the intellect, under the command or direction of the will"[38] is excellent, if it is detached from Thomistic empiricism and incorporated into an Augustinian philosophy. Unfortunately some Reformed theologians, if indeed they wish to do so, are not completely successful.[39]

*Since man is God's image, man's language is God's language, and we think God's thoughts after him – not some different analogical thoughts, but God's thoughts themselves.*

35. D'Arcy, 296.
36. D'Arcy, 297.
37. D'Arcy, 300.
38. D'Arcy, 213.
39. See my *Language and Theology.*

## 5. Biblical Data

Although a Christian does not ask for any extended argument defending the appropriateness of using Scriptural data, he might be encouraged by the fact that the secular investigations of belief are so various and inconclusive, depending as they do on experience, that even the secular writers themselves ought to welcome divine revelation. God created man and therefore knows more about human nature than any psychologist could ever discover experimentally. Then, too, the Romanist writers, even though they believe that the Bible is infallible, use it insufficiently and often misinterpret it by reason of tradition, papal pronouncements, and what may be called fallacious scholastic arguments. The Reformers, on the other hand, not only appealed to Scripture, as opposed to the secularists, but to *sola Scriptura*, as opposed to the Romanists.

For this reason it is appropriate at this point to insert a preliminary amount of Scriptural data. Later the discussion of each theologian in turn will also be studded with Biblical citations; but a sample here will serve as an acceptable foundation.

Seminaries have traditionally divided theology into two courses. The more elementary one is called Biblical Theology; the more advanced is called Systematic Theology. The first collects all the Biblical data, usually in the order of its temporal disclosure to man: *Genesis*, then *Malachi*, then the *Gospels* and *Apocalypse*. After this fund of information is laid on the table, the theologian reorganizes it systematically. That is, he first collects all the information on God's nature, then all the information on God's rule over the universe, then sin, redemption, and so on. The result is a logical system. This procedure is here followed within a narrower range. First the Biblical data will be collected, perhaps not exhaustively, nor altogether in strict historical order, but a sample of what is meant will be given. Then some systematic and general inferences will be attempted.

First, then, the references. God told Noah that there would be a great flood. *Genesis* 6 may not use the word *faith*, but it makes clear that Noah believed what God said. Abraham is sometimes called the father of the faithful. Not only does the Old Testament describe how firmly he believed God's prophecies, but *Galatians* in the New Testament identifies Christian faith with the faith of Abraham. *Romans* 4, *Hebrews* 11, and *James* 2 also make Abraham's faith a part of their argument.

The role of faith in the Old Testament should not be minimized. One could use Jacob, Joseph, Moses, Gideon, David, and Daniel (to name only a few) as examples. Sometimes disbelief, the absence of faith, is mentioned; and in *Psalm* 78:21-22, 32, in addition to the merely historical event, the consequences of unbelief are stated: "And anger also came up against Israel because they did not believe in God.... Instead of this they still sinned and did not believe in his wondrous works."

*Secular investigations of belief are so various and inconclusive, depending as they do on experience, that even the secular writers themselves ought to welcome divine revelation.*

The word *believe* in this quotation is a Hebrew term only twice translated *faith*, sometimes translated *truth* or *truly*, but frequently translated *believe*.

One can learn about the fact of faith, *i.e.*, the instances, the nature of faith, its importance and its various relations, from negative as well as from positive examples. *Isaiah* 7:9 says, "If you will not believe, truly you shall not be established." This is not now the place to consider whether the *King James* translation *will* means that belief is voluntary assent; here we are merely collecting examples of data. *2 Chronicles* 20:20 states the converse: "Believe in the Lord your God, so shall you be established; believe his prophets, so shall you prosper."

Since this is not a textbook on Old Testament Biblical theology – Oehler-Day produced a volume of 593 pages – the verses picked must be taken as simply samples. The theme of Biblical data is even more difficult when we come to the New Testament. A short list must suffice. A verse often quoted is

> *Hebrews* 11:1: Faith is the substance of things hoped for, the evidence of things not seen.

Some people take this as a definition of faith. It is no more a definition than "A triangle is something one studies in geometry courses." It is not even so clear. Most people know what a geometry course is – though with the serious deterioration of public education in the United States fewer people have a satisfactory notion – but hardly anybody knows what the word *substance* means. Is it a substance in the sense that wheat is the substance out of which bread is made? The *New American Standard* tries to clarify the verse by translating it

> Faith is the assurance of things hoped for, the conviction of things not seen.

*Arndt and Gingrich's Lexicon* gives both meanings for *hypostasis*: *substance* and *conviction*. It also gives *reality* and *actual being*. The more complete *Liddell and Scott* lists the *act of standing under, sediment, abscess, soup, duration, origin, courage, resolution, real nature,* as well as *substance, actual existence, wealth,* and *title deed to property*. The other word in the verse, *evidence* or *conviction* (*elegchos*), means *proof, reproof, correction* (*Arndt and Gingrich*) and *disproof, refutation, scrubbing, catalogue, inventory* (*Liddell and Scott*). This information should warn the reader that although quoting verses is an indispensable prerequisite for formulating Christian doctrine, much more is required.

Nor is the exact meaning of individual Greek words the only difficulty. It is possible to know accurately every word in a sentence without knowing the meaning of the sentence. For example, *James* 2:20 speaks of a dead faith. James also says that Abraham was justified by works and not by faith alone. How does this fit in with what Paul says? However, let us quote half a dozen verses or so as a small sample of the data necessary to a study of faith.

> *Mark* 11:22: Have faith in God.

*It is possible to know accurately every word in a sentence without knowing the meaning of the sentence.*

*John* 6:29: This is the work of God, that you believe in whom he has sent.

*Acts* 20:21: Repentance toward God and faith in our Lord Jesus Christ.

*Romans* 4:19: Not being weak in the faith....

*Ephesians* 2:8: By grace you have been saved through faith.

*Hebrews* 12:2: Looking to Jesus, the leader (ruler, prince) and perfector of the faith....

*Jude* 20: Building up yourselves on your most holy faith....

*Revelation* 2:13, 19: You...have not denied my faith.... I know your faith.

*Revelation* 13:10: Here is the patience and the faith of the saints.

*Revelation* 14:12: They keep the commandments of God and the faith of Jesus.

*The term* faith *has two very distinct meanings.*

These arbitrarily selected verses all contain either the noun *faith* or the verb *believe* from which root the noun gets its meaning. This is a very small sample because the verb *believe*, by rough count, occurs 248 times in the New Testament and the noun *faith* or *belief* occurs 244 times. No doubt the reader will be glad that not all 492 passages were quoted.

Here is as good a place as any to sound a warning. The term *faith* has two very distinct meanings. Sometimes it means the mental activity of believing. Indeed it is this meaning which is the subject of the present study. In the list just quoted this meaning occurs in *Mark* 11:22, *John* 6:29, and *Acts* 20:21; while the second meaning, namely the propositions believed, occurs in *Revelation* 2:13, 19 and 14:12. This second meaning is prominent in the pastoral epistles. Although many people confuse the two and slip from one to the other without realizing what they are doing, this warning should enable an attentive reader to identify each throughout the present monograph.

Before we leave the sphere of Biblical data and proceed to something more systematic, it may be well to discuss a difficult verse in anticipation of further troubles. The end in view, viewed perhaps from afar, is the definition of *faith*. Examples of difficulties will help us find the definition. Now, *James* 2:20 is a puzzling passage. He speaks there of a dead faith and describes it as a faith unproductive of good works. Precisely what a man of dead faith actually believes is not too clear. One thing, however, is clear: The word *faith* here cannot mean "personal trust" in the sense that some popular preachers impose on it in distinction to belief. "Dead trust" would be an unintelligible phrase. Clearly James means a belief of some sort; and the only belief James mentions is the belief in monotheism. Islam therefore would be a dead faith.

There are some other varieties of faith which may be mentioned as this subsection concludes. *Matthew* 13 apparently refers to what some theologians call "temporary faith." Charles Hodge writes, "[N]othing is more common than for the Gospel to produce a temporary impression....Those thus impressed, believe."[40] But Hodge does not say precisely what they believe. He hardly acknowledges that the person in the parable who is represented by the stony places believes anything, even though we read that he "hears the word and anon with joy receives it."This sounds as if the stony man believed some or even all of the Gospel. However, the previous verses describe such men as "seeing, see not; and hearing, hear not; neither do they understand"; following which Jesus quotes Isaiah. A person can indeed hear words without understanding them, but can he thus believe them, and can he receive them with joy? Clearly there are troubles here that we must ponder.

Other theologians speak of an "historical" faith, by which, strangely, they do not mean only a belief in the truth of historical events recorded in the Bible, but also in some, many, or perhaps all the Biblical norms of morality. Possibly the rich young ruler would exemplify this sort of faith. He certainly believed that he had kept all the Commandments, but unfortunately this was a mistaken belief. How much else of the Old Testament he believed (*Genesis* 17?) is not clear.

One further point may be made before the systematic exposition begins. It has more to do with church history than exegesis. In the second century a widespread heresy almost engulfed and destroyed the church. It was Gnosticism. The name comes from the word *gnosis, knowledge.* Later theologians have sometimes contrasted faith with knowledge. This is the wrong contrast, for two reasons. First, *2 Peter* 1:3 says that everything pertaining to godliness comes to us through knowledge. There are many supporting references. The pastorals have several. The second reason is that the knowledge of which the Gnostics boasted was a theory of cosmology, including highly imaginative accounts of what happened before *Genesis* 1:1.

Admittedly, the Gnostics were devoid of Christian faith; but the contrast is not between faith and knowledge – it is a contrast between the different objects known or believed. The Gnostics knew, or believed in, thirty eons, a docetic incarnation, and a pseudo-atonement. The Christians believed a different set of propositions. Since, however, some students of evangelistic zeal may question the value of a "merely secular, psychological" analysis of belief, it is best to show the importance and necessity of saving faith. Then as saving faith is recognized as a species of generic faith, the analysis will have its proper setting.

The reader will doubtless be disappointed at the inadequacy and inconclusiveness of the previous paragraphs. But in a sense that was their purpose: They gave a sample of the Biblical data and by indicating a few of the problems showed the need of a more systematic procedure. One might think that a systematic exposition of faith would now begin with a definition of *faith*. This would indeed be proper; but the reader would immediately ask, "How do you get that definition from the Bible?" This is what we shall attempt to show, and we shall begin with a survey of Reformation views.

*2 Peter 1:3 says that everything pertaining to godliness comes to us through knowledge.*

40. Charles Hodge, *Systematic Theology*, III, 68.

*36*

## 6. John Calvin

The section on "Roman Catholic Views" contained some of Calvin's attack on the doctrine of implicit faith. A continuation of this subject will show that arguments which some people dislike as negative – it is unpopular to be negative – are logically as positive and as constructive as any others. To assert that some books are not interesting is to deny that all books are interesting. Denials and assertions, positives and negatives, are inseparable. When Calvin attacks implicit faith, he proclaims the Protestant doctrine of explicit faith. Therefore, we shall continue to quote some lines from the *Institutes*. One must realize, of course, that Calvin is discussing saving faith, for which reason not everything he says is true of generic faith. This is rather obvious and need cause no confusion, for the differences between Islamic, Jewish, or Communistic faith and Christian faith can hardly escape notice.

Now, Calvin:

> Paul makes faith the inseparable attendant of doctrine, in these words..."as the truth is in Jesus...[and] the words of faith and good doctrine".... There is an inseparable relation between faith and the word...."These are written, that you might believe"....Take away the word, and no faith will remain.... [W]e must still consider what it is that faith properly has respect to in the word....When our conscience sees only wrath and indignation, how can it but tremble and be afraid?... But faith ought to seek God, not shun him....

> But suppose we substitute benevolence and mercy [and Calvin quotes a number of verses]....We shall have a full definition of faith, if we say that it is a firm and sure knowledge of the divine favour toward us, which, founded on the truth of a free promise in Christ, and revealed to our minds, and sealed to our hearts, by the Holy Spirit.[41]

*This emphasis on doctrine, the truth, the Word, the promise, sets the standard for Reformation theology.*

This emphasis on doctrine, the truth, the Word, the promise, sets the standard for Reformation theology. With due respect to Calvin, however, one may ask whether or not the concluding definition tends to confuse faith with assurance. More on this later. It may also be doubted whether the definition is "complete." At least there is more to be said. It is clear, however, that Calvin emphasizes knowledge, in particular the knowledge of God's promise. Hence the object of belief is a proposition.

In reading Calvin one must consider the date of the *Institutes*. This work was first published in 1536. The final edition, much enlarged, came in 1559. The Council of Trent was called in 1542; it recessed in 1547 and resumed in 1551. It recessed again from 1552 to 1562; and its final decisions were confirmed by the pope in 1564. Thus, Calvin began writing before the Council convened; he finished his work before the Council concluded; and hence his description of Romanism could not be accurately based on the Council's conclusions. He had to use concrete examples from actual authors and preachers. The result is that some of his descriptions of Romanism are not true of what later became the official Roman position.

41. John Calvin, *Institutes of the Christian Religion*, III, ii , 6-7. See also paragraphs 2-5.

For example, in III, ii, 8, he says, "They insist that faith is an assent, with which any despiser of God may receive whatever is delivered by Scripture." Now, maybe some brash Schoolman or stupid monk said this; but it is not the post–Tridentine official position. In the twentieth-century *Catholic Encyclopedia*, faith is stated to be "fiducial assent." Nor is it clear that a despiser of God can receive as true whatever – some things no doubt, but everything? – is contained in Scripture.

However much we oppose the Roman Church, even to asserting the Reformation view that the papacy is the Antichrist, it is unnecessary, and we do our cause no good, to misrepresent these idolators. Hence, since it was impossible to include everything about Catholicism and exclude everything about Calvin in the earlier section, so too in this section they are again intermingled. As a matter of history, therefore, a few paragraphs on the decrees of Trent follow. These decrees contain much that is wrong. They teach that baptism is the instrumental cause of justification and that in justification God makes us just. They assert human cooperation and deny irresistible grace; and many other things, including of course the abominations of the Mass. However, and nonetheless, there are some remnants of Christianity. The quotation following concerns faith, and though mixed with stultifying error, there are some good phrases.

Sixth Session, chapter VIII:

> [W]e are therefore said to be *justified by faith* because faith is the beginning of human salvation…. *without which it is impossible to please God*…. [W]e are therefore said to be justified *freely*, because that none of those things which precede justification – whether faith or works – merit the grace itself of justification…otherwise…*grace is no more grace.*

Then follow a repudiation of Reformation heretics (chapter IX), the increase of justification (chapter X), then on keeping the Commandments, presumption, predestination, and perseverance (chapters XI, XII, XIII), etc.

After chapter XVI come some Canons opposing the Reformation view of justification. For example, "If any one says, that men are justified, either by the sole imputation of the justice of Christ…to the exclusion of [infused] grace and the *charity which is poured forth in their hearts by the Holy Ghost*, and is inherent in them…, let him be anathema."

Even here this is not so bad as it sounds to post-Reformation ears; or at least the error is often incorrectly identified. The Romanists included in their term *justification* what the Reformers and the Bible call *sanctification*. This latter, of course, requires infused holiness and love. A more accurate identification of the Romish error would be their complete blindness to Biblical justification. They used the term, but they omitted and denied God's judicial, justifying acquittal.

In addition to the decrees of Trent, something from the *Dogmatic Decrees of the Vatican Council* (A.D. 1870) forms an interesting historical note:

*A more accurate identification of the Romish error would be their complete blindness to Biblical justification.*

Chapter III: *On Faith*. Man being wholly dependent upon God, as upon his Creator and Lord…we are bound to yield to God, by faith in his revelation, the full obedience of our intelligence and will. And the Catholic Church teaches that this faith, which…is a supernatural virtue, whereby, inspired and assisted by the grace of God, we believe that the things which he has revealed are true…because of the authority of God himself.…

But though the assent of faith is by no means a blind action of the mind, still no man can assent to the Gospel teaching, as is necessary to obtain salvation, without the illumination and inspiration of the Holy Spirit, who gives to all men sweetness in assenting to and believing in the truth. Wherefore, faith itself, even when it does not work by charity, is in itself a gift of God, and the act of faith is a work appertaining to salvation, by which man yields voluntary obedience to God himself, by assenting to and cooperating with his grace, which he is able to resist.

This is certainly not Reformation theology, and some of its phrases clearly contradict the teaching of Scripture. Nevertheless it may appear that Calvin did not correctly anticipate the Tridentine Symbol when he gave the Romish definition of faith as "a mere assent with which every despiser of God may receive as true whatever is contained in the Scripture."

In addition to the fact that Calvin wrote before the Council of Trent assembled, and finished writing before it concluded, misunderstandings, especially on our part today, can arise because of changes in the meanings of words over four centuries. Calvin says "that assent itself…is more a matter of the heart than the head, and of the affection than the intellect." *Since the Scripture never contrasts the head and the heart, but frequently contrasts the heart and the lips, one ought to suppose that by head Calvin meant the understanding and by heart the will.* Nor is "the obedience of faith," which he quotes in the very next sentence, an "affection": It is a volition. Obedience is always voluntary. A few lines below Calvin speaks more clearly: "They talk absurdly when they maintain that faith is formed by the addition of pious affection to assent, since assent itself…consists in pious affection, and is so described in the Scriptures."[42]

If much that Calvin says exposes the errors of Rome, these last words should warn evangelicals not to belittle assent, "mere" assent of the mind, for this voluntary acceptance of the truth is itself a pious action (if not an "affection").

The *Larger Catechism* (Question 72) will serve as a conclusion for this contrast between Romanism and Calvinism.

Justifying faith is a saving grace, wrought in the heart of a sinner, by the Spirit and Word of God, whereby he, being convinced of his sin and misery, and of the disability in himself and all other creatures to recover him out of his lost condition, not only assents to the truth of the promise of the Gospel, but receives and rests upon Christ and his righteousness, therein held forth, for pardon of sin, and for the accept-

42. Calvin, *Institutes*, III, ii, 8.

ing and accounting of his person righteous in the sight of God for salvation.

Unfortunately there is one phrase in this answer that seems to deviate from Calvin, and for which the prooftext follows an inaccuracy in the *King James* translation. The phrase is "not only assents…but receives and rests." The addition of these words seems to be a denial that the assent itself can be "pious." Not to extend this subsection unduly, for some of the later discussion will cover the point, one may study the exegesis of *Ephesians* 1:13 in Hodge and other commentators. Though it differs somewhat from Hodge, the student may consider this translation: "In whom also you received an inheritance, having heard the Word of truth, *i.e.*, the Gospel of your salvation, in which [neuter] also having believed, you were sealed." The emphasis here is on having believed the good news.

The relation between faith and knowledge had been a matter of discussion long before Calvin. Not to mention Clement's *Stromata* (V, 1) or Cyril of Jerusalem (*Catechetical Lectures*, V, 4), we note that Augustine took as a sort of motto "*Credo ut intelligam*," and Aquinas held that "*Intelligo ut credam*." But the seeming sharpness of the disagreement is modified by the consideration that the two theologians did not use *intelligo* in the same sense. The empirical Aristotelianism of Thomas and the rational Platonism of Augustine separate before questions of faith can be considered. Calvin in general follows Augustine, and his view of Scripture differs from that of Aquinas.

It is true that Calvin seems to place some reliance on the cosmological argument, compromising *Sola Scriptura*; and he also seems to prove or at least to support the truth of Scripture by evidential reasons in the *Institutes* I, viii, whose title is "Rational Proofs to Establish the Belief of the Scripture." A better title would have been, "Historical Evidences of the Bible's Divinity." Indeed, the *Westminster Confession* (I, v) correctly evaluates these evidences and accurately reproduces Calvin's view that the Scriptures are self-authenticating. In fact, in his preceding chapter Calvin so declares. He says explicitly that the Scriptures "ought not to be made the subject of demonstration and argument from reason."[43] Therefore he should not have used the misleading title of I, viii. We ought to understand likewise the intended force of his so-called cosmological arguments, though admittedly they are more embarrassing than chapter eight.

In recent years some disciples of Søren Kierkegaard, and many sincere, though inadequately educated, apologetes, have misinterpreted Calvin's view, and especially some of his still medieval terminology. Perhaps "Thomistic terminology" would be a better expression, for though medieval it remains in common use today. The misapprehension is that when Calvin rejects "reason," and belabors secularists as proud and high-minded, and warns against "curiosity," he means to reject logic. This is a rather strange misapprehension, for Calvin is widely castigated as being all too logical. The word *reason* therefore should be

*Calvin says explicitly that the Scriptures "ought not to be made the subject of demonstration and argument from reason."*

43. Calvin, *Institutes*, I, vii, 5.

understood to mean sensory experience, on which, according to Aquinas, all knowledge is based. The contrast is not between reason and revelation, as if revelation were irrational, but between ordinary human experience with its implications and, on the other hand, divinely revealed information. As for logic, we appeal a second time to the "good and necessary consequence" of the *Westminster Confession*. Those authors who speak of Calvin's "abdication of reason from its sovereignty" either misunderstand or use language almost certainly to be misunderstood in the twentieth century.

Consider this passage which concludes a well-written page: "[I]t is impossible for any man to obtain even the minutest portion of true and sound doctrine without being a disciple of the Scripture. Hence the first step in true knowledge is taken.... For not only does faith, full and perfect faith, but all correct knowledge of God, originate in obedience...."[44] The following section details the aberrations of a mind that depends on natural resources. This explains Calvin's antagonism toward "curiosity," as mentioned just above – an antagonism that secular thinkers identify as Calvin's original sin. But though he could not include the necessary context in every instance, it is clear enough in some: "[L]et us here remember that on the whole subject of religion one rule of soberness is to be observed, and it is this – in obscure matters not to speak or think or even long to know more than the Word of God has delivered."[45] This advice may indeed put astronomy and botany beyond our interest, but in view of Calvin's enormously extensive commentaries, he opened up spacious vistas for "curiosity." There is a great scope for faith and knowledge.

In this Scriptural context, not in the context of Aristotelian empiricism, we can formulate a proper view of faith and its relation to knowledge, volition, or anything else pertinent. With our basis in Scripture we need not accept the Thomistic position that we cannot know what we believe and cannot believe what we know.

T. H. L. Parker is the author of a very fine study on *Calvin's Doctrine of the Knowledge of God*.[46] If Warfield's *Calvin and Calvinism*[47] is a must, Parker's book is so likewise. But both these authors flounder on occasion. No doubt the present writer does so too: Each reader must judge for himself where. But with whatever confusion he may be tainted, Parker's is one he wishes to avoid.

Parker writes:

> The knowledge of God cannot be regarded as one of the branches of epistemology, but differs fundamentally from all other forms of knowing.... Not only is the object of this knowledge different from other objects of his [man's] knowledge, but because the object of this knowledge is God, whose difference from man is such that there exists a religious discontinuity between man and Him, the knowing itself is not of the same kind as those acts of knowing which have for their object something in the same dimension as man.... Knowing God is a unique activity in man's experience, having its own categories. It runs the risk, if it borrows from the categories of general epis-

*"[I]t is impossible for any man to obtain even the minutest portion of true and sound doctrine without being a disciple of the Scripture."
— John Calvin*

44. Calvin, *Institutes*, I, vi, 2.

45. Calvin, *Institutes*, I, xiv, 4.

46. Eerdmans, revised 1959.

47. Oxford University Press, 1936.

temology, of destroying itself by turning its direction from its true object, God, to an idol fabricated by itself.[48]

After carefully reading this paragraph one must conclude that the confusion is substantial and not merely verbal. Note that Parker assigns to the knowledge of God categories that are different from those of general epistemology. God is not merely a different object of knowledge: Our activity of knowing is epistemologically different. Now, Parker does not enumerate the categories through which other objects are known. Worse, he does not enumerate the categories through which God is known. If he cannot state these two lists of categories, how can he discover that they differ? Of course, if Kantian space and time were categories, which they are not, they would not be applicable to God. But if unity, plurality (trinity), reciprocity, and others are categories, and if these are not applicable to God, how can we assert of God the clearly expressed Scriptural descriptions? If the forms of logic are, or are dependent on, the categories, and if they are excluded from the knowledge of God, then we must conclude that God can be both omnipotent and limited, both omniscient and ignorant, both spiritual and corporeal. Why is it permissible to say that a cat is not a dog, yet impermissible to say that God is not Satan? When man's knowing straddles two mutually exclusive epistemologies, he must be beside himself.

If one is less than enthusiastic about this criticism through a distaste for Kant, the objection can be restated in Aristotelian terms. His categories included substance, quality, relation: Athanasius thought that the category of *substance* was necessary; surely the three Persons have *relations* to one another, and to us as well; and is Parker willing to assert that God has no *qualities*? Mercy, for instance? Surely if a theologian wants to maintain that the human mind uses other categories when thinking about God, he ought to name them. To refuse to name them is impolite. To be unable to name them is disastrous.

In spite of some appearances to the contrary, Calvin really restricts knowledge to the Scriptures, and so avoids Parker's irrationalism. Calvin says, "By knowledge, we do not mean comprehension such as that which we have of things falling under human sense."[49] But in doing so, he is not suggesting different categories; he is not denying the law of contradiction; he is, rather, rejecting Aristotelian empiricism.

In the *Institutes* he also says that "when we are drawn [to Christ by the Spirit of God]…we are both in mind and spirit exalted far above our own understanding. For the soul, illumined by him, receives, as it were, a new eye, enabling it to contemplate heavenly mysteries, by the splendor of which it was previously dazzled. And, thus, it is only when the human intellect is irradiated by the light of the Holy Spirit, that it begins to have a taste of those things which pertain to the kingdom of God."[50] This language is too figurative for us to pin down its exact meaning, but at least there is no hint in it that the illumination of the Holy Spirit produces an activity apart from the *apriori* law of contradiction. Indeed, Parker inconsistently admits it, for he says, "This must

*When man's knowing straddles two mutually exclusive epistemologies, he must be beside himself.*

*"By knowledge, we do not mean comprehension such as that which we have of things falling under human sense."*
— *John Calvin*

48. T. H. L. Parker, *Calvin's Doctrine of the Knowledge of God*, 106.

49, Calvin, *Institutes*, III, ii, 14.

50. Calvin, *Institutes*, III, iii, 34.

not be taken literally, however; Calvin did not mean that our natural faculties are destroyed when we believe and new faculties given to us by the Spirit."[51] What is given to us is not a new and different set of categories, but *faith*. "It is man who knows, but his knowledge is faith – by virtue of the supernatural gift of God."[52] Calvin in many places denies that the fall made man an irrational being. So far from this is he that his wording sometimes reminds us of the Romanist view that in the fall man lost a *donum superadditum*. Man's

> soundness of mind and integrity of heart were...withdrawn.... [R]eason, by which man discerns between good and evil, and by which he understands and judges [in matters of mathematics and cosmology], is a natural gift, it could not be entirely destroyed.... In this sense John says, "the light still shines in darkness."[53]

Calvin with his consuming interest in saving faith does not write at length on general epistemology; but it is fair, I believe, to say that for him man frequently fails to use the laws of logic properly. Not only are the laws themselves untouched by sin, but also man's obligation to use them is in no sense diminished. Calvin is no anti-intellectual or irrationalist. His comment on *Acts* 17:22 says, "The mind of man is His [God's] true image."

One author tries to complicate Calvin's theory by distinguishing between *scientia* and *cognitio*. In his *Commentary* on *John* 10:38 Calvin writes,

> Though he [John] places knowledge [*scientia*] before faith,[54] as if faith were inferior, he does so, because he has to do with unbelieving and obstinate men...for rebels wish to know before they believe. And yet our gracious God...prepares us for faith by a knowledge [*notitia*] of his works. But the knowledge [*cognitio*] of God...comes after faith.

This distinction should not be pressed as if it were a formal theoretical difference. Calvin does not uniformly preserve this distinction. And in this passage from *John* the *notitia* is the sensible cognition of Christ's miracles. Furthermore, Calvin seems to have stumbled when he concludes that a prior *notitia* must be superior to a temporally later faith.

## 7. Thomas Manton

Was it not Aristotle who said that after a great thinker had laid down the main lines of a system, inferior minds could easily work out the details? There is some truth in this, but it does an injustice if the second thinker happens to be a genius too. Even if not a genius, the later thinker merits the credit of explaining the matter more fully and answering questions that readers of lesser intelligence ask. Now, Thomas Manton (1620-1677) was no genius, but he and others of his age are mistreated when liberals haughtily refer to them as the later scholastic exponents of Protestantism.

*"The mind of man is His [God's] true image."*
*– John Calvin*

51. Parker, 108.
52. Parker, 109.
53. Calvin, *Institutes*, III, ii, 12.
54. Of course, to the confusion of American college students, *scientia* does not mean what they mean by *science*.

Thomas Manton, though vulnerable to several criticisms, nevertheless expresses a view that has often been repeated in evangelical productions. His analysis of belief, expounded in his commentary on *James*,[55] separates it into three parts: *notitia*, *assensus*, and *fiducia*, or understanding, assent, and trust. Perhaps even theologians who favor this analysis of belief might omit *fiducia* if they confined themselves to belief as such; for in colloquial language a person who believes that Columbus discovered America in 1492 is not taken as an example of trust. Yet, even so, is he not actually an example of *confidence*? The word *trust* is a peculiar word, as the word *confidence* has just shown. There is further discussion of *trust*.

Quoting *James* 2:19 Manton remarks that the faith here is a "bare speculation" and cannot possibly save anyone.

*That this faith cannot save is very true. It is no more than a belief in monotheism.*

That this faith cannot save is very true. It is no more than a belief in monotheism. This the Muslims possess. But however it may be with Muslims, it seems incorrect to call the faith of devils a bare "speculation." This word often is used to refer to some proposition that is so unverifiable as to be more likely false than true. Granted, Manton also calls it a *knowledge*; and this is better, because on this point, if on nothing else, the devils believe the truth.

He continues: "'Thou believest'; that is, assentest to this truth." Belief, therefore, is an act of assent to the truth. Yet, Manton adds, believing is the "lowest act of faith."

Is there a higher act of faith? If so, is it higher because it has a more detailed object, *i.e.*, a greater number of propositions? But in this case it would still be an ordinary act of believing. Or is it higher because some psychological element beyond the act of believing is present? What would that element be?

Manton continues with the object of this belief. "*There is one God.* — He instanceth in this proposition, though he doth limit the matter only to this." This is a now rare usage of the verb, not noun, *to instance*. It means, to give an instance; the proposition, "there is one God," is therefore an instance or specification of what the man believes. Manton suggests that the man believes or assents to "other articles of religion." This is doubtless true, for nearly everyone who believes in any sort of God believes something else about him beyond bare existence. That the man has an extensive Jewish or Christian theology, however, is not clear.

"Thou dost well," quotes Manton; "It [the Scriptural phrase] is an approbation of such assent, so far as it is good, and not rested in...."

Again Manton has described the act as voluntary assent...naturally, all assent must be voluntary. But what also needs to be noted here are the words "rested in." When we say we rest in, or should not rest in, this or that, do we mean that in addition to *notitia* and *assensus* there is some other psychological element in saving faith called "resting"? Or does it mean that saving faith, rather than being psychologically different, must be an assent to other propositions in addition to monotheism? The latter seems to be the case, whether or not Manton meant it

55. Thomas Manton, *An Exposition of the Epistle of James*. The National Foundation for Christian Education, no date.

so. We should not "rest in," *i.e.*, be satisfied with, the single proposition, "There is but one God." This proposition even the devils accept. But for salvation men must not only accept the monotheistic proposition, but as well other propositions relating to the atonement.

On the next page Manton notes that the devils assent to this one truth and to other truths revealed in the Word, even to "many truths in the Scriptures" (on the following page). But how much of the Bible the devils believe, justification by faith perhaps, is a question that we in our ignorance of satanic psychology cannot answer. Manton apparently wants to maximize the devils' orthodoxy.

"Bare assent," says Manton, "to the articles of religion doth not infer true faith. True faith uniteth to Christ, it is conversant about his person...."[56] Two factors seem to be confused in Manton's mind: the psychology and the propositions. Does this quotation mean that saving faith, in addition to belief in monotheism, must also include the Chalcedonian Christology? Certainly an assent to Chalcedon, however "bare," is "conversant about his person." Or does Manton's statement mean that the devils themselves subscribe to Chalcedon, and that "conversant" is a psychological element in addition to assent? It would seem so because otherwise no contrast could be made between "*assent* to the articles of religion" and "*conversant* about his person."

Faith "is not only *assensus axiomati*, an assent to a Gospel-maxim or proposition; you are not justified by that, but by being one with Christ. It was the mistake of the former age to make the promise rather than the person of Christ, to be the formal object of faith...."[57]

The mention of the person of Christ is pious language. Similar expressions are common today. One slogan is, "No creed but Christ." Another expression, with variations from person to person, is, Faith is not belief in a proposition, but trust in a person.[58]

Though this may sound very pious, it is nonetheless destructive of Christianity. Back in the twenties, before the Methodist Church became totally apostate, a liberal in their General Conference opposed theological precision by some phrase centering on Christ, such as, Christ is all we need. A certain pastor, a remnant of the evangelical wing of the church, had the courage to take the floor and ask the pointed question, "Which Christ?"

The name Jesus Christ, at least since 1835 in Strauss' *Leben Jesu*, has been applied to several alleged persons. Strauss initiated the "Life of Jesus Movement." It ran through Ernest Renan to Albert Schweitzer.[59] But the persons described are nothing like the person described in the Creed of Chalcedon, nor, for that matter, are they alike amongst themselves. It is necessary therefore to ask, Which Christ? or, Whose Christ? The Christian or Biblical answer is the Creed of Chalcedon. A person can be identified only by a set of propositions.

This is what Manton refers to as the "mistake of the former age." Thomas Manton was a Puritan of the seventeenth century, and when he speaks of "the former age," he is not referring to apostate Romanism, but to the Reformers themselves. Hence he is a witness that they

*A person can be identified only by a set of propositions.*

56. Manton, 240.
57. Manton, 240.
58. In recent years both the Neo-orthodox and the pseudo-evangelicals have propounded the pious nonsense that the Greek word for faith (*pistis*) should be understood by its use for a Hebrew term and not in its Greek meaning. The Hebrew term or terms mean trust or faithfulness and not belief. James Barr, who can in no sense be thought favorable to what Manton calls "the mistake of the former age" *i.e.*, "the mistake" of the Protestant Reformers, in his superbly scholarly volume, *The Semantics of Biblical Language* (Oxford University Press, 1961), reduces the pseudo-evangelical view to unscholarly ruins.
59. Compare Geerhardus Vos, *The Self-Disclosure of Jesus.* George H. Doran, 1926.

FAITH AND SAVING FAITH

defined faith as an assent to the promise of the Gospel. By the same token, he wishes to introduce some other element into faith in addition to this act of will. What is it? He answers, "[T]here is not only *assent* in faith, but *consent*;[60] not only an assent to the truth of the word, but a consent to take Christ.... True believing is not an act of the understanding only, but a work of all the heart."

A careful study of these words, and of the complete context in Manton, plus a comparison with the Scripture, should conclude that Manton is confused. The first point is that the word *consent* receives no explanation. It makes a pleasant alliteration with *assent*, but literary style is no substitute for analysis. Is "consent" an act of will? Ordinary language would make it seem so; but if so, how is it different from assent? If "consent" is not voluntary, and if it cannot be an act of the understanding either, what sort of mental state is it? Then too, when he says that "true believing is not an act of the understanding only, but a work of all the heart," he is not accurately confronting "the former age." The former age never said that true believing, or false believing either, is an act of the understanding only. The former age and much of the later ages too specify assent in addition to understanding. They make this specification with the deliberate aim of not restricting belief to understanding alone. One can understand and lecture on the philosophy of Spinoza; but this does not mean that the lecturer assents to it. *Belief is the act of assenting to something understood. But understanding alone is not belief in what is understood.*

Manton himself acknowledges,

> I confess some expressions of scripture seem to lay much upon assent, as *1 John* iv.2 and v.1; *1 Corinthians* xii:3; *Matthew* xvi.17; but these places [Manton strangely says] do either show that assents, where they are serious, and upon full conviction, come from some special revelation; or else, if they propound them as evidences of grace, we must distinguish times....[61]

Now, *Matthew* 16:17 is not clearly a special revelation. It can well be, and more probably is, an illumination such as God gives to every believer. Nor is *1 Corinthians* 12:3 a special revelation: It refers to all men – it is a completely general statement – and cannot apply only to the few recipients of special revelation. Unless, therefore, one wishes to be very dogmatic about Peter in *Matthew*, all of these verses, in Manton's opinion, are to be set aside, are to be explained away, by "distinguishing the times." True enough, God administered the covenant in the Old Testament in a manner different from his administration of the New. Then too, but the differences are much less important, the apostolic age, and the following two centuries, faced difficulties that do not so directly trouble us now. But such historical differences are entirely irrelevant to the present discussion. Whether the propositions and promises of the Old Testament were more vague and less specific than those in the New, and whether the truths of the Gospel seemed more "con-

*Belief is the act of assenting to something understood. But understanding alone is not belief in what is understood.*

60. Perhaps the first systematic theologian to use this term was John of Damascus or Damascene: *fides est non inquisitus consensus; i.e.,* "faith is an unquestioned consent."

61. Manton, 240-241.

trary to the ordinary and received principles of reason" there than now (which is much to be doubted), all this is irrelevant because the mental act of believing is the same in every age and every place. Manton's account of faith is therefore confused, and it has led him to set aside some instructive New Testament material.

The crux of the difficulty with the popular analysis of faith into *notitia* (understanding), *assensus* (assent), and *fiducia* (trust), is that *fiducia* comes from the same root as *fides* (faith). The Latin *fide* is not a good synonym for the Greek *pisteuoo*. Hence this popular analysis reduces to the obviously absurd definition that faith consists of understanding, assent, and faith. Something better than this tautology must be found.

## 8. John Owen

If now Thomas Manton has deserved mention, all the more so does his greater contemporary, John Owen (1616-1683), who, among other things, wrote a four-thousand page commentary on *Hebrews*. Here his smaller four-hundred-fifty page book on *Justification by Faith* compels our attention.[62]

On page 70, Owen begins an examination of the nature of faith. But the reader must take care. The examination is introduced thus: "Of the nature of faith in general, of the especial nature of justifying faith, of its *characteristical* distinctions from that which is called faith but is not justifying...."[63]

No objection can be made to such an examination; but the student should take care to understand what the nature of faith is in general. Justifying faith is a species of faith, and if one does not know what faith in general is, one cannot know what the faith is that justifies. Does Owen keep this distinction clear?

Unfortunately, he does not make it sufficiently clear to us. In fact he says, "The distinctions that are usually made concerning faith...I shall wholly pretermit; not only as obvious and known, but as not belonging to our present argument."[64] Owen seems to have had an optimistic view of his generation. But even if these distinctions were as obvious and well known then as he says, they are not so today. But even "pretermitting" much, Owen cannot escape giving some indication of what the act of believing is.

His very next paragraph speaks of a non-justifying "historical faith." It is not because this faith has much to do with history that it is called historical. In addition to events of history, this faith believes the promises of the Gospel. "But it is so called from the *nature of the assent* [italics his] wherein it doth consist...."[65] Apparently, then, there are two kinds of assent. All faith is assent; but justifying faith is a different variety of assent. What this difference specifically is, Owen does not say. He indeed says the difference does not lie in the object of the faith, the proposition believed, but in the nature, or psychological characteristics of this particular type of assent. We would like to know what this different psychology is.

*Justifying faith is a species of faith, and if one does not know what faith in general is, one cannot know what the faith is that justifies.*

62. John Owen, *The Doctrine of Justification by Faith*. Volume V of *The Works of John Owen*. The Banner of Truth Trust [1965] 1981.
63. Owen, 71.
64. Owen, 71.
65. Owen, 72.

Owen is quite clear that "all faith is an assent upon testimony, and divine faith is an assent upon a divine testimony." Obviously divine testimony is different from human testimony; and, as the great Puritan said, the effects of some beliefs differ vastly from the effects of other beliefs. But differences in effects as well as in objects are irrelevant to the question whether there are species of believing. It is to be feared that some notion of "species of beliefs" has been confused with "species of believing." Nor is a reference to a temporary faith as opposed to a permanent faith any more relevant. In fact Berkhof, who follows Owen, adds that temporary faith may last all through one's life, that it is not necessarily hypocritical, and that it includes a stirring of the conscience. No wonder he remarks that "Great difficulty may be experienced in attempting to distinguish it from true saving faith."[66] This view also bears on the doctrine of assurance. Yet Owen says, "Justifying faith is not a higher, or the highest degree of this faith, but is of another kind or nature."[67] Yet all his evidence shows not a different type of believing, but a different object of belief. He refers to: (1) different causes; (2) different objects of a previous or preparatory belief; and (3) different objects of faith,[68] though he had previously ruled out objects as the difference.

> *Berkhof, who follows Owen, adds that temporary faith may last all through one's life, that it is not necessarily hypocritical.*

As Owen's account continues, the confusion grows worse. Not only does he misunderstand the Roman position, describing their faith as an assent that does not produce obedience; but also he is dissatisfied with "such a firm assent as produceth obedience unto all divine commands"[69]: dissatisfied because something further is necessary. For Owen, faith seems to have three main characteristics, the third of which has eight subdivisions.

> *As Owen's account continues, the confusion grows worse.*

The first of these three is assent to the truth: "all divine faith is in general an assent unto the truth that is proposed unto us upon divine testimony." The second point is rather a reassertion of the first. The only difference seems to be that the first refers to some limited number of truths a given individual happens to know, while the second includes "all divine revelation," or even "all divine truth," a phrase that includes divine truth that God has not revealed. Presumably Owen did not mean what he said. But even with the proper restriction, it is not likely that a new Christian, recently justified, understands and assents to every proposition in the Bible. After a lifetime of study a learned theologian could hardly know so much. But, one may say, even the new Christian assents to Biblical infallibility. Quite so, that is a single proposition. Does he then have implicit faith in all the other Biblical propositions? On the contrary, Evangelicalism excludes the Romish doctrine of implicit faith. Hence justification cannot depend on our assent to all revealed truth. Justifying faith must be an assent to some truths, not all. Even Owen himself, after having said "all divine revelation," restricts justifying faith to some truths only. But in addition to whatever, all or some, is believed, Owen insists that justifying faith must include certain *causes* and *adjuncts* beyond assent.

His third paragraph begins with an explicit denial that faith is an

66. Louis Berkhof, *Systematic Theology*, 502.
67. Owen, 72.
68. Owen, 80.
69. Owen, 81.

*48*

assent, "be it never so firm and steadfast, nor whatever effects of obedience it may produce."[70] Nor does it equally respect all divine revelation, but only some. Then follow eight points, mainly negative.

(1) Assent is not "an act of the understanding only." Owen's immediate refutation is hardly pertinent; but since no one ever held the point he opposes, for everyone adds something to simple understanding, one may take Owen's first subpoint merely as an attempt to be complete.

(2) Here Owen objects to the proposition that "*All divine truth* is equally the object of this assent."[71] If it were, so his refutation goes, the proposition that Judas was a traitor would as much effect our justification as that Christ died for our sins. Near the end of this monograph an attempt will be made to specify what proposition or propositions are essential to saving faith. Owen's adverb equally justifies his assertion, though he might have added (if it were his opinion) that the proposition about Judas can be a part of justifying faith.

(3) He next denies that "This assent unto all divine revelation may be true and sincere, where there hath been no previous work of the law, nor any conviction of sin."[72] Owen may well be correct in making this denial, even though the sudden conversion of Paul seems to conflict with it. But in any case and no matter how true, the paragraph contributes nothing to an analysis of the act of believing.

(4) Point four is very confused, and point (5) asserts, what is at best doubtful, that the devils in *James* assent to everything in the Bible. Point (6) asserts that hope and trust are not contained in a "mere" assent to the truth, "but they require other actings of the soul than what are peculiar unto the understanding only."[73] But is not Owen off the track? Of course hope and trust require the volition of assent as well as an understanding of the promise or hope.

Point (7) strays completely away from Scripture and depends entirely on introspective experience. Thus his objection to assent here is given solely on his own authority, rather than upon the authority of Scripture. It should be obvious by now that Owen has neither refuted the position that saving faith is a volitional assent to an intellectual proposition, nor presented any alternative analysis of its nature.

(8) Point 8, however, is indubitable because it is a puerile tautology. "That faith alone is justifying which hath justification actually accompanying of it.... To suppose a man to have justifying faith, and not to be justified, is to suppose a contradiction." Of course it is; but for that very reason it is a fallacy to conclude "Wherefore it is sufficiently evident that there is somewhat more required unto justifying faith than a real assent unto all divine revelations...."[74]

Owen continues for several difficult pages. He objects to identifying the object of faith with Christ's promise of forgiveness. Instead he maintains that Christ himself is the object of justifying faith. Although this sounds very pious, Owen and others might not have said this, if instead of the term *faith* they had used the Scriptural word *believe*. When we believe a man, we believe what he says. Nor does it help Owen's

*Owen has neither refuted the position that saving faith is a volitional assent to an intellectual proposition, nor presented any alternative analysis of its nature.*

70. Owen, 81.
71. Owen, 82.
72. Owen, 82.
73. Owen, 83.
74. Owen, 83.

*Belief must always have a proposition as its proper object, and therefore must be assent.*

view to insist on the Scriptural phrase, *believe in Christ*, as something essentially different from believing Christ. As we said before, believing-in a man may indicate a willingness to believe what he will say in the future as well as what he has said in the past. But belief must always have a proposition as its proper object, and therefore must be assent. Owen, let it be repeated for the sake of clarity, does not deny that assent must always somehow be included in faith. Speaking of the promises of forgiveness he says, "[I]t cannot be but that, in the actings of justifying faith, there is a peculiar assent unto them. Howbeit, this being only an act of the mind, neither the whole nature nor the whole work of faith can consist therein."[75] Now it may well be said that the work or results of faith are several, but such results, such as the preaching of the Gospel by an evangelist, are not justifying faith – they are works of righteousness, none of which justify; but if faith or believing itself is not an act of the mind, there remains no hope for finding it anywhere else. Dare we suggest that it is the work of the fingers, lungs, or stomach?

All the foregoing comes from Owen's chapter on the causes and object of justifying faith; and this may to a certain extent excuse the confusion. The following chapter is the nature of justifying faith; and it would seem better to have described what belief is before specifying the object of particular beliefs.

At the beginning he remarks that the faith he is discussing is a sincere faith. So be it. Assent is always sincere. No matter what a person believes, he believes it sincerely. A person does not always sincerely state what he believes. He may obscure or even deny his beliefs. But assent to a proposition is *ipso facto* sincere.

*Assent is always sincere. No matter what a person believes, he believes it sincerely.*

Owen then gives negative as well as positive examples.

> The unbelief of the Pharisees…is called the "rejecting of the counsel of God…."
>
> Most of those who rejected the gospel by their unbelief, did it under this notion, that the *way of salvation* and blessedness proposed therein was not a way answering divine goodness….[76]

Surely this quotation is a statement of truth; but it confutes much that Owen has said, for whereas the disciples assented to Christ's statements when they understood them, the Pharisees assented to or believed contradictory propositions. Therefore, one must reject what Owen says a few lines below, to wit, "unbelievers…may give an *assent* unto the truth of it [the Gospel], so far as it is a mere act of the mind." This is logical nonsense, psychological impossibility, and theological confusion. His only defense here, just a few lines below, is that he is no longer talking about sincere faith but only insincere faith.

However severe this criticism of Owen may seem, let not the student suppose that Owen is to be despised. He is one of the greatest Puritans, and we should be extremely happy if we could make as few mistakes as they did. Furthermore, for all the confusion on this point, Owen nonetheless seems to acknowledge that believing is voluntary assent to an understood proposition. Put aside questions as to the ob-

75. Owen, 86-87.
76. Owen, 94-95.

ject or objects believed, recognize that phrases not containing the words *voluntary* or *assent* may nonetheless have the same meaning, and realize that the act of belief is psychologically the same no matter what is believed, and it is hard to find a phrase descriptive of belief better than voluntary assent.

Thus in his great commentary on *Hebrews*, at chapter 11, verse 3, Owen says,

> "By faith we understand," that is, by faith we assent unto the divine revelation.... [W]e come not only to assent unto it as true, but to have a due comprehension of it [creation] in its cause, so as that we may be said to understand it.... Those who firmly assent unto divine revelation, do understand the creation of the world, as to its truth, its season, its cause, its manner, and end.

Perhaps Owen is too optimistic as to the extent of our understanding; but, again, faith or belief is a volitional assent to an understood proposition.

## 9. Charles Hodge

Charles Hodge, on all counts, is a theologian whose views must be considered. He is the soul and center of American Presbyterianism, properly so-called. His discussion of faith begins in Volume III, page 41, of his *Systematic Theology*, with the words, "The first conscious exercise of the renewed soul is faith.... [I]n the order of nature [the stages in which salvation advances] it must precede repentance." Though the first of these two sentences shows that Hodge is chiefly interested in saving faith, he must perforce say something about generic faith in order to produce any respectably comprehensive theory. The second sentence is doubtful. When such doubtful, vague, or puzzling statements appear, it is worth the time and trouble to analyze them. In this case the difficulty lies in the colloquial use of these terms. Presumably Hodge means that one must believe the Gospel (faith) and by so doing learn that repentance from sin is necessary. But etymologically *repentance* means a change of mind, not necessarily restricted to specifically moral matters. It can include a change of mind with reference to all theology, and that too beyond a simple understanding of the doctrines such as any infidel may easily achieve, so as to take in the belief that those understood doctrines are true. In this sense faith and repentance, both gifts of God, are the same thing. Hodge lacks clarity here because he separates faith from repentance by imposing unacceptable limits on both. Faith includes the moral precepts; and repentance, though not colloquially, surely includes the belief that Jesus is Lord. If they are separated, and if repentance is limited to sin and morality, it becomes a subdivision of faith; but if repentance has the broad meaning of any change of mind, faith is its subdivision. What then is the precise nature of faith?

"Faith...is assent to the truth."[77] Here and elsewhere in this section Hodge emphasizes trust as being the meaning of the Greek word.

*Etymologically, repentance means a change of mind, not necessarily restricted to specifically moral matters.*

77. Hodge, III, 42.

Some authors and many preachers contrast *trust* in a person with *belief* in a proposition. They often disparage "intellectual belief." They must then disparage all belief, since there is no other kind. But if trust and belief are different things, even if not antithetical things, how is trust defined? When a preacher does not tell his congregation what he means by his main terms, the people are confused, often without realizing it. But Hodge does better. He speaks most frequently of trusting that a statement is true, rather than trust in a person. In fact, on the same page he adds that faith is "that state of mind in which a man receives and relies upon a thing as true." He connects this with trust by saying, "To regard a thing as true, is to regard it as worthy of trust";[78] and so he does not divorce trust from truth, but continues with a quotation from Augustine, "To believe is nothing else than to think with assent." Some of his following pages seem inconsistently to modify this view, but, as we shall see, this is, all in all, Hodge's basic position.

Speaking more particularly of saving faith, but with explicit references to generic faith also, Hodge admirably rejects the flowery rhetoric of those platform theologians who call "faith a 'special organ for the eternal and holy.' It is not necessary [says Hodge] to assume a special organ for historical truths, a special organ for scientific truths, and another for the general truths of revelation, and still another for 'the eternal and holy.'"[79] Even "limiting it to a consciousness of reconciliation with God [as J. E. Erdmann did] is contrary to the usage of Scripture and of theology."[80] Inadequate also are those views which try to define faith as intermediate between opinion and knowledge. For example,

> Locke defines faith to be the assent of the mind to propositions which are probably, but not certainly true.... To believe is to admit a thing as true, according to Kant, upon grounds sufficient subjectively, insufficient objectively.... In all these cases the only difference between opinion, belief, and knowledge is their relative strength.[81]

Presumably Hodge means to reject any view that depends on relative strength, even if opinion and knowledge can be clearly defined.

A puzzling paragraph comes a little later, for on pages 51 and 52 Hodge describes several psychological variations of faith, concluding that faith is not always a voluntary assent, on the ground that sometimes people believe against their will, and in other instances wish they could believe, but cannot. These two cases supposedly show that belief is not within the power of the will. The argument is of course fallacious, for even if a person strongly dislikes a theory or doctrine, and reluctantly considers it carefully, perhaps with a view to refuting it, the evidence for it may prove overwhelming and with pain and regret he accepts it, against his previous will, but nevertheless voluntarily.

Under the heading "Definitions Founded on the Objects of Faith," there is likewise some confusion. Actually Hodge does not discuss the objects of faith, but reverts to the accompanying circumstances, in particular the distinction between faith and knowledge. If we believe a

*When a preacher does not tell his congregation what he means by his main terms, the people are confused, often without realizing it.*

78. Hodge, III, 43.
79. Hodge, III, 44.
80. Hodge, III, 45.
81. Hodge, III, 46-47.

certain proposition because someone informs us about it, we have faith; but if we prove it for ourselves, we have knowledge. Note that it is the same proposition in both instances. Faith is not distinguished from knowledge by its object, as the subhead promised, but by our method of learning it. "When he understands the demonstration of that proposition, his faith becomes knowledge."[82] A more consistent dependence on the object believed would result in a more consistent solution of the problem. But when Hodge, by making knowledge depend on demonstration, concludes that "faith means belief of things not seen, on the ground of testimony,"[83] a curious situation has arisen. Stated in other words, Hodge is saying that we believe the "thing" because we believe the testimony. This reduces to the position that "faith or belief is a belief by means of belief."

A few pages ago Hodge seemed to have rejected the notion that the distinction between faith, opinion, and knowledge was based on their relative "strength." But now the rejection is not so clear. Echoing some Thomistic sentiments, he explains that faith is not knowledge because we believe what we cannot prove. To quote: "Reason begins… with taking on trust what it neither comprehends nor proves…."[84] In one sense of the words this is utter nonsense. Reason or no reason, a person cannot take on trust what someone states in an incomprehensible foreign language. Hodge is not guilty of nonsense such as this. He means that we may believe a geometrical theorem without having deduced it ourselves. This is not nonsense: It is tautology. It merely means that we have not demonstrated what we have not demonstrated. His following sentence is, "Faith is a degree of certainty less than knowledge and stronger than probability."[85]

One must ask, By what thermometer are these degrees measured? Are the units centimeters or ounces? One must also ask, What is probability? The probability of shooting twelve with two dice is one over thirty-six. Then further, are there not students who, after demonstrating a theorem, are more certain of some teen-age superstition than of Euclid's reasoning? Much, nearly all, of Hodge's confusion arises from his empirical epistemology. "The ground of knowledge is sense or reason."[86] He thinks that science proves the truth of its laws, *demonstrates* them, with the result that the laws of physics are not tentative hypotheses but eternal truths. This was of course the commonly accepted Newtonian position of the nineteenth century; but the twentieth century has almost without exception rejected it. Einstein replaced Newton, and no one yet knows who will replace Einstein in the twenty-first century.[87]

Hodge holds that science depends on "sense and reason;" but if sense is unclear, reason is more so. This monograph is far from denying that "faith is founded on the testimony or authority of God."[88] But the axiom that the Bible is the Word of God does not justify Hodge's notion of what he calls knowledge. Whereas Hodge seems to limit *reason* to the deduction of physical laws from sensory observations, one might better define *reason* as the deduction of theology from Scrip-

*Much, nearly all, of Hodge's confusion arises from his empirical epistemology.*

82. Hodge, III, 54.
83. Hodge, III, 63.
84. Hodge, III, 62.
85. Hodge, III, 62.
86. Hodge, III, 75.
87. See my *Philosophy of Science and Belief in God.*
88. Hodge, III, 64.

ture; or, still better, simply the deduction of conclusions from premises. Antichristian scientists take advantage of Hodge's phraseology, even though few have ever heard of Hodge, and conclude that faith is unreasonable, irrational, and that we all should adopt "scientism" as the true philosophy. On the contrary, the present writer holds that it is *rational* to believe what God reveals. Hodge's seeming limitation of reason to physics is unfortunate. Nevertheless, Hodge agrees that "Faith is the reception of truth…the record which God has given of his Son,"[89] and he quotes *1 John* 5:10 in Greek.[90] Hodge adds, "Its [faith's] object is what God has revealed." Then below, on the same page, "faith is a reception of truth…."[91]

Unfortunately, the confusion as to kinds of faith soon reappears.[92] Of course, Jewish faith is not Islamic faith, nor is either of these Christian faith. One might also list political faith and a faith in AT&T stock. But this is not a difference in the definition of faith: It is a difference in the object or propositions believed. They are still all assents. Many theologians fall into this confusion.

*He obscures his good theology by setting it in a background of false philosophy, and this obscures the truth and confuses the reader.*

These criticisms do not mean that Hodge's theology is bad. On the contrary, it is very good. Every man makes mistakes, but in theology Hodge makes fewer and those less in importance than any other I have read. The criticism is that he obscures his good theology by setting it in a background of false philosophy, and this obscures the truth and confuses the reader. No doubt he would direct the same criticism against me, for he is very convinced of the Scottish Common Sense philosophy, which I regard as horrible.

However, he is not so irrational as my criticisms may have suggested. He probably had not heard of Kierkegaard, but he answers him clearly and bluntly:

*No one can deny the law of contradiction and defend Christianity.*

> The assumption that reason and faith are incompatible; that we must become irrational in order to become believers is, however it may be intended, the language of infidelity; for faith in the irrational is of necessity itself irrational. It is impossible to believe that to be true which the mind sees to be false. This would be to believe and disbelieve the same thing at the same time…. Faith is not a blind, irrational conviction. In order to believe, we must know what we believe, and the grounds upon which our faith rests.[93]

Here we have a perfectly clear assertion of the universal rule of logic. No one can deny the law of contradiction and defend Christianity. Later on, after one or two confusing sentences, Hodge says explicitly, "The cognition of the import of the proposition to be believed, is essential to faith; and consequently, that faith is limited by knowledge. We can believe only what we can know, *i.e.*, what we intelligently apprehend."[94]

This is an admirable statement, even though it obviously uses the term *knowledge* in a sense different from that which he previously used. It also becomes clouded over when he wonders "Whether faith is a purely intellectual exercise."[95] If by these words he meant to suggest

89. Hodge, III, 65.
90. See my *Commentary on 1 John*.
91. Hodge, III, 66.
92. Hodge, III, 67.
93. Hodge, III, 83.
94. Hodge, III, 84.
95. Hodge, III, 90.

that faith is a volitional as well as an intellectual activity, there could be no criticism; but when he explicitly mentions "affections," the introduction of an emotional element seems to be intended.[96] That emotions sometimes accompany volitional decisions cannot be denied; but this is far from insisting that an intellectual decision has emotion as a necessary ingredient. In connection with Romanism Hodge says,

> Regarding faith as a mere [pejorative language] intellectual or speculative act [though Thomas did not regard faith as a speculative or philosophical act], they consistently deny that it [faith] is necessarily connected with salvation. According to their doctrine a man may have true faith, *i.e.*, the faith which the Scriptures demand, and yet perish.[97]

To support this statement Hodge quotes the Council of Trent, Session VI, Canon 28. But the Canon says no such thing. It errs in the opposite direction, for it says that though grace (not as Protestants define it) be lost, faith remains and the person does not perish.

In contrast with Romanism, as Hodge understands it, he says, "Protestants with one voice maintain that the faith which is connected with salvation is not a mere intellectual exercise."[98] And he quotes Calvin, *fidei sedem non in cerebro esse, sed in corde* (*Commentary on Romans* 10:10). He also quotes the *Institutes* III, ii, 8, "the heart rather than the brains, and the affections rather than the intelligence." There are two or three difficulties in this section from Calvin. First, *cerebri*, brains, is the language of behaviorism and should never be thus used in the twentieth century. In the sixteenth century, however, it was a metaphorical term for the mind or intellect. Second, and more seriously, the Scriptures make no distinction between the head and the heart, as if mathematics came from the head and faith from the heart. The Old Testament frequently contrasts the heart and the lips – sincerity versus hypocrisy – but the term *heart*, at least seventy-five percent of the time in the Old Testament, means the mind or intellect.

## Interlude on the Head and the Heart

It may seriously deface the organization of this monograph, and it certainly interrupts the account of Charles Hodge, but because of its importance, including the fact that Calvin seems involved too, not to speak of hundreds of present day pastors, it seems essential to include an awkwardly lengthy interlude on the alleged contrast between the head and the heart – an interlude devoted to Biblical exegesis.[99]

The aim of citing the following Biblical data – an unusually extended list for such studies as this, but only a small fraction of the textual instances – is to show as clearly as possible what the term *heart* means. Were the misunderstanding less pervasive, were the pastors less Freudian and more Biblical, were the congregations less confused and misled, a much briefer list would have sufficed. Present ignorance, however, would justify even a more extensive documentation than that which now follows.

96. Not so in Jonathan Edwards' *Treatise Concerning Religious Affections*. Toward the end of Part I, Section I, he says, "The *will* and the *affections* of the soul are two faculties; the affections are not essentially distinct from the will, nor do they differ from the mere *actings* of the will." Similarly, Thomas Goodwin (1600-1679) in his *An Exposition of Ephesians*, at *Ephesians* 1:14 (Sovereign Grace Book Club, 1958, 259, bottom paragraph) states as an accepted fact that "You know the soul of man hath two great faculties…he hath an understanding, he hath a will and affections." Since the soul is said to have two functions, it is clear that affection and volition are synonymous.

97. Hodge, III, 89.

98. Hodge, III, 90.

99. Anyone who wishes to write or preach on Biblical psychology must, really must, read *The Bible Doctrine of Man* by John Laidlaw, second edition, T & T Clark, Edinburgh, 1895. The present paragraphs use, add to, and subtract from Laidlaw's superb study.

*Genesis* 6:5: The Lord saw…that every intent of the thoughts of his heart was only evil continually.

Here the heart is connected with thinking. Whatever emotions the sons of God may have had upon seeing the daughters of men, the verse refers to their thoughts – and not merely thoughts with regard to ungodly marriages, but with reference to their conduct in general. Their thoughts surely included thoughts on finances and most certainly thoughts on theology. They thought it useless to think of God.

*Genesis* 8:21: The intent [*King James:* imaginations] of man's heart is evil from his youth.

*This is not emotional, for the verse pictures a settled, lifelong philosophy. Emotions are sudden, transient upheavals.*

This verse, like the preceding, indicates theological thinking. The activity of intellection is clear. A second activity is also implied in both these verses: the word *intent* in the phrase "the intent of the heart" seems to indicate volition. The Hebrew word means both *concept* and *purpose*. Very obviously this is not emotional, for the verse pictures a settled, lifelong philosophy. Emotions are sudden, transient upheavals. Since men's conduct is governed by these lifelong principles, the term *heart* also indicates volition as well as intellection.

*Genesis* 17:17: Abraham fell on his face and laughed and said in his heart, Will a child be born to a man one hundred years old?

Perhaps Abraham felt some emotion of contempt at God's stupidity, but his heart raised an intellectual objection to God's promise. He said, because he thought in his heart, that a man of 100 cannot engender, nor can a woman of 90 give birth to a child. This is biological intellection; and it is sound thinking, except when God miraculously intervenes.

*Genesis* 20:6: Yes, I know that in the integrity of your heart you have done this.

No doubt Abimelech experienced sexual emotions upon seeing beautiful Sarah, but in this verse and in the preceding the heart is described as thinking that Sarah was Abraham's sister and not his wife. This was an intellectual judgment, and it is the judgment, not the emotion, that is assigned to the heart.

*Exodus* 4:21: I will harden his heart so that he will not let the people go.

Here the intellectual judgment is in the background. Of course, Pharaoh had judged or thought that the Israelite slaves were financially valuable to Egypt; but the point of this verse has to do with volition rather than with intellection. God would harden or strengthen Pharaoh's will to refuse Moses' demand. Perhaps fifteen or twenty percent of the Old Testament instances of the term *heart* refer to volition rather than to intellection. Naturally, as we shall see, volition always depends on a prior intellection. Very few instances of the term *heart* refer distinctly to emotions. *Exodus* 7:3 says the same thing.

*Exodus* 35:5: Whoever is of a willing heart, let him bring...[a] contribution: gold, silver, bronze.

The Hebrew term for *willing* can be translated *voluntary* or *magnanimous*. The term *heart*, therefore, stands for volition and not emotion.

*Deuteronomy* 4:9: Keep your soul diligently, lest you forget the things which your eyes have seen, and lest they [the things] depart from your heart all the days of your life.

Here the heart is described as the repository of historical information, which information includes the Ten Commandments and the subsidiary laws. No doubt Moses here commands voluntary obedience, but the contents of the heart are propositions concerning historical events. The heart knows. There is nothing emotional here.

*1 Samuel* 2:1: My heart exults in the Lord.

It is true that sometimes the term *heart* refers to emotions. Here, rather clearly, Hannah is emotional. Of course she is also theological, especially if we hold that she prefigures the virgin Mary's *Magnificat*. Nevertheless, Hannah and Mary both spoke emotionally. In about ten percent of the Old Testament instances of the word *heart* emotions are definitely indicated.

*1 Samuel* 2:35: I will raise up for myself a faithful priest who will do according to what is in my heart and in my soul [*King James:* mind].

The terms *heart* and *soul* here are presumably synonyms, as in the New Testament "heart, soul, strength, and mind" are synonyms for the purpose of inclusiveness. Here *soul* (Hebrew *nephesh*) does not mean what it means in *Genesis* 2:7, where God formed man of the dust of the ground, breathed into him the breath or spirit of life, and man became a living soul. In *Genesis* and generally in the Old Testament, *soul* is a composite or compound of clay and spirit, incarnate man. This is not true in *1 Samuel* 2:35, for God is not a compound of earth and spirit. "What is in my heart and in my soul" refers to God's plans for the future. They cannot be emotions because the immutable God is impassible and no more has emotional ups and downs than he has arms and eyes.

*2 Samuel* 7:3: Go, do all that is in your mind [*King James:* thine heart], for the Lord is with you.

The *King James* is the accurate translation; the *New American Standard* is the correct interpretation. David had plans for building a temple. God, as we know, cancelled these plans, but nonetheless the contents of David's heart were architectural propositions.

*Psalm* 4:4: Meditate in your heart upon your bed and be still.

Here intellection is commanded and emotions are explicitly forbidden. Meditation is a strictly intellectual activity. It requires quiet and stillness. Emotion hinders, distorts, or almost eradicates thinking.

*The contents of the heart are propositions concerning historical events.*

*The immutable God is impassible and no more has emotional ups and downs than he has arms and eyes.*

Acting under the stress of emotion we usually act blindly. An emotionally overwrought student, having had a spat with his sweetheart, can't memorize the Greek irregular verbs or solve a problem in physics. Nor can he do theology. We must meditate and be still. This command displeases pragmatic Americans.

*Meditation is a strictly intellectual activity. It requires quiet and stillness. Emotion hinders, distorts, or almost eradicates thinking.*

> *Psalm* 7:10: Who saves the upright in heart.

The context rather clearly specifies righteous conduct; that is, the *heart* here chiefly refers to volition. Unhypocritical assent to God's commands is presupposed as a background.

> *Psalm* 12:2: They speak falsehoods to one another; with flattering lips and with a double heart they speak.

Obviously this is an intellectual activity. The heart, that is, the intellect, has devised false statements for the purpose of flattering. To utilize deceit requires at least a modicum of intelligence. Also note the contrast between the lips and at least one heart, the heart that knows its purpose and recognizes the falsehoods.

> *Psalm* 14:1: The fool has said in his heart, There is no God.

The man may be a fool for thinking so, but nonetheless he thinks in his heart – it is the heart that thinks. The context which follows speaks of corrupt and abominable deeds, but these have their origin in the heart that thinks.

> *Psalm* 15:2: He who…speaks truth in his heart.

*He thinks in his heart – it is the heart that thinks.*

Unlike the fool of *Psalm* 14, the man here thinks and speaks the truth. The remainder of the *Psalm* describes some of his actions, none of which is emotional. He speaks to himself in his heart and what he says is the truth. The term *heart* obviously means the mind or intellect.

> *Isaiah* 6:10: Make the heart of this people dull…and their eyes dim…lest they see with their eyes…understand with their heart, and repent and be healed.

Explicitly the heart is here described as the organ of understanding. Repentance, mentioned in the final phrase, is a change of mind. How can so many preachers who claim to be Biblical have missed so much in the Old Testament? They speak with devout fervor, but their message owes more to Freud than to the Scriptures. Also note parenthetically that the eyes mentioned here are not the two orbs in the front of the face. It is not sensation that is alluded to; the *seeing* is also an intellectual *seeing*, as when one "sees" the solution of a problem.

> *Isaiah* 10:7: [God uses Assyria for his own purpose] Yet it does not so intend, nor does it plan so in its heart.

The General Staff of the Assyrian Army works out military plans in its heart. It is unaware that God is using them for his purpose. Nevertheless, they do the planning and thinking in their hearts. This takes intelligence. The heart therefore is the mind or intellect.

*Isaiah* 33:18: Your heart will meditate on terror.

Not only is meditation referred to the heart, but the context specifies counting and weighing. This heart will no longer be baffled by "unintelligible speech which no one comprehends or a stammering tongue which no one understands." Presumably the converse, comprehension and understanding, will be the case. This is what the heart does.

> *Isaiah* 44:18-19: They do not know nor do they understand, for he has smeared over their eyes so that they cannot see and their hearts so that they cannot comprehend…. Nor is there knowledge or understanding.

Note again that the eyes and the seeing have nothing to do with literal sensation, but with comprehension. The Scriptural evidence that the term *heart* means the mind, the intellect, the understanding, is becoming tedious in length. But the emotional error is so widespread that it ought to be buried under a thousand verses. We shall, however, add only another half dozen to the Old Testament list.

> *Jeremiah* 3:17: Nor shall they walk any more after the stubbornness of their evil heart.
> *Jeremiah* 5:23-24: A stubborn and rebellious heart…they do not say in their heart, Let us now fear the Lord our God.
> *Jeremiah* 9:26: Uncircumcised of heart.
> *Jeremiah* 23:16: They speak a vision [revelation] of their own heart.

The last of these references envisages the mind or understanding. The others seem to refer more directly to the will or volition. Yet there can be no volition without a prior intellection.

> *Zechariah* 7:10: Do not devise evil in your hearts.

*Jeremiah* 3:17 more directly indicated the volition, with the understanding presupposed. This verse indicates the intellect, with later volition implied.

Now, just in case some enthusiastic evangelist should say that the emotional New Testament contradicts and supersedes the intellectual Old Testament, we shall supply another tedious list.

> *Matthew* 5:8: Blessed are the pure in heart.
> *Matthew* 5:28: …has committed adultery with her already in his heart.

If these two verses do not clearly refer to intellection or comprehension, they at least and clearly enough refer to volition. Even if adultery includes emotions, as it does, the emphasis here is on the decision or volition.

> *Matthew* 6:21: Where your treasure is, there will your heart be also.

Depositing one's treasure in a safe place requires first a judgment of evaluation and then a volition that places the treasure there. Depositing one's paycheck in a bank is not usually an emotional affair.

*The Scriptural evidence that the term* heart *means the mind, the intellect, the understanding, is becoming tedious in length.*

*Matthew* 9:4: Why are you thinking evil in your hearts?

The men whom Jesus here castigates had been guilty of drawing some invalid inferences. Their inferences were indeed fallacious, or at least based on a false premise; but their activity was nonetheless ratiocination.

*Matthew* 11:29: I am meek and lowly of heart.

In this situation emotion is completely ruled out. Meekness and lowliness do not comport with emotional outbreaks. The mind must be calm.

> *Matthew* 12:34, 40: Out of the abundance of the heart the mouth speaks...for as Jonah was three days and three nights...so shall the Son of Man be in the heart of the Earth.

Verse 40 is quoted here to show how the term *heart* can be used metaphorically, and also because the list is to contain every instance of Matthew's use of the word. This assumes that the term is missing from verse 35. It is verse 34 that advances the argument. When a man thinks, meditates, ponders, and arrives at well-thought-out ideas, he speaks them. He speaks with his mouth, but the organ of thinking is the heart.

> *Matthew* 13:15, 19: This people's heart is waxed gross [*New American Standard*: has become dull]...lest they should understand with their heart....When anyone hears the word of the kingdom and does not understand it, the evil one comes and snatches away what has been sown in his heart.

*(margin note:)* Could it be any more clearly expressed that understanding is the function of the heart?

Could it be any more clearly expressed that understanding is the function of the heart? Someone hears the Gospel for the first time and does not understand it. The words remain in the mind for a time; but since he does not understand, the evil one easily erases even the words.

> *Matthew* 15:8, 18, 19: This people...honors me with their lips, but their heart is far from me....Those things which proceed out of the mouth come forth from the heart...for out of the heart come evil thoughts, murders....

The contrast of verse 18 is that between the heart and the lips. It is not the now popular contrast between the head and the heart. The people in question are hypocrites. After a short conversation with his disciples, Jesus, speaking more generally, teaches that what a man says originates in his heart. This is true even of the hypocrite, for he has already thought in his heart that it would be best to say what he does not believe. Thus, though he speaks well, he plans murder in his heart. Emotions do not plan murder.

> *Matthew* 18:35: If you from your hearts forgive not....

Jesus here contrasts, at least by implication, an insincere forgiveness with a sincere forgiveness. One might speak words of forgiveness, yet harbor deep resentment. To *forgive from the heart* indicates a forgiveness that is one's basic intent and thought: The words correctly represent the mind. The heart is the mind.

> *Matthew* 22:37: You shall love the Lord your God with all your heart, and with all your soul, and with all your mind.

This is not a metaphysical trichotomous theory of human personality. The three terms are synonymous, joined together for emphasis. They do not separate the heart and the mind: They identify them.

> *Matthew* 24:48: If that evil slave says in his heart....

Here the slave, having concluded that his master will not return for a long time, hatches a plan to defraud the inferior slaves. He hatches this plan in his heart. He has thought out all or most of the details. The function of the heart is to think and plan. The heart is the intellect.

This has been, I believe, a complete list of every instance of the term *heart* in Matthew's *Gospel*. Confused Calvinists should now adjust the thoughts of their hearts to conform with Scripture, even if Arminians find it impossible to do so.

But wait. It may resemble continuing blows on one who is already knocked out on the canvas, but some later books of the New Testament must be mentioned.

The *Book of Acts* contains about twenty instances of the word *heart*. The first occurrence is in 2:26 and can very plausibly refer to the emotions. It is quite true that the term *heart* in a few instances refers to the emotions. In the same chapter, verse 37, "Pierced to the heart," or "smitten in conscience," may include a tinge of emotion, and verse 46, "gladness and sincerity of heart" may have an emotional overtone.

*Acts* 4:32 concerns a judgment on economic policy that eventually became a disappointment; while *Acts* 5:3-4 refer to the heart of Ananias as having planned to lie to the Holy Ghost. It was deliberate economic planning, an activity of the mind, without a trace of emotion. In *Acts* 7:23 Moses, when forty years of age, decided – "it entered his heart" – to inspect the condition of the Jews in Egyptian slavery. This was a considered political step that turned out otherwise than Moses had planned. Verses 39 and 51 also refer to political planning, with a religious decision involved in the latter verse. *Acts* 8:21-22 as well refer to personal gain or prestige; no emotional element is obvious. *Acts* 8:37, even if spurious, is still Greek, and it identifies the function of the heart as believing that Jesus Christ is the Son of God. This is a theological judgment. There are eight additional instances of the term *heart* in *Acts*, and the reader is encouraged to look them up.

*Romans* seems to have fifteen instances of the term. In *Romans* 1:21 the heart is connected with a false theology, and three verses later this results in immorality. The immorality included sexual emotions, but it also included idolatry and the worship of animals. This is theology too. *Romans* 2:5 refers to an unrepentant heart, more theological than emotional; *Romans* 2:15, as I see it, asserts certain *apriori* principles derived

*The three terms – heart, soul, and mind – are synonymous, joined together for emphasis. They do not separate the heart and the mind: They identify them.*

from the creation of Adam. This is the structure of the human mind. The last verse of the chapter contrasts purely external conformity to religious tradition with the sincere theology of a regenerate Israelite. There is an intellectual difference.

Some people may want to see emotions in *Romans* 5:5. It would be hard to prove. *Romans* 6:17, speaking of obedience, uses the term *heart* for volition. *Romans* 8:27 is another instance. If "unceasing grief" is indeed an emotion, then 9:2 uses the word in this sense. But I cannot see that "my heart's desire and prayer" in 10:1 is an emotion. It is rather a fixed determination. The instances in 10:6, 8, 9, 10 are indisputably intellectual, or volitional in the assent of verses 9 and 10. The final reference in *Romans* is 16:18 in which the subject is intellectual deception.

*First Corinthians* has five references: 2:9; 4:5; 7:37 twice; and 14:25. The first of these refers to theological doctrines underivable in empirical philosophy, but received, understood, and believed through revelation. Note the emphasis on mind (Greek *nous*) at the end of the chapter. *First Corinthians* 4:5 has nothing to do with emotion. Chapter 7:37 refers to a principle of parental control; and 14:25 concerns a knowledge of one's previous conduct, now recognized as sinful.

If any reader finds this list tedious, let him consider how tedious it is for the present author to check it out and write it down. The term *heart* occurs about 160 times in the New Testament. The instances now given, both from Old and New, conclusively show that the basic meaning of the word is mind or intellect. Volition, usually the assent to intellectually understood propositions, is also a meaning, and emotion is rarely the point of the passage. Suppose we agree not to complete the enumeration, but just stop right here.

Before the intrusion of this material on the head and the heart, the argument had begun with "two or three difficulties in this section from Calvin": First, the unfortunate behavioristic overtones of some of Calvin's language; second, the defective grasp of Biblical psychology in many writers; and now we proceed to the third point. The context in Calvin from which the unfortunate language was quoted insists that "it is an absurdity to say that faith is formed by the addition of a pious affection to an assent of the mind; whereas even this assent is a pious affection." Calvin uses the term *affection* to denote a voluntary intellectual assent. Not all assents are pious. Not only may one assent, unknowingly, to a falsehood; but also an assent to a proposition of geometry is not a "pious" assent. Here Hodge with many others confuses the nature of the assent with the propositions assented to.

The effect, indeed the unwitting acknowledgment, of this type of confusion comes on the next page.

> That saving faith is not a mere speculative assent of the understanding, is the uniform doctrine of the Protestant symbols. On this point, however, it may be remarked, in the first place, that...the Scriptures do

*The term* heart *occurs about 160 times in the New Testament.... [T]he basic meaning of the word is mind or intellect. Volition, usually the assent to intellectually understood propositions, is also a meaning, and emotion is rarely the point of the passage.*

not make the sharp distinction between the understanding, the feelings, and the will, which is common in our day.[100]

Is this not an acknowledgment that Hodge and others have imposed a foreign psychology on the Scripture? Hodge continues, "A large class of our inward acts and states are so complex as to be acts of the whole soul, and not exclusively of any one of its faculties." Here again the distinctions are assigned in the wrong direction. Faculty psychology, largely abandoned now, invented parts or faculties of the soul for various acts, while the Scripture, as I understand it, has the unitary soul or mind acting on various objects. For example, conscience is not a faculty of the soul for morality and intellect a separate faculty for geometry. Rather, the distinction is that in the first case the mind studies matters of morality, while in the second the same unitary mind studies geometry. This view is consonant with the idea that faith in pickles and faith in God are psychologically identical; the difference lies in the object. If, further, the older term *affection* (which in Greek used to mean something like being hit with a hammer) means what we today call *emotion*, it must be described as a sudden disturbance in the mind's normal intelligence. Most sins, perhaps not all, occur because an emotion has disturbed the mind's rationality. That is why the New Testament so often condemns desire or lust.

Hodge's account of faith, though deformed by his empirical philosophy, is nonetheless correct in the main. The same page continues,

> If we take that element of faith which is common to every act of believing; if we understand by it the apprehension of a thing as true and worthy of confidence…then it may be said that faith in its essential nature is intellectual or intelligent assent.

Granted, Hodge does not finish his paragraph consistently, but his final words, if we take the term *heart* in its Scriptural sense, are good: "the faith which is required for salvation is an act of the whole soul, of the understanding, of the heart, and of the will."[101] All that remains to be done is to clarify the relation between the understanding and the will, which together are actions of the heart or mind.

## 10. B. B. Warfield

The great Princeton theologian Warfield[102] begins his chapter on faith with a study of the Hebrew word we may transliterate into the English *amen*, which the verb *believe* in the *King James* uniformly represents. Yet he says that *believe* is a weaker and dilute meaning of the Hebrew verb. The stronger meanings denote *fixedness, steadfastness*, and *reliability*. Just why *fixedness* is strong and *believe* is weak, Warfield does not explain. The Hiphil form of the verb, with one exception, means "'to trust,' weakening down to the simple 'to believe.'" With the prefix *beth*, "It is probably never safe to represent the phrase by the simple 'believe.'"[103] Warfield, without denying that the object of this verb

*Conscience is not a faculty of the soul for morality and intellect a separate faculty for geometry.… Most sins, perhaps not all, occur because an emotion has disturbed the mind's rationality. That is why the New Testament so often condemns desire or lust.*

100. Hodge, III, 91.
101. Hodge, III, 91.
102. "The Biblical Doctrine of Faith" in *Biblical Doctrine*. Oxford University Press, 1929, 467-508.
103. Warfield, 468.

can be a theological proposition, stresses a personal object more than Hodge did. He repeats the unfortunate pejorative claim that "This faith...is obviously no mere assent."[104] Yet to do him justice one must note also that "The thing believed is sometimes a specific word or work of God...the fact of a divine revelation...or the words or commandments of God in general," as well as "God's prophets" and "God himself." He rather stresses the latter, for he continues: "The object of Abram's faith...was not the promise...what it [Abram's faith] rested on was God himself....To believe in God, in the Old Testament sense, is thus not merely [pejorative] to assent to His word, but...to rest...upon Him."[105]

Warfield then tries to preserve this alleged Hebrew meaning for the Greek *pisteuoo* (*believe*) by connecting the latter to the former through the usage of the *Septuagint*. This background in the *Septuagint* was necessary because "it [*pisteuoo*] had the slightest possible connection with religious faith in classical speech."[106] Here again is the confusion of meaning with the object. Had *pisteuoo* in classical Greek a strong religious connotation, its meaning might have been too much colored by pagan superstitions. But without such pagan connotations its common usage can be taken over in the New Testament. Indeed, Warfield's attempt to justify his view by an appeal to Xenophon's *Memorabilia* undermines rather than establishes his position. If the Greek *pisteuein* was so far removed from the Old Testament *amen*, how was it that the Seventy chose it as the best translation?

Similarly, his argument based on Philo's use of *pistis* (*faith*) is vitiated by the same confusion. Philo's *faith* may have been naturalistic, not even synergistic, while New Testament faith is a gift of God's grace; but these differences are irrelevant. We are not here concerned with the cause of faith, nor with the different objects of faith, but with the nature of faith. Whether Zeus or Jehovah, whether botany or astronomy or mathematics be the object, the question is, Is faith an *assent*? Note too that any pagan influence that Philo might have absorbed – less than many people think – could not have affected the Seventy, who came about two hundred years earlier.

But for all Warfield's aversion from assent, he clearly admits that "When construed with the dative, *pisteuein* in the New Testament prevailingly expresses believing assent, though ordinarily in a somewhat pregnant sense," whatever this last phrase may mean. "When its object is a thing, it is usually the spoken...or written...word of God."[107] With respect to *pisteuein* and the accusative he says, "With these weaker [why weaker?] constructions must be ranged also the passages, twenty in all..., in which what is believed is joined to the verb by the conjunction *oti*."

A "deeper sense of the word" is indicated when the verb is followed by prepositions, even though the preposition in *Mark* 1:15 governs the "gospel."[108] There are of course many instances when the grammatical object is a person. The exegesis of these passages has already been hinted at and will be further discussed later.

*Warfield, without denying that the object of this verb can be a theological proposition, stresses a personal object more than Hodge did.*

104. Warfield, 470.
105. Warfield, 471.
106. Warfield, 472.
107. Warfield, 475.

When Warfield takes up "The Historical Presentation of Faith," he acknowledges that "the first recorded acts after the Fall – the naming of Eve, and the birth and naming of Cain – are expressive of trust in God's promise."[109] In the following sentence he speaks of Noah's "trust in God and His promises." At least twice on page 486 he describes the patriarchal religion as a "religion of promise." It is impossible for any honest student of the Old Testament to avoid the idea of promise, and this requires the object of faith to be a proposition. Continuing his historical survey Warfield writes, "The law-giving was not a setting aside of the religion of promise."[110]

It is necessary to remind the reader that these criticisms of Warfield and other Calvinistic theologians with reference to the nature of faith as assent do not derogate from the excellence of their exposition of Biblical faith as soteric, as an endowment from God, and whatever force and value the Scriptures assign to it. The point of the criticism is that these spiritual qualities belong to an act of assent, rather than to a very vague something else. This confusion mars Warfield's otherwise fine discussion of faith in *James*.[111] Contrary to what he says, James did not "rebuke the Jewish tendency to conceive faith…as a mere [the pejorative word again] intellectual acquiescence." In addition to Warfield's pointing out that James wrote, "If a man says he have faith, can the [that sort of] faith save him?" one must note that their "intellectual acquiescence" had a different object; and it was the difference in object, not the similarity in intellectual assent, that deprived their faith of soteric efficacy. Warfield also falls into the error of supposing that *Hebrews* 11:1 is the definition of faith,[112] while the remainder of the chapter is a description. It is all a description. And it is incredible that he says, "Least of all the New Testament writers could John confine faith to a merely [!] intellectual act: his whole doctrine is rather a protest against the intellectualism of Gnosticism."[113] Warfield seems to suppose that if John combatted the intellectualism of the Gnostics, he had to oppose all intellectualism.[114]

In his final section on "The Biblical Conception of Faith," Warfield again takes *Hebrews* 11:1 as "almost [!] a formal definition…it consists neither in assent nor in obedience."[115] But try as he may to make God rather than a proposition the object of faith, he must include a belief in "the forgiveness of sins…the revelations of this grace, and the provisions of this mercy."[116] These terms indicate certain propositions to be believed, accepted as true, given our assent.

> Such a faith, again, could not fail to embrace with humble confidence all the gracious promises [!] of the God of salvation…nor could it fail to lay hold with strong conviction [though one man said, "Lord, I believe, help my unbelief"] on all [does anyone know them all?] those revealed truths ….[117]

Nonetheless, a few lines farther down the page he denies that faith terminates on the promise, namely, those "propositions which declare God's grace and willingness to save."

*It is impossible for any honest student of the Old Testament to avoid the idea of promise, and this requires the object of faith to be a proposition.*

108. Warfield, 476.
109. Warfield, 485.
110. Warfield, 486.
111. Warfield, 495.
112. Warfield, 498.
113. Warfield, 500.
114. As for John's intellectualism, see *The Johannine Logos* and my commentary on *1 John*. These two and the one on *Colossians* also present a view of the relationship between Christianity and Gnosticism rather different from the view popular in Warfield's day.
115. Warfield, 501.
116. Warfield, 502.
117. Warfield, 503.

## 11. Minor Men: John Anderson and J. H. Bavinck

During the lifetime of Charles Hodge, John Anderson wrote a good book on *Saving Faith*. [118] A short summary will be sufficient to outline his views. "He who is the object of our faith is called Christ." [119] There follow several pages on the offices of Christ. Coming to the object of faith he asks,

> Whether such principles as the being of God, the immortality of the soul, a future state of rewards and punishments, as they are known by human reason in its present corrupt state, are to be considered as objects of faith?

And he answers,

> It is absurd to call such truths…objects or matters of faith, while they are known and considered no otherwise than as matters of reason. [120]

Note the phrase, "as they are known by human reason in its present corrupt state." This phrase prevents the passage from being pertinent to the question of this study. It even seems as if Dr. Anderson thinks it possible to prove the truth of these propositions by "human reason" (never defined) apart from revelation. For example, he speaks of "These truths, not as matters of faith, but as dictates of reason…and whoever is an enemy [of these "rational" truths] must be much more an enemy of the latter [truths of revelation]." [121] Of course this is false, as anyone with a knowledge of Aquinas, or of non-Thomistic presuppositionalists, recognizes.

More to the point for the present study, Anderson acknowledges that "The whole word of God is indeed the object of faith… [though] in the word, which is its general object, it seeks a special object." [122]

In Discourse II Anderson examines "the ACT of believing in the name of Jesus Christ, abstracted from such things as accompany or follow it." [123] This faith is not "a resolved subjection to, or compliance with, what they call the precepts of the gospel." [124]

> The following [is the] definition of saving faith: "that it is a real or unfeigned persuasion, wrought in my heart by the Holy Ghost, that, in the gospel record,… God gives his Son Jesus Christ, with his whole salvation, to sinners of mankind indefinitely, and to me a sinner in particular." [125]

How much of the record one must believe, he does not say; and unless *I* know what to believe, how can I know that anything applies to *me*? On the following page he seems to include the knowledge of "the all-sufficiency of his Son Jesus to accomplish our salvation." Since this requires several pages to explain, including 20-25 Scripture verses, from the Old Testament as well as from the New, the object to be believed seems to be a somewhat extensive theology. Indeed, Scriptural exposition continues for pages, and there is no clear indication of how much is essential to saving faith. In this exposition, too, the *act* of faith, though it was the chapter heading, seems to have been forgotten.

*"The whole word of God is indeed the object of faith…"*
*— John Anderson*

118. United Presbyterian Board of Publication. Fifth edition, 1875.
119. Anderson, 18.
120. Anderson, 31.
121. Anderson, 22-23.
122. Anderson, 38.
123. Anderson, 46.
124. Anderson, 50.
125. Anderson, 54.

But he returns to it on page 82.

He states,

> To consider the ACT of saving faith…we must observe that it is a persuasion wrought in our hearts by the supernatural operation of the Holy Spirit.… Secondly, we observe that it is a SURE persuasion…it must carry in it real assurance.[126]

Though this contradicts the *Westminster Confession*, he continues saying that "true and saving faith evidences assurance to be its nature."[127] It is "a belief of the gospel record."[128] It includes "all the purposes of justification and salvation." Then later he adds,

> There is an appropriation in nature of saving faith, from its correspondence with the record of God concerning his Son Jesus Christ.[129]
>
> Faith is further distinguished…by its hearty approbation of…the whole device of salvation through Christ crucified, as well ordered in all things and sure.[130]

This surely takes in a great amount of theology.

Anderson frequently mentions belief in the promise. A promise, and the particular promise he mentions of a son to Abram, is a proposition; but he does not specify any particular promise to us, speaking only generally of "the word of the gospel."[131] "The appropriation …arises from the matter believed, or from the records that God hath given us.…"[132] "Strong faith…is that which proceeds most singly upon the ground of God's word of promise."[133] This is in general true, and in the main Anderson seems to hold that the object of faith is propositional.

Johan H. Bavinck, another minor writer, is the author of a book whose title is *Faith and Its Difficulties*.[134] It may not be his best work, but its title brings it within the scope of this investigation.

A man's publications must in some way reveal what we may call his psychological constitution. Bavinck's is evident on his first page: "One is possessed with a feeling of awe when one begins to talk about God." Perhaps this ought to be so. Trying to imagine what that omnipotence is which could create *ex nihilo* the galaxies astronomy talks about, should discourage us from trying to imagine. But Bavinck's anxiety before God seems to stem from a less justifiable anxiety before his human friends:

> Even when I talk with a friend about my fellow man, who has the same peculiarities and weaknesses that I have, I realize that at any moment I run the danger of doing him an injustice…that I will attribute ulterior motives, while in reality there are none.

Though this is a danger in published works – I have misrepresented D'Arcy by summarizing only a part of his book – and while the attribution of ulterior motives to others than authors is possible, it occurs in only a small, a very small proportion of conversations, and is certainly not an important factor to govern a study of faith. But Bavinck is so gripped by anxiety that he denies what many Reformed theolo-

*Trying to imagine what that omnipotence is which could create* ex nihilo *the galaxies astronomy talks about, should discourage us from trying to imagine.*

126. Anderson, 83.
127. Anderson, 84.
128. Anderson, 86.
129. Anderson, 121.
130. Anderson, 129.
131. Anderson, 137.
132. Anderson, 146.
133. Anderson, 146.
134. Wm. B. Eerdmans Company, 1959.

gians assert, namely, that we can think God's thoughts after him. After denying this he adds, "I am convinced that no language has the word power adequately to express the ineffable majesty of His Being. We wish to speak about the unknown God."[135]

Since language is a gift from God with the purpose of enabling us to speak about him and to him, and since the Bible contradicts the idea of God's being unknown or "totally other," Bavinck's theory of language should be viewed with suspicion. Of course no one denies that we are ignorant of what God has not chosen to reveal. The well-known verse in *Deuteronomy* (29:29) is explicit and in thinking it we think that thought of God after him. Further, if God is unknown, there is no good reason for writing a book on faith. Even if we often misunderstand, yet we must sometimes get the truth, for that is why God gave us a book that is profitable for (true) doctrine, for reproof, and instruction in righteousness. Even when Bavinck acknowledges that "This does not mean that there is no way by which we may learn to know him," he adds that for many people of our generation "He is nothing else but the UNKNOWN." Granted, he does not use the term *unknowable* in this sentence; but he has capitalized UNKNOWN, and this after saying that language is (inherently) inadequate.

Bavinck, of course, wants to make this unknown God somewhat knowable.

> Nature's overwhelming greatness [leads man] irresistibly...forced to confess that there must be SOMETHING, [though] Nature in itself is an unfathomable riddle.... That God of nature is for us the Unknown God.

Then "guidance and direction" occurs to us on our "good days and bad days...and in all these things the great Ruler of our lives speaks to us." He is now seen as "the Regent of our life." Finally "we meet God...in Jesus Christ." Then apparently by faith we merge the SOME-THING, the Regent, and Christ into one. But still "we shudder at the appalling unknownness of God." Bavinck speaks of being "oppressed with fear and anguish," and he "shudders." Several times he uses the phrase "the mysterious Other."

Can such a disturbed mentality give us a clear concept of faith?

Of course, Bavinck believes that this Unknown Something has spoken in Jesus Christ. But if language is inadequate, do Christ's words give us any knowledge? Are Christ's words only unintelligible pointers to Something that soothes our disturbing emotions? Bavinck indeed says that "God revealed his eternal and holy will of salvation through the Cross of Christ."[136] But is the Cross a symbol, a myth, or inexplicable fact? Or did God through Matthew, Paul, and John give an intelligible explanation of the significance of Christ's death? And do we, when we read words, obtain knowledge thereby? Bavinck presumably believes that Christ's death was a vicarious and propitiatory sacrifice, but these pages do not show how his presuppositions justify the possibility of such information.

*If language is inadequate, do Christ's words give us any knowledge?*

135. Bavinck, 9.

A few pages later he gives other criteria of faith: "If the palace of Caiaphas would have collapsed in the night of Jesus' condemnation, or if Pilate had been struck dead in the midst of the hearing – faith would not be faith anymore.... Everyone would be forced to bend and give in. The facts would force us, against our wills, to agree with God."[137] This is unsatisfactory for several reasons. First, there is still no definition of faith. Second, in Old Testament times there were events as spectacular as the collapse of Caiaphas' palace would have been, and it was not true that "faith would not be faith any more." Third, Jesus said that even if some people would return from Hell and tell their brothers of the penalties beyond the grave, they would not "be forced against [their] wills to agree with God." An author should not allow fervent devotion or literary charm to hide the truth. On the next page, Bavinck describes a mustard seed as something "infinitesimally small," which visibly it isn't. Now, no doubt some readers will consider such objections as nit-picking. Yet it is not an infinitesimally small point: It is symptomatic of carelessness. If, however, I seem severe, let me say that pages 33-36, though too rhetorical to suit my taste, are nonetheless very true.

*An author should not allow fervent devotion or literary charm to hide the truth.*

Eventually Bavinck gives what seems to be intended as a definition of faith: "Faith really is nothing else but the courageous decision that I will no more indulge in self-contemplation and speculation."[138] Obviously this statement is unacceptable. First, it does not apply to many of the beliefs which the secular writers enumerate. Nor is it Biblical. Surely to confess that Jesus is the Messiah and that God raised him from the dead is more than "nothing else but a courageous decision...no more [to] indulge in self-contemplation." Not only is there something else, but what Bavinck says is excluded is actually included, unless self-examination, which Scripture commands, is not self-contemplation.

The remainder of the book leads to our conclusion that its title is a misnomer. It deals with cares of temptation and spiritual struggle, but has little to do with faith. As such it probes the sinful tendencies of even the best Christians and may prove of great help to many people. But it will impede rather than enlarge one's understanding of the Gospel message.

## 12. John Theodore Mueller

After the earlier sections of this study, sections on secular views of belief, and after the Roman Catholic views, the material has been limited to the Calvinistic tradition. Obviously the present writer is a Calvinist, writing chiefly for Calvinists, with some pious hopes that others also may be influenced. Now, there is nothing wrong in confining one's attention to Calvinism. But since it was Luther, and not Calvin, who first brought the doctrine of justification by faith to the attention of Europe, and since Lutheranism is the numerically largest division of evangelicalism, we ought gratefully to acknowledge the fact, even though the reference be inadequate.

136. Bavinck, 27.
137. Bavinck, 28.
138. Bavinck, 45.

John Theodore Mueller is a recent and excellent Lutheran theologian. In his *Systematic Theology* he uses the common three-fold division of *knowledge, assent*, and *confidence*. But he seems – and this puzzles a reader – to restrict knowledge and assent to uninterpreted historical events. Surely he cannot have meant this, for obviously a person can believe a doctrine as well as an historical event. Some modification, fortunately, occurs on the next page, where he says, "However, if the term *notitia* is understood in the sense of true spiritual knowledge of Christ...and the term *assensus* is conceived as spiritual assent to the promises of the Gospel..., then both of these terms include the *fiducia cordis.*"[139] This, of course, makes *fiducia* redundant. Even on the puzzling page he said, "Faith which justifies is not merely a knowledge of history...but it is assent to the promise of God...." And two pages earlier he had asserted, "Saving faith is always *fides actualis* [not the Romish implicit faith], or the apprehension of the divine promise by an act of the intellect and will."[140]

*Though we hold Martin Luther in highest honor, later Lutheranism has been more Melanchthonian than Lutheran.*

Though we hold Martin Luther in highest honor, later Lutheranism has been more Melanchthonian than Lutheran. Even so, the Missouri Synod and Concordia Seminary are to be admired for turning back the assaults of liberalism in the past decade. Yet, if the present study has taken some Calvinists to task on this or that point, it is permissible to state some difficulties found in Professor Mueller's learned tome. These difficulties are not so much located in the psychology of believing, for Mueller is very clear on the basic evangelical doctrine of assent, widely forgotten by non-Lutherans who still call themselves evangelicals. The difference to be noted in the interest of a more balanced though still inadequate presentation has to do with the permanence of belief.

At first sight Mueller seems to be very Calvinistic. He writes,

> It is clear that a believer is in full possession of divine pardon, life, and salvation from the very moment in which he puts his trust in Christ.... For this reason the believer is also certain of his salvation, for saving faith is in its very nature the truest and greatest certainty. If [any groups] deny that the believer may be sure of his salvation, it is because they teach that salvation in part at least depends upon the believer's good works....[141]

These words could easily be taken to imply the Calvinistic doctrine of the perseverance of the saints, if not that of irresistible grace. But later, on page 436, Mueller denies that all persevere and rejects Calvin's teaching that faith cannot be lost. "The Calvinistic doctrine of final perseverance is unscriptural."[142] "Calvinism cannot comfort a believer with real assurance of salvation."[143]

Yet, strange to say, on the next page he states that "As God did not omit anything to prepare salvation for [the believer], so also he omits nothing by which this salvation is *finaliter* attained."[144]

Now, an astute theologian may see more clearly than a layman who would be deceived how this wording can escape Calvinism. Even some

139. John Theodore Mueller, *Systematic Theology*, 326.
140. Mueller, 323.
141. Mueller, 329.
142. Mueller, 437.
143. Mueller, 438.
144. Mueller, 439.

Arminians assert assurance – in the sense that they are sure they would be taken to Heaven if they should die right now, though if they live longer they may lose their faith and be lost. Similarly Mueller said, "Every true believer in Christ therefore is sure of his [present!] state of grace and salvation."[145] But many of us will indeed live until tomorrow. Therefore Mueller's rejection of Calvinistic comfort cannot be of much comfort to Lutherans.

## 13. The End of History

Some of the more professorial readers of this book may be disappointed that so little attention is paid to current authors and so much to earlier theologians. There is a simple explanation. The earlier theologians, as the quotations indicate, wrote rather extensively on the subject, whereas during the second and third quarters of this century the material has been shorter in length and poorer in quality. One example illustrates both deficiencies. In *The Presbyterian Journal* (November 26, 1980) Stephen M. Reynolds had an article titled "Justification – Faith and Works." Particularly noticeable is his failure to define his terms. To quote:

> The message of *James* becomes especially important when the teaching of bare faith-justification, or even assent-justification, arises to trouble the church, as it evidently was doing in his day, and as it is certainly doing in ours. This is the view that justifying faith does not necessarily include obedience or good works.
>
> The man who relies on assent-justification claims he has justifying faith when what he has is no more than intellectual assent to the Gospel and a desire to escape eternal damnation. The one who relies on assent-justification says, "I accept Christ as Savior, but not yet as Lord." He thinks he is assured of salvation because he has faith, but he does not understand what faith truly is.
>
> To understand the words of *James*, "a man is justified by works," to mean no more than that he demonstrates his justification by his works, leaves the one who relies on assent-justification a false way of feeling that all is well with his soul.[146]

In addition to his loose terminology the writer depends on false assertions. The end of the first quoted paragraph insists that "assent-justification" "does not necessarily include obedience or good works." The word *necessarily* perhaps saves the paragraph from being outright false, provided the writer can quote an exponent of assent who explicitly says that good works are not included. Or, perhaps the truth of the statement can be defended by insisting that those who defend assent do not include good works in assent – they only say that good works follow. But without even this excuse the next-to-last sentence in paragraph two, namely "The one who relies on assent-justification says, 'I accept Christ as Savior, but not yet as Lord,'" cannot escape the charge of outright falsehood. None of the Calvinistic theologians quoted above ever said any such thing. It is regrettable that a periodical, supposedly

*Mueller's rejection of Calvinistic comfort cannot be of much comfort to Lutherans.*

145. Mueller, 332.
146. Reynolds, 9.

71

Calvinistic, should print such incompetent drivel. The Apostle Paul in his day met the essentially similar objection that justification by faith alone encouraged immorality. He defended his position in *Romans 6, 7,* and *8.*

## 14. The Necessity of Faith

To this point the discussion has been centered on the history of the doctrine. The objections to some parts of the various views, though in appearance negative, were, as earlier indicated, actually positive and constructive. Turning now from the historical matrix, the study will try to collect and somewhat organize these previous conclusions. Then, too, although there was a section on "Biblical Data," more Biblical data are to be added. To begin with, a relatively non-controversial point will be made, not only to round out the exposition, but also because it leads into a most embarrassing puzzle. The thesis is that faith is necessary to salvation.

*It is regrettable that a periodical, supposedly Calvinistic, should print such incompetent drivel.*

One difficulty in the doctrine of justification by faith alone has to do with infants and imbeciles. Most Christians believe that some who die in infancy are saved, and many believe that all who die in infancy are saved. But if faith is necessary, and if infants are incapable of believing anything, what happens to Calvinistic theology? The usual answer is to deny that faith is universally necessary and that infants and some others are justified without faith. The Lutherans, however, are more consistent. They hold that infants can exercise faith even before birth. Of course, how they can believe the Gospel which they cannot possibly have heard remains a mystery, for the Scripture says, Faith comes by hearing. On the other hand, Lutherans have a powerful point in their favor as they cite the case of John the Baptist, who was filled with the Holy Ghost while yet in his mother's womb.

The Antichristian Supreme Court should consider this when they legalize the murder of babies on the ground that they are not yet human beings.

Be this all as it may, Supreme Court, Calvinism, and Lutheranism, each reader must decide for himself whether the following Biblical passages require the conclusion that faith is a necessity for salvation. And if faith is necessary to salvation, it is necessary for theology also. We must understand what the Scriptures say. The following verses, or at least some of them, seem to teach that faith is necessary. Assuredly they teach more than this, and references to them must later be made in explanation of other phases of the doctrine. But they are given here for the sole purpose of pointing out the necessity of faith.

*John* 3:15-16: Everyone who believes in him has everlasting life.... He who believes in him shall not perish.

*Acts* 16:31: Believe on the Lord Jesus, and you shall be saved.

Strictly speaking, these two verses do not show that faith is necessary to salvation. They show that faith is sufficient. If someone believes, he has eternal life. No one is lost who believes. But these two verses, if taken alone, allow for the possibility that something else could be substituted for faith. Suppose I am driving south on Interstate 65, and in Kentucky I come to Cave City. The attendant at the gas station says, "If you take Routes 9 and 231 you will surely get to Murphreesboro." True enough. But it is also true that if I continue on I-65 and 24 I shall get to Murphreesboro just as well.

Now…

> Mark 16:16: He who believes and is baptized shall be saved, but he who does not believe shall be condemned.

teaches not only that faith is sufficient, but also that without faith salvation is impossible. However, since some scholars do not regard this as part of the canon, three other verses follow.

> John 3:18: He who believes in him is not judged; he who does not believe is judged already.

> John 3:36: He who believes in the Son has eternal life; but he who disobeys the Son shall not see life.

> Hebrews 11:6: Without faith it is impossible to please him [God].

*Without faith salvation is impossible.*

These verses are sufficiently explicit; but the general doctrine of justification by faith alone is a stronger proof than a few sample verses. The passages on justification may not singly be so explicit: It is necessary to combine them and draw inferences. But in view of the last half of *Romans* 3, and for that matter of the last half of *Romans* 5, the conclusion is the more compelling because the base is broader.

## 15. The Language

Since faith is of such importance, and even if it were not of such importance, theology must determine its meaning. Those who wish to talk about it ought to know the nature of that particular kind of faith which is necessary for salvation. Herman Hoeksema begins his chapter on "Saving Faith" with this paragraph:

> Saving faith is that work of God in the elect, regenerated, and called sinner whereby the latter is ingrafted into Christ and embraces and appropriates Christ and all his benefits, relying upon him in time and eternity.[147]

*Theological terms need to be defined; they need to be understood; or else we do not know what we are talking about.*

Aside from the fact that some of the verbs in this sentence are too vague to be useful, one may admit that the sentence is true. But it is not a definition of faith. To say that faith ingrafts us into Christ says less than to say roast beef gives us nourishment. The latter does not tell us what beef is. Nor does the former tell us what faith is. Theological terms need to be defined; they need to be understood; or else we do not know what we are talking about. To make progress toward a definition, we begin with the usage of the language.

The Greek verb means *believe*. So it was translated in the previous

147. Herman Hoeksema, *Reformed Dogmatics*, 1966, 479.

verses quoted. Here will follow some instances of its ordinary use, both in pagan sources and in the Bible. The Biblical verses from the *Septuagint* are not chosen because they are Biblical, but, like the pagan sources, they show how the word was used in pre-Christian times. When the New Testament authors began to write, they perforce used the common language.

Aristotle, *De Anima* 428b4: The Sun is believed to be larger than the Earth.

Aristotle, *Meteorologica* 343b10: [On a certain point] it is necessary to believe the Egyptians.

Thucydides I, 20: It is hard to believe every bit of evidence about them.

*Psalm* 78:22 in the Septuagint translation says that the Israelites "did not believe in God."

*Isaiah* 53:1: Who has believed our report?

> *A number of theologians give the impression that the translation* believe *is misleading. They want to make "faith" something other than "mere belief."*

Even though this is the common usage – and in a moment a large number of New Testament passages will show the same thing – a number of theologians give the impression that the translation *believe* is misleading. They want to make "faith" something other than "mere belief." The following lengthy list has some bearing on this conviction.

*John* 2:22: They believed the Scripture.

*John* 3:12: If I told you about earthly matters and you do not believe, how shall you believe if I tell you about heavenly things?

*John* 4:50: The man believed the word that Jesus had spoken to him.

*John* 5:47: If you believe not that man's writing, how shall you believe my words?

*John* 6:69: We have believed and know that you are the Holy One of God.

*John* 8:24: If you believe not that I am [what I claim to be] you shall die in your sins.

*John* 8:45: Because I tell you the truth, you do not believe me.

*John* 9:18: But the Jews did not believe...that he had been blind.

*John* 11:26: Do you believe this?

*John* 11:27: Yes, Lord, I believe that you are the Christ.

*John* 11:42: I said it that they may believe that you have sent me.

*John* 12:38: Who has believed our report?

*John* 13:19: You may believe that I am he.

*John* 14:29: Now I have told you before it happens, so that when it happens you might believe.

*John* 16:27: And have believed that I came out from God.

*John* 16:30: We believe that you came forth from God.

*John* 17:8: have believed that you did send me.

*John* 17:21: that the world may believe that you have sent me.

*John* 20:31: These are written that you might believe that Jesus is the Christ, the Son of God.

*1 Corinthians* 13:7: Love believes everything.

In reading over these verses carefully, the student should note that the object of the verb is sometimes a noun or pronoun denoting a statement (*word, this, things, writings*), and sometimes a person (in this list, *me*; in other verses, *God*), and sometimes there is no explicit object at all. The significance of this will become apparent in a moment.

To be specific and to make the New Testament data clear, note that the object of belief in *John* 2:22 is the Scripture; in *John* 3:12, earthly and heavenly things, *i.e.*, information concerning earthly and heavenly society; in *John* 4:50 the man believed the word, not a single word like *Sun, rain,* or *Jerusalem,* but rather a sentence. The Greek word *logos* hardly ever means a single word, and the usual translation of *John* 1:1 is a mistake that has befuddled nearly everybody. In *John* 6:69 the object of the verb *believe* is the phrase "that you are the Holy One of God." Other cases of *believe that* are *John* 8:24, 9:18, 11:27, and at least eight others in the list.

It is clear that the Greek verb *pisteuo* is properly translated *believe*; and it would have been much better if the noun *pistis* had been translated *belief.* An English novel, *The Way of All Flesh,* indicates that in the late eighteenth and early nineteenth centuries the evangelical Anglicans recited the *Belief,* rather than the *Creed.* The author seems to assume that the congregations did not know that *credo* means *I believe.* The partial examination of the verses just above shows what the object of belief is. Usually it is the truth. Even where the grammatical object is not a phrase, the sense requires it.

The Scriptures contain many instances of the verb with the noun *God* as their explicit object. Though none of the verses in the last group quoted has *God* as the explicit object, everyone remembers that "Abraham believed God." The verb here should not be taken to mean something different from its other instances. What Abraham believed was the promise of God. God said, "I am your shield. . . . This shall not be your heir. . . . So shall your seed be. And he [Abraham] believed in the Lord" (*Genesis* 15:1-6); and "Abraham believed God" (*Romans* 4:3). In English too, when we say we believe a person, we mean we agree that his statement is true.

If this is now settled, still some people assert that there is a distinct and important difference between believing a statement or even believing a person and believing in a person.

Before the argument resumes, it is best to collect some more Scriptural data.

*Matthew* 18:6 and *Mark* 9:42: one of these little ones who believe in [*eis*] me.

*John* 1:12: He gave power to them who believe in [*eis*] his name.

*It is clear that the Greek verb* pisteuo *is properly translated* believe; *and it would have been much better if the noun* pistis *had been translated* belief.

*John* 2:11: His disciples believed in him.

*John* 2:23: Many believed on [*eis*] his name.

*John* 7:5: Neither did his brothers believe in him.

*John* 9:35-36: Do you believe on the Son of God? …Who is he, Lord, that I may believe on [*eis*] him?

*John* 12:36: Believe in [*eis*] the light.

*John* 14:1: You believe in [*eis*] God, believe also in me.

*Acts* 16:31: Believe on [*epi*] the Lord Jesus and you shall be saved and your house.

*Romans* 4:18: Who against hope believed in [*epi*] hope.

*1 Timothy* 1:16: Believe on [*epi*] him to life everlasting.

*1 Peter* 1:21: Who are believers [noun] in God.

> Ephesians *1:1 is better translated "to the believers in* Christ Jesus," *as also in* Colossians *1:2 and a dozen other places.*

The first reference in this last list speaks of young children. They cannot have had much theological education. The passage of course does not mean that we should be like children in respect of their ignorance, nor, as is sometimes wrongly assumed, in respect of their innocence. But rather they believed that Jesus would somehow bless them. If anyone wish to say the children *trusted* in him, well and good; to trust is to believe *that* good will follow.

The contrast between *John* 2:11, 23 and *John* 7:5 is that some believed Jesus was the Messiah and some did not.

*John* 12:36 and its context speak of light. The light seems to be the Old Testament in verse 34. It may also be Christ's interpretation of the Old Testament prophecies. Later Christ would be taken away and the Old Testament would be darkness to them. Verses 35 and 36 need not be translated "*While* you have light," but equally good grammar allows "As you have light, *i.e.*, use whatever degree of light you now have." Here, as often, the contrast between light and darkness is the contrast between truth and falsehood.

The final verse in the list uses the noun *believers*, or a substantive adjective if you wish. It does not mean trusting or faithful; but believer. *Acts* 16:1 refers to Timothy's mother as a believer (feminine form). *Ephesians* 1:1 is better translated "to the believers in Christ Jesus," as also in *Colossians* 1:2 and a dozen other places.

These references are cited because some people find a great difference between *believing* a person and *believing in* him. There is no doubt a difference, but it is quite different from the difference these people think they have in mind. Attentive readers who read their publications will conclude that very likely they have nothing in mind, for they regularly avoid stating what the difference is. Let us use a human example, for if we begin by talking about believing in God, our sense of piety may deceive us. Any ordinary instance will do. I meet a stranger on the plane and we begin to talk. His conversation indicates that he is a chemical engineer. Somewhere along the line he remarks that a certain chemical process does so and so. I believe him; I accept his statement as true. But I do not for that reason believe *in* him. He may be a scoundrel. Occasionally engineers are. On the way home I sit next to a very good friend of longstanding. He is a lawyer. He tells me about some legal matter. But now I not only believe this one statement: I believe *in* him because I believe that anything he will tell me in the future, especially if it concerns law, will be true. I believe he always tells the truth and always will. Of course, since he is a sinner, he may make a mistake. But when we believe *in* God, we believe *that* he will never make a mistake. *To believe in* is simply a reference to the future beyond the present single statement.

Then too some preachers who have had a year or two of Greek make allegedly scholarly remarks about a difference between a New Testament belief and a pagan Greek belief. Better scholars, Gerhard Kittel, Gerhard Friedrich, and Rudolph Bultmann, have these things to say:

> From a purely formal standpoint there is nothing very distinctive in the usage of the NT and early Chr. writings as compared with Gr. usage.... Πιστεύ εἰς is equivalent to πιστεύειν ὅτι..."to regard as credible, as true." Πιστεύειν εἰς Χριστον Ιησοῦν (Col. 2:16), εἰς αὐτόν and εἰς ἐμέ (often in Jn.) etc. simply means πιστεύ ειν ὅτι Ιησοῦς ἀπέθανεν καὶ ἀνέοτη.... In Jn. esp. πιστεύειν εἰς and πιστεύειν are constantly used interchangeably in the same sense. [Note: Cf. also Ac. 8:37E...][148] This is proved also by the poss. expression ἐπιστεύθη (sc. Ιησοῦς Χριστός, 1 Tim. 3:16) and the fact that πιστις is equivalent, not to πίστις c. dat., but to πίστις c. gen. obj....[149]

Two pages later they write,

> πιστεύω often means to believe God's words. Belief is thus put in Scripture (Jn. 2:22), in what is written in the Law and the prophets (Ac. 24:14), in what the prophets have said (Lk. 24:25)...in Moses and his writings (Jn. 5:46f), also in what God is saying at the moment, e.g., through an angel (Lk. 1:20, 45; Ac. 27:25). [See also pages 208 and 222.]

To translate or to summarize a little, these three language scholars said: *To believe in* is equivalent *to believe that. To believe in* Christ Jesus simply means *to believe that* Jesus died and rose again. In *John* especially *to believe in* and *to believe that* are constantly used interchangeably.

In opposition to these linguistic studies, some theologians and many ministers wish to minimize belief and detach faith from truth. Louis Berkhof strangely tends in this direction. Since at this time he commands widespread respect, and since many schools use his book, it proves profitable to conclude this subsection with a few paragraphs concerning his views.

Berkhof admits that *John* 4:50 uses the verb *pisteuo* in the literal sense of believing that a proposition is true. Naturally; for the explicit object is the *word* or *sentences* that Jesus had just spoken. Similarly *John* 5:47. Berkhof even allows *Acts* 16:34, *Romans* 4:3, and *2 Timothy* 1:12 to mean belief in the truth of a proposition, although the explicit object of the verb is *God* or *Christ*.

*To believe in* is *equivalent to* believe that. To believe in *Christ Jesus simply means* to believe that *Jesus died and rose again.*

148. Even if the verse is spurious, the Greek is genuine.

149. Gerhard Kittel and Gerhard Friedrich, editors. *Theological Dictionary of the New Testament*, Volume VI, 203.

In spite of these instances, where the predicate is the noun *God*, though the actual and immediate object is a proposition, and particularly in contrast with the instances where the object is explicitly a proposition, Berkhof says, "On the whole this construction is weaker than the preceding,"[150] where *pisteuoo* means "confident trust in a person." But why weaker? Would it not be more accurate to say that this construction with a proposition as the object is more literal and accurate than the preceding abbreviated expressions? Berkhof continues, "In a couple of cases the matter believed hardly rises into the religious sphere, *John* 9:18, *Acts* 9:26...." But if these are instances of ordinary usage, and not particularly religious, such as "The Jews did not believe that he had been born blind," it should show all the more clearly what the ordinary meaning of *believing* is. No religious motif is there to distract one's understanding. It is true that the object of belief in such instances does not rise into the religious sphere; sometimes the object may be banal or trivial; but the point at issue is not the object of belief or faith, but the nature of faith and the meaning of the verb *pisteuoo*.

From page 493 on, Berkhof speaks as follows. *Pistis* (the noun) and *pisteuein* (the verb) "do not always have exactly the same connotation." He specifies two meanings of the noun *pistis* in classical Greek.

> It denotes (a) a conviction based on confidence in a person and in his testimony, which as such is distinguished from knowledge resting on personal investigation; and (b) the confidence itself on which such a conviction rests. This is more than a mere intellectual conviction that a person is reliable; it presupposes a personal relation to the object of confidence, a going out of one's self to rest in another.

The lexical information of this quotation is accurate enough; but the comments are groundless. Why is confidence in a person's truthfulness more than "a mere intellectual conviction that a person is reliable"? What is intended in the pejorative use of the word "mere"? Why is a conviction of another person's honesty and reliability not a "personal relation"? And can any intelligible sense be found in the phrase "a going out of one's self to rest in another"?

However, to continue the quotations from page 494 on, we read that in the New Testament

> the following special meanings [of the noun *pistis*] should be distinguished: (a) an intellectual belief or conviction, resting on the testimony of another, and therefore based on trust in this other rather than on personal investigation,[151] *Phil.* 1:27 [which rather obviously refers to the doctrines of the Gospel], *II Cor.* 4:13; *II Thess.* 2:13 [the object here is truth], and especially in the writings of John; and (b) a confiding trust or confidence...*Rom.* 3:22, 25; 5:1, 2; 9:30, 32....This trust must be distinguished from that on which the intellectual truth mentioned under (a) above, rests.

But why? No reason is given. Is it not true that "a confiding trust or confidence" depends on previous instances of being told the truth?

---

*Why is confidence in a person's truthfulness more than "a mere intellectual conviction"?*

150. Louis Berkhof, *Systematic Theology.* Fourth edition, 494.

151. Though it is not necessary to the main argument, one may note that the phrase "rather than on personal investigation" conflicts with actual usage. A scientist personally investigates this or that phenomenon; he accepts a great deal of evidence in favor of a certain hypothesis; and he believes that this equation is the correct explanation. That belief may depend on the testimony of someone we think competent goes without saying; but this condition should not be made part of the definition of faith.

The first time I meet a man and hear him speak – unless he comes already highly recommended, which merely pushes the illustration one step backwards – I cannot reasonably grant him a confiding trust or confidence. After I have observed his habit of always telling the truth, I can have confidence in him. But this is also an intellectual belief that he constantly tells the truth. It differs from the former only in the circumstance that the object of the belief is a different proposition. First, I believed the proposition *a chemical formula would do so and so*; now I believe the propositon *he always tells the truth*.

Berkhof cited some references to support his contention. But *Romans* 3:22 does not support him. It merely mentions, in four words, "faith in Jesus Christ." The immediately following words are "to all who believe." What they believe is more explicitly stated in 3:25, which Berkhof also lists. The phrase is "through faith in his blood." Clearly this is not baldly literal. *Blood* is a symbol for the atonement. It cannot even be restricted to Christ's death, for the Pharisees themselves believed that Christ died. What the Pharisees did not believe was the significance of Christ's death, namely, that he paid the penalty of our sin. Verses 25 and 26 are the best summary in the New Testament of the core of the Gospel: the doctrine of justification by faith; and this doctrine – a set of propositions – is the object of belief. Nor do Berkhof's other citations (*Romans* 5:1, 2; 9:30, 32) support his conclusion. They make no distinction such as Berkhof makes. They simply speak of faith. By saying five lines below that "The last [yielding of Christ and trusting in him] is specifically called saving faith," Berkhof implies that the conviction of the truth of the Gospel and "intellectual trust" is not saving faith. *Romans* is a great book, and we are willing to quote it, more than willing, anxious: *Romans* 10:9 says that "if you confess with your mouth that Jesus is Lord, and believe in your heart that God raised him from the dead, you shall be saved." As the Old Testament has made abundantly clear, the heart is the mind; and believing that God raised Christ from the dead is as intellectual an exercise as believing that two and two are four.

On page 495 Berkhof continues, Faith "is also represented as a hungering and thirsting…. In eating and drinking we not only have the conviction that the necessary food and drink is present, but also the confident expectation that it will satisfy us…."

There is a major flaw in this paragraph: It misapplies a metaphorical expression. Hungering and thirsting are figures of speech, as is nourishment also. Of course having food present before us does not nourish us. It must be eaten. Now, Berkhof compares the uneaten food before us with believing the Gospel. This requires, in the spiritual application of the metaphor, an additional factor beyond believing. A proper application of the metaphor would compare looking at the food before eating it with hearing the Gospel before believing it. In neither case is there nourishment. Nourishment comes, literally, when we eat; spiritually, when we believe the good news. Understanding the words of the evangelist is an intellectual act and it does

*Verses 25 and 26 are the best summary in the New Testament of the core of the Gospel: the doctrine of justification by faith; and this doctrine – a set of propositions – is the object of belief.*

not save; believing those words after having understood them saves. But this too is an intellectual act. The objects or propositions are different. The first act, in unbelief, is, "I understand that the evangelist thinks Christ died for man's sins." The second act is, "I believe that it is true that Christ died for man's sins." These are both cases of intellectual or volitional assent; but the objects, *i.e.*, the propositions, differ immensely.

*Christ's promises of salvation are vastly different from the propositions of botany; but believing is always thinking that a proposition is true.*

There are, he says, other instances of the verb *believe* where "the deeper meaning of the word, that of firm trustful reliance, comes to its full rights." But Berkhof, like others, fails to show how this "deeper meaning" differs from the straightforward literal meaning. Among the many instances of the verb *believe*, there is, to repeat, a difference of objects. One may believe that two and two are four, and this is arithmetic; one may also believe that asparagus belongs to the lily family, and this is botany. Botany is not mathematics, of course; but the psychology or linguistics of believing is identical in all cases. Therefore, one should not confuse an analysis of belief with an analysis of numbers or plants. Christ's promises of salvation are vastly different from the propositions of botany; but believing is always thinking that a proposition is true. The further development will also support this conclusion.

## 16. Person or Proposition?

While Professor Berkhof serves as a good example, many other Protestant theologians also, both Lutheran and Reformed, tend to make a sharp distinction between "a confident resting on a person" and "the assent given to a testimony." "Confident reliance" is supposed to differ from "intellectual assent."

*To believe in a person is to be confident, i.e., to believe that he will continue to tell the truth.*

The term *resting* or *reliance* is seldom if ever explained in theology books. One is left in the dark as to what it means. An illustration may furnish a clue and make the words intelligible. Suppose a high school student is assigned a problem in geometry. He works out a solution, looks at it from all angles, perhaps he corrects a small detail and then tests each step again to see if he has made a mistake; seeing none, he now puts down his pencil and rests. That is to say, he has assented to his argument. He believes he now has the truth.

But most theologians are not so clear, nor can they, as earlier indicated, bolster up their imagined distinction with references to *pisteuein eis*, for a few paragraphs back Kittel disposed of such a contention. English also has the same usage. As Modernism developed in the 1920's and suspicion attached to this or that minister, people would ask, Does he believe in the virgin birth? Does he believe in the atonement? They did not ask, Does he believe the virgin birth? The preposition *in* was regularly used. But of course the meaning was, Does he believe *that* the virgin birth is true? Does he believe *that* Christ's death was a substitutionary sacrifice? Thus, to believe *in* a person is to be confident, *i.e.*, to believe *that* he will continue to tell the truth.

In spite of the popularity and supposed superior spirituality of the contrast between a mere intellectual proposition and a warm, living person, it rests on a mistaken psychological analysis. Even Berkhof admits, with at least an appearance of inconsistency, that "As a psychological phenomenon, faith in the religious sense does not differ from faith in general.... Christian faith in the most comprehensive sense is man's persuasion of the truth of Scripture on the basis of the authority of God."[152]

This is an excellent statement and should be defended against Berkhof's previous contrary assertions.

## 17. The Object

Still a most embarrassing question has not yet been answered, nor even asked. It is this: If the object of saving faith is a proposition, what is that proposition? Surely no one is justified by believing that Abraham lived about 2000 B.C., or that Saul was the first King of Israel, though both of these propositions are completely Scriptural. Nor can we as Protestants believe implicitly whatever the Bible says. Calvin put it tersely: Implicit faith is ignorance, not knowledge. What one has never heard or read cannot be believed, for faith comes by hearing. Hearing what? We do not hear or read the whole Bible every day; we cannot remember it, if we read it through once a year. And a recent convert has probably never read it all. Then which verse, of the several an evangelist might quote, is the one which, believed, justifies the sinner? Has any reader of this study ever heard a minister answer or even ask this question?

When this subject was touched on many pages back, it was said that repentance was necessary. "Repent and be baptized" is a well-known command. But it does not answer the present question. To repent is to change one's mind. But in what respect? Beliefs, resolutions, ideas come and go. We are always changing our minds, and obviously there are many changes of mind that have nothing to do with justification. The question presses upon us: Which change of mind?

Among the theologians previously quoted, Owen's discussion stimulates this question. Any attentive reader – there are many inattentive – must face the problem. But though the question is so obvious, the answer is not. Indeed, the question has no answer; that is, it has no single answer. Centuries ago a somewhat similar situation and difficulty arose and was given an impossible answer. Years after Athanasius wrote the Nicene Creed, a so-called Athanasian Creed was formulated that pronounced damnation on everyone who did not believe its numerous propositions on the Trinity. The propositions themselves are on the whole very good; but less than one percent of the Christian community can recite them from memory. Possibly not more than twenty-five percent have even heard them. No Calvinist would assert that salvation requires us to believe them explicitly. On the opposite end of the scale from those who would insist on the wording of the

*"As a psychological phenomenon, faith in the religious sense does not differ from faith in general.... Christian faith in the most comprehensive sense is man's persuasion of the truth of Scripture on the basis of the authority of God."*
*– Louis Berkhof*

152. Berkhof, 501.

Athanasian Creed, some independent churches write their own creed of five or six articles with fewer words than this one article on the Trinity. But are these few the irreducible minimum for salvation? The question above asks for precisely those beliefs which are necessary for justification.

Consider the case of Justin Martyr, one of the earliest heroes of the faith. Did he really have saving faith? He was a Christian, was he not? He died for the name of our Lord and Savior. He must have been regenerated and justified, must he not? But it is doubtful that any strong Lutheran or Calvinistic church would have admitted him even to communicant membership. His view of the atonement was abysmal. Quite possibly the strife-torn church in Corinth, troubled with fornication, law-suits, and idol-worship – its members do not seem to have denied Christ's resurrection, but they had denied the resurrection of believers – had a better theology than Justin Martyr. But to what justifying propositions did he or they assent?

*The Church is neither commanded, encouraged, nor even permitted to be satisfied with a bare minimum of half a dozen doctrines.*

Now, Justin Martyr was not a moron. Morons have doubtless been regenerated and justified. Some members of extremely primitive tribes also, with their minds incredibly confused. What propositions did they believe? Is there any passage in Scripture that identifies, in a scale of decreasing knowledge, the very minimum by which someone can still be justified?

But even if a minimum of propositions could be listed, below which number justification were impossible, it would still be the wrong question with a perverted outlook. This is the basic weakness contributing to the low spiritual level of most so-called fundamentalist congregations. The Church is neither commanded, encouraged, nor even permitted to be satisfied with a bare minimum of half a dozen doctrines. Historic Presbyterianism is in a much better position with its multi-paragraph thirty-three chapters of the *Westminster Confession*. The Bible commands the maximum, not the minimum. Jesus said,

> Matthew 28:19-20: Teach all nations... instructing them to observe *all things* that I have commanded you.

There seems to be no other conclusion but that God justifies sinners by means of many combinations of propositions believed. For which reason a minister should not confine himself to topics popularly thought to be "evangelistic," but should preach the whole counsel of God, trusting that God will give someone the gift of faith through sermons on the Trinity, eschatology, or the doctrine of immediate imputation.

## 18. A Conclusion

The sections of this monograph have presented some of the history of the doctrine of faith and have explained a fair amount of its Scriptural basis, along with a few Calvinistic implications. That the drawing of valid implications is justified, the *Westminster Confession* asserts in I, 6: "The whole counsel of God, concerning all things necessary for his own glory, man's salvation, faith, and life, is either expressly set down in Scripture, or by good and necessary consequence may be deduced from Scripture." Obviously; for otherwise how could any orthodox minister preach a sermon? This dependence on implication, deduction, and necessary consequence is indispensable for the propagation of the Gospel. Those "religious" people who decry logic lack every basis for proclaiming any message at all. No declarative sentence can have a meaning except in virtue of the law of contradiction. See St. Aristotle, *Metaphysics*, Book Gamma. Or if the *Metaphysics* is not on your night table, read the *Gospel* and *First Epistle of John*.

The present theological climate, however, is inimical to clear thinking. Intellectualism is in disgrace. Even such a conservative, orthodox theologian as G. I. Williamson, though he does not deny the section of the *Confession* just quoted, passes over the matter of deduction in one sentence.[153] He then immediately tries to restrict its application by saying, "The Mosaic Law, for example, is not expressed by way of abstract principles. Moses declared the law in terms of concrete instances." This is ridiculous. The Ten Commandments do not include a single concrete case. They forbid all murder: They mention neither Cain nor Lamech. They condemn all adultery: They do not specify any single instance. They prohibit all theft: Rachel's particular example is missing. Of course, Williamson is not consistently opposed to deductive logic. He rather represents those conservative theologians who have not completely escaped the influence of contemporary irrationalism.

By and large, twentieth-century religion is irrational and anti-intellectual. The earlier Modernism was covertly so; the later Humanism, Neo-orthodoxy, or Existentialism are violently so. Anti-intellectualism has no place for Biblical and Calvinistic faith. Scriptural "information," or historical statements as Kierkegaard put it, have nothing to do with salvation; and salvation itself is sometimes reduced to an earthly life minus anxiety. Karl Barth, for example, ridicules the empty tomb and talks vaguely about "the Easter event." Instead of preaching propositions, these men recommend an irrational experience, an encounter, a wager, a confrontation. If anything is to be believed, it is that authentic Christianity is self-contradictory.[154]

This religious Neo-orthodoxy is paralleled by atheistic Existentialism. And modern culture as a whole is impregnated with Freudian irrationalistic emotionalism. Even if the temper of the times cannot be altered, maybe a few ministers who want to be orthodox can be shown how much their secular education, not only in the schools but also through the press, has diluted their Gospel, and thus be persuaded to return to Calvin and Paul.

Saving faith as assent, truth as propositions (there is no other kind of *truth*), the inerrancy of Scripture, with the outright rejection of all irrationalism, are integral parts of a single system.

*Those "religious" people who decry logic lack every basis for proclaiming any message at all.*

*Saving faith as assent, truth as propositions (there is no other kind of truth), the inerrancy of Scripture, with the outright rejection of all irrationalism, are integral parts of a single system.*

153. G. I. Williamson, *The Westminster Confession of Faith for Study Classes*, 11.

154. See my *Karl Barth's Theological Method* and Paul K. Jewett's *Emil Brunner's Concept of Revelation*.

On one or the other of these several points, consider Calvin once more.

In his *Commentary* on *John* 3:33 Calvin wrote, "…giving their assent to God…. [T]o believe the Gospel is nothing else than to assent to the truths which God has revealed."

On *John* 6:40 he says, "[T]hat man offers an aggravated insult to the Holy Spirit, who refuses to assent to his simple testimony…. Faith proceeds from the knowledge of Christ."

At *John* 6:69 we read, "….*we believe and know*…. [F]aith itself is truly the eye of the understanding…. *Knowledge* is connected with faith, because we are certain and fully convinced of the truth of God…."

Then on *John* 17:8, "[N]othing which relates to God can be known aright but by *faith*, but that in *faith* there is such certainty that it is justly called knowledge."

Commenting on *Ephesians* 4:13, which states the goal of a unity of faith and a mature knowledge of the Son of God, Calvin teaches that

> Enthusiasts [Pentecostals, *et al.*] dream that the use of the ministry ceases as soon as we have been led to Christ [because we can now depend on guidance and visions]…. Paul maintains that we must persevere…make progress till death…that we must not be ashamed to be the scholars of the church, to which Christ has committed our education.

The epistle and the commentary continue by warning us not to remain children, deceived by every wind of false and deceitful doctrine, but to become mature.

Note too how maturity is described in *Hebrews* 5:11-6:2. The babe in Christ, who has been nourished on milk, must now eat solid food and become a teacher. The doctrines of repentance and faith, of baptism and ordination, of the resurrection and the final judgment, are elementary. One must press on to the maturity of more complex theology: namely, all three volumes of Charles Hodge.

Foundational to this intellectualism, this rationalism, or however anyone wishes to name this emphasis on truth, is the doctrine that man is the image of God. One should not try to dilute this doctrine by picturing man as a container somewhere within which the image of God may be found. *1 Corinthians* 11:7 does not say that man *has* the image of God; it says that man *is* the image of God. This image, which distinguishes man from animals, is rationality. It was not destroyed by the fall, for we are still human beings and not animals. We are still generically rational, though sin has considerably damaged our use of reason. We add up our check stubs incorrectly, and our emotions drive us into foolish conduct (or worse). But we are still human because we are the created image of God. Though we often believe falsehoods, we are still obligated to believe the truth. And if God causes us to believe, since faith is the gift of God, then we are slowly renewed in the knowledge and righteousness of our original creation.

Incidentally, this is a further reason for rejecting the empirical epis-

> "[T]o believe the Gospel is nothing else than to assent to the truths which God has revealed."
> —John Calvin

temology of Thomas and some Protestants. Adam was created, having knowledge. The Thomists go so far as to say that Paul in the first chapter of *Romans* placed his stamp of approval on empiricism and the cosmological argument. There is a different interpretation of chapter one; but *Romans* 2:15 is a sufficient refutation of the *tabula rasa* theory. In the split second of his creation, Adam, before he could rub his eyes and see the Sun, had a knowledge of God, and of logic too.

If any reader is disturbed by the present author's insistence on logic, reason, intellect, and knowledge in comparison with his lack of emphasis on righteousness, it should be remembered that (1) there can be no righteousness without knowledge; (2) American evangelicalism puts most of its emphasis on conduct, morality, the fruits of the Spirit, and "practical" Christianity; (3) there is a woeful lack of emphasis on truth, theology, the teachings of Scripture. Of course these teachings have moral implications, but the righteousness enjoined in *Romans* 12-15 plus some in chapter 16 has as its foundation the eleven preceding chapters. Does it not follow, therefore, that a minister should preach eleven sermons on deep doctrine to every six or five-and-a-half on conduct? The latter should by no means be omitted: The crime and depravity of American society is without parallel in history since the time of the Roman Empire. Nor has the church itself much to be proud of. But a one-sided preaching of righteousness will have little effect on Las Vegas or New York. Not until this alcoholic, drug-ridden scum hears and believes – faith comes by hearing, not by mystic encounters – hears and believes the doctrines of the Trinity, the Incarnation, the atonement, justification by faith, and the Second Advent, will there be any moral improvement. It is justification alone that produces sanctification, and justification occurs by means of faith alone.

The present writer, I hope evidently, does not disparage righteousness; but the topic of the monograph is faith, and to the main conclusion the argument now returns.

The most common analysis of personality among conservative Christians today is the three-fold division into intellect, will, and emotions. As a matter of fact, a two-fold division into intellect and emotion is probably more common, for a Freudian, sexually-oriented society has discarded the will. It was not always so. Whedon's *The Freedom of the Will* was published in 1864; Girardeau's *The Will in Its Theological Relations* was published in 1891; and in 1898 came Archibald Alexander's *Theories of the Will.* The first two are Arminian, and no doubt Arminians, if asked, will still assert the freedom of the will, but you have to ask them; for the Nazarenes, the Pentecostals, the Holiness groups give me the impression of having forgotten the will in their constant stress of emotion. Henry B. Smith, a Calvinist of last century, divided "the whole soul" into intellect, will, and sensibilities.[155] Strange, even the empirical theologians of today hardly ever mention sensation in this connection, however much they make use of it in epistemology.

A paragraph on Augustine will prove profitable. Since he thought of man as a replica of the Trinity, he needed a threefold division, but he

*A one-sided preaching of righteousness will have little effect on Las Vegas or New York.... It is justification alone that produces sanctification, and justification occurs by means of faith alone.*

155. H. B. Smith, *System of Christian Theology,* 1884, 540.

did not always come up with the same three. Sometimes it was *mens, notitia,* and *amor* (mind, knowledge, and love); more frequently it was *memoria* – Augustine defended the continuity of the resurrected saint with his earthly life on the basis of a continuing memory – *intelligentia,* and *voluntas.* He also enumerated *memoria* (not of oneself, as above, but "memory" of God), *intelligentia,* and *amor.*

Those who know little about the Bible and less about the history of theology will delightedly grasp at Augustine's love, with the remark, "There you have emotion, and the Bible surely says a lot about love." In answer, one must admit that Augustine not only stressed love, but even placed it in a position superior to intellect. But the love August-ine had in mind, and love as considered in Scripture, is a volition, not an emotion. The Scripture commands love. Commands are addressed to the will. Emotions are involuntary. One should not interpret, misin-terpret, Scriptural love in terms of the secular psychology of the twen-tieth century. God has no emotions, and his image, man, in his unfallen state, may have been analyzed into intellect and will, knowledge and righteousness. Emotion and disease came in with the fall.

Earlier in this century J. Gresham Machen defended, and suffered for, the primacy of the intellect.

> To the pragmatist skepticism of the modern religious world, there-fore, the Bible is sharply opposed; against the passionate anti-intellec-tualism of a large part of the modern Church it maintains the primacy of the intellect; it teaches plainly that God has given to man a faculty of reason which is capable of apprehending truth, even truth about God.[156]

To summarize a few thoughts from his introductory chapter is not so much plagiarism as a recommendation that the population of this ninth decade return and read this classic of the third.

Machen begins by noting that some devout souls regard an analysis of faith as

> impertinent and unnecessary. Faith…cannot be known except by ex-perience, and…logical analysis of it…will only serve to destroy its power and its charm…. Religion is an ineffable experience; the intellectual expression of it…theology may vary and yet religion may remain the same.[157]

Those who entertain this view avoid defining their terms. They

> are greatly incensed when they are asked to tell in simple language what they mean by these terms [*atonement, redemption, faith*]. [They find it] disconcerting to be asked what faith is.[158]

The same anti-intellectualism is evident in secular education also. Machen lived before the invention of the phrase, "Johnny can't read;" but he could say, "The undergraduate student of the present day is being told that…the exercise of the memory is a rather childish and mechanical thing, and that what he is really in college to do is to think for himself and to unify his world." Later this phrase became "to do one's own thing."

*One should not interpret, misinterpret, Scriptural love in terms of the secular psychology of the twentieth century.*

156. J. Gresham Machen, *What Is Faith?* 51.

157. Machen, 13.

158. Machen, 14.

He usually makes a poor business of unifying his world. And the reason is clear…. [H]e has no world to unify. He has not acquired a knowledge of a sufficient number of facts in order even to learn the method of putting facts together….[159] A mass of details stored up in the mind does not in itself make a thinker; but on the other hand thinking is absolutely impossible without that mass of details…. [I]t is impossible to think with an empty mind.[160]

The decline of intellectualism, if

lamentable in secular education, is tenfold worse in the sphere of the Christian religion…. Bible classes today often avoid a study of the actual contents of the Bible as they would avoid pestilence or disease; to many persons in the Church the notion of getting the simple historical contents of the Bible straight in mind is an entirely new idea.[161]

In addition to secular education and the Church, anti-intellectualism has invaded the Christian home.

I did not get my knowledge of the Bible from Sunday School, but…[from] my mother at home. And I will venture to say that although my mental ability was certainly of no extraordinary kind [a statement proved false by his extraordinarily competent publications] I had a better knowledge of the Bible at fourteen years of age than is possessed by many students in the theological seminaries of the present day.[162]

The present writer too memorized the *Shorter Catechism* by that age. But "the lamentable fact is that the Christian home [two exceptions are my daughters and their children], as an educational institution, has largely ceased to function." Now, fifty years later, home and family have been largely aborted. This educational, religious, and moral decline, Machen attributes to anti-intellectualism.

He gives an example – Goodspeed's mistranslation of the verb *dikaioō* Another example is Ellwood's perversion of history by saying that "Jesus concerned himself but little with the question of existence after death." Then Machen states his purpose for writing his book:

As over against this anti-intellectual tendency in the modern world, it will be one chief purpose of the present little book to defend the primacy of the intellect, and in particular to try to break down the false and disastrous opposition which has been set up between knowledge and faith.[163]

This introductory chapter continues for another twenty pages, but these excerpts form a sufficient recommendation that the book be read again.

Let other books detail the humanistic degradation of the public schools under the National Education Association; let the pastors point out the Antichristian bigotry of the present Secretary of the federal Department of Education; let a Moral Majority mount an attack on corrupt and prodigal Congressmen. In the study at hand the subject is saving faith.

> *"It will be one chief purpose of the present little book to defend the primacy of the intellect, and in particular to try to break down the false and disastrous opposition which has been set up between knowledge and faith."*
> – J. Gresham Machen

159. Machen, 16.
160. Machen, 20.
161. Machen, 20-21.
162. Machen, 21-22.
163. Machen, 26.

Faith, by definition, is assent to understood propositions. Not all cases of assent, even assent to Biblical propositions, are saving faith; but all saving faith is assent to one or more Biblical propositions.

*Faith, by definition, is assent to understood propositions.... all saving faith is assent to one or more Biblical propositions.*

# The Johannine Logos

## 1. Introduction

The *Gospel of John* is the most hated book of the Bible, and the most beloved – for the same reason, namely, that it was written that you might believe that Jesus is the Christ, the Son of God, and that believing you might have life through his name. If the contents of a book were not important, it could not be very much hated or very much beloved. The contents of this *Gospel* are extremely important. Therefore it abounds with points suitable for discussion and controversy. The point for discussion here, as the title indicates, is the Johannine *Logos*. As a most important point it has been discussed in many volumes. They usually restrict themselves to the first few verses of the first chapter and ignore, for a reason but an inadequate reason, how John used the word *logos* in the remainder of the *Gospel*. This additional material will not be ignored here.

In studies on *John* or on the New Testament as a whole, it is customary to begin with what is called *Introduction*. The word is used in a more technical sense than is found in most other subjects. College curricula have courses called Introduction to Psychology, Introduction to Botany, Introductory Logic, and so on. These courses give their students the first and easiest parts of the subjects indicated. But an Introduction to the *Gospel of John* is not very easy, and it is so far from summarizing the main contents of the book that it gives its readers hardly any notion of what the *Gospel* is all about. Introduction discusses questions such as authorship and date. It asks, Was the author a disciple who ate the last Passover with Jesus and participated in the first Lord's Supper, John, the son of Zebedee? Or was he someone else of the same name? Or perhaps the author was an unknown person in the late second or early third century who, with a good imagination, wrote a fantasy and attached John's name to it. If this be the case, then the book has no historical importance for the years A.D. 27-30 or thereabouts. It would be completely untrustworthy as a source of knowledge concerning what Jesus said and did. In this case it would be a book to be despised.

This study of the *Gospel* is particularly concerned with the substantial contents of the *Gospel*, the intellectual or doctrinal teaching of the book, the truth that it proclaims, and is not much concerned

*The* Gospel of John *is the most hated book of the Bible, and the most beloved – for the same reason.*

with matters of higher criticism or Introduction. The questions about the author, date, and so on will not be discussed very thoroughly. However, they cannot be entirely omitted. Some of the evidence will occur incidentally as the contents are considered. For example, on several occasions the text shows that the author had to have been an eyewitness: Geographical detail, temporal succession, and minute bits of information are evidences to which historians give weight.

During the last hundred years, and even before 1870, destructive critics have dated the *Gospel* in the late second century. Bruno Bauer, a New Testament critic of the middle of the nineteenth century, declared that *Mark* was the first *Gospel* to be written and that it was written during the reign of Hadrian, 117-138. Consequently he dated John's *Gospel* later, about A.D. 165. Now, this dating presents a puzzle when one remembers that the *Muratorian Canon*, a document of A.D. 170, shows that the *Gospel* was universally accepted; for between Bauer's date and that of the *Canon* there is not time enough for a fraudulent document to overcome suspicion and be accepted as canonical. If, on the other hand, the *Gospel* had been published between A.D. 110 and 140, the hundreds of Christians who knew John personally would have denounced it as a forgery. The conclusion is that the *Gospel* must have been written in the first century.

The late date is no longer so widely held. One of the first scholars to react against this destructive criticism, and one of the best, was my professor of Hebrew in the University of Pennsylvania, James Alan Montgomery, to whose very slender six feet five we students all looked up. The year I began Hebrew with him he published an article, "The Origin of the Gospel According to St. John," and gave me a copy. After twenty-nine pages of solid argument the pamphlet concludes:

> The end of my argument is this: That the Gospel of St. John is the composition of a well-informed Jew, not of the Pharisaic party, whose life experience was gained in Palestine in the first half of the first century, whose mother tongue was Aramaic, and that this conclusion alone explains the excellence of the historical data and the philosophical phenomena of the book — unless indeed, with Burney, we must argue to a translation of an Aramaic original.

One reason, in addition to its scholarly contents, for mentioning this article is Dr. Albright's comment thirty-one years later.[1]

> We have seen that both narratives and logia of John's Gospel certainly or presumably date back to oral tradition in Palestine before A.D. 170.... [The oral tradition has been rearranged and edited].[2] But there is absolutely nothing to show that any of Jesus' teachings have been distorted or falsified, or that any new element has been added to them.... There is no reason to suppose that the needs of the Church were responsible for any inventions or innovations of theological significance. Whether the Gospel was edited by John the Presbyter or Papias...or whether some other reconstruction is more probable, we may rest assured that it contains the memories of the Apostle John – regardless of

---

*During the last hundred years, and even before 1870, destructive critics have dated the* Gospel *in the late second century.*

---

1. "Recent Discoveries in Palestine and the Gospel of John," *The Background of the New Testament and Its Eschatology*, ed. by Davies and Daube. Cambridge University Press, 1954, 170-171.

2. Albright has a strange fondness for oral tradition, even when none is needed.

whether he died in Jerusalem or in Ephesus, though the latter is so well attested by tradition that it remains most plausible.[3]

In a footnote Albright continues, "In this connection I should like to direct attention to an excellent book by the lamented J. A. Montgomery…which deals very intelligently with the limited material then available for the background of the Gospel. I subscribe unreservedly to his conclusions" (30).

Twelve years later Albright wrote,

> All the concrete arguments for a late date for the Johannine literature have now been dissipated, and Bultmann's attempts to discern an earlier and later form of the Gospel have proved to be entirely misleading….The date which I personally prefer is the late 70s or early 80s, *i.e.*, not more than thirty or forty years after the composition of the earliest Pauline epistles.[4]

For these reasons and arguments suggested in these quoted paragraphs, one need give no credence to the accusation of Benjamin W. Bacon, in his *The Gospel of the Hellenists*, that the tradition in favor of the Apostle's authorship is "naturally suspect." What is suspect is Bacon's imaginations. He systematically disparages external evidence and accepts as historical his own subjective fancies. For example, he claims that *John* 1:6-8 was not in the original, but was inserted by an editor (243). No manuscript evidence supports this invention. Similarly with *John* 7:37-44 and 10:7-10. Not willing to search for the meaning of the text, as the manuscripts have it, he devises his own meanings and rearranges the order of passages to suit his idea of what an editor would do. Some of his deletions are parenthetical remarks – as if the original author could not have made parenthetical remarks.

The dating, and the significance of the dates, of the extant manuscripts can well be omitted from a study of John's theology. But one point may be included. A tiny scrap of papyrus, called P[52], has three verses of *John* on one side and two verses on the other. It cannot have been written after A.D. 150, possibly earlier. Because of evidence such as this, even a radical critic like R. H. Fuller has said of John's *Gospel*, "The date is certainly not later than 100, as the Roberts fragment P[52] shows."[5]

A second subject of discussion has to do with the words we read in our printed *Gospels*, *i.e.*, the words we read in the printed Greek editions. Are these the words of the original manuscript? Or have they been so altered by copyists over the centuries that there is no reason to suppose that John wrote them? This is a very professorial question, even for those who know Greek. Fortunately, the professors with their papyri sheets and vellum codices can answer this question with comparative ease. But the manifold details are not for the general reader.

A third subject of discussion is the question whether the *Gospel* pictures Jesus the Messiah, divine, the Son of God, and the Second Person of the Trinity. The initial question is not whether Jesus is the Messiah. It is not even whether Jesus claimed to be Messiah. These

*Are these the words of the original manuscript? Or have they been so altered by copyists over the centuries that there is no reason to suppose that John wrote them?*

3. The remark on John's dying in Jerusalem is directed against R. H. Charles' assertion, in his work on *Revelation*, that the Apostle John was martyred before A.D. 70. Charles, of course, is intent on denying the *Gospel's* authenticity. But even if John had been martyred at that date, he could still have written the *Gospel* because there is no internal evidence against dating it before the destruction of Jerusalem. This consideration meets Charles' position, for if he rejects the external evidence putting John in Ephesus twenty years later, he leaves for himself only internal evidence for the date.

4. *New Horizons in Biblical Research.* Oxford University Press, 1966, 46.

5. *A Critical Introduction to the New Testament.* London, 1966, 177.

matters are later implications; but the initial question is, Does this *Gospel* present Jesus as Messiah? Geerhardus Vos in his *Self-Disclosure of Jesus* examined these matters thoroughly. His discussion covers all four *Gospels* and he analyzes all the nineteenth-century theories on these points. One of his conclusions is that these theories exhibit a strong and suspicious bias. The present study pays little attention to these nineteenth-century details. The text is quite clear on the main issue. Nevertheless, there remain questions of exegesis and inference. Of course, parts of the story are so clear that misunderstanding is almost impossible. Therefore, this present book will not be a commentary. There is little use heaping up comments about the obvious; and there are enough commentaries. But many of the puzzling passages can well be examined over again. This sort of discussion will form a large part of what follows. It cannot all be original. Nothing written on *John* today can be original, unless it be something very bad. But what is written here will be about as original as most studies of John, and may prove somewhat helpful. At least the writer hopes so.

Critical problems (author, date, and historicity) and the interpretation of puzzling passages overlap. Is the author a Jew? Does he talk from an Old Testament background? Or does he introduce Greek philosophical speculation into the Christian church? For example, why did he begin with the Prologue, and what does it mean? Did he reject or aim to correct the accounts of Matthew, Mark, and Luke? In this last question matters of historicity and interpretation are intertwined.

Or, further, maybe the question of historicity should not be raised at all. Maybe it does not matter. The *Gospel* can be an impressionistic picture, the result of a mystical, nonverbal revelation. Its aim may not be to convey to us any information, but to produce impressions on us. The accuracy is irrelevant. All that counts is the subjective emotions that are stimulated. Albert Schweitzer proposed a Christianity that lives out of the experiences and energies of an immediate religion that is independent of every historical ground. Emil Brunner wrote, "The witness to the resurrection is not an eye-witness but a faith-witness. It does not inform us of the resurrection, it attests it." Brunner makes even more puzzling statements: "The account of the apostle of his meeting with the risen one is not the basis of the revelational witness, but a phase of it. This phase is the basis of our belief in Christ and therefore of our belief in the resurrection." He continues, "We could believe in the resurrection even if there were no reports of it, so long as we remember that we have the apostolic testimony only because the apostle met the risen Lord, and without that testimony we could not believe."[6]

This raises the whole question of what revelation is. Did Jesus tell us the truth? Did John write the truth? What is truth? Well, John has something to say about what truth is. Maybe some people will not believe what John says; but it is neither scholarship nor honesty to make him say what he does not say. The first thing to do here is to examine the text. And this will be done.

*Albert Schweitzer proposed a Christianity that lives out of the experiences and energies of an immediate religion that is independent of every historical ground.*

6. *Die christliche Lehre von Schöpfung*, 439-441.

The scope of these problems is ample and profound. Some very elementary remarks will also be included, even some sermonic material. For that matter, why should not scholarly exegesis be sermonic material? Most humble believers do not have the opportunity to study the destructive critics. But they must meet their influence. It is pervasive. Popular attacks on Christianity are based on the theories of Strauss, Renan (to mention some antiques), Brunner, and Bultmann. The background should be made known. But elementary material is also necessary for background. Over the past twenty years I have quoted a Bible verse as the basis of an exercise in logic. In all these college classes, I think I have found only one student who knew that the statement came from the Bible. I hope that people who attend church, or at least good churches, know a little more. But for the sake of college students, this book will contain some elementary material. Each reader must take what suits him.

Before plunging into anything difficult or profound, one does well to note in a general way what John's purpose was in writing this *Gospel*. To be sure there is no doubt about the purpose, for John states it clearly: "These things are written that you may believe that Jesus is the Christ, the Son of God, and that believing you might have life through his name." Although this statement of purpose is so explicit, still a little preparatory explanation will provide the background for the study of the details to come.

*"These things are written that you may believe that Jesus is the Christ, the Son of God, and that believing you might have life through his name."*

For one thing, could not this statement of purpose be made of *Matthew*, *Mark*, and *Luke*? Was John the only disciple who wanted to convince people that Jesus was the Son of God? Hardly; and yet there is a difference in emphasis and in execution, a difference that makes the purpose especially appropriate for John. There are several differences.

The first difference, and the most obvious, is that Matthew, Mark, and Luke all give a somewhat extended account of the three years of Christ's ministry. They may not have written what nineteenth-century historians would call a Life of Jesus, but in their fulness they approximate a biographical account. John, on the other hand, does not give an extended account; although it is he rather than the others who makes it clear that Jesus' ministry covered a three-year period. Yet John selects out of these three years only about twenty days. In fact, one third of the *Gospel*, chapters 13-19, occurs all in one day. Naturally the day of crucifixion must loom large in any *Gospel*. Therefore, there is a certain amount of overlapping between John and the other three. But as for the other nineteen days, John seems to have deliberately avoided (with one main exception) repeating the events recorded in *Matthew*, *Mark*, and *Luke*. There was, of course, no need to repeat. Therefore Bultmann's argument is valueless, when he says that John either never heard of the virgin birth, or, if he had, repudiated it. When John came to write his *Gospel*, late in the first century, the other *Gospels* were already well-known and widely circulated. A comparison will show that aside from the passion week, which obviously no *Gospel* writer could omit, there are only two clear contacts with the other three *Gospels*, namely, the feeding of the five thousand and the walking on the sea. This difference shows John's independence of the other writers. He did not intend to set them aside, to correct them, nor even to supplement them. Of course, he does supplement them, but that is not his purpose, nor does his method imitate theirs.

The second difference between John's *Gospel* and the others (which are in technical language called "Synoptics" because they have the same point of view) is a difference in method or procedure. John relied on personal reminiscences. He was an eyewitness, and he wrote about what he saw and heard. The other *Gospel* writers were not eyewitnesses, or at least were not to the same extent. Matthew no doubt observed nearly everything after the time he became a disciple, but Mark could have seen only a little. The *Muratorian Canon* says that Luke never saw Jesus. John, however, depends on a vivid memory and reports many apparently trivial details. These are signs of an eyewitness. He notes accurately the passage of time (something Matthew is not interested in at all); he gives precise geographical locations; he tells us that the water pots at Cana were made of stone. He tells us what he saw; and, of course, and above all he saw Jesus – but he does not say it just that way. He says (1:14) "We beheld his glory, the glory as of the only begotten of the Father, full of grace and truth." And through the *Gospel* he tells us what he and the other disciples saw with their eyes, what they heard, and what their hands handled of the Word of Life.

A third difference between John's *Gospel* and the Synoptics has already been implied. In limiting his personal reminiscences to the events of twenty days, John fills his *Gospel* with a different content. As was said before, there are only two clear points of contact (not counting the last week). The difference in content lies in this: The Synoptics, with their more extensive coverage of Christ's ministry, give a more public view of Christ. They show us Christ before the multitudes. John, too, in certain places speaks about the crowds; but he chiefly describes lone individuals before Christ. The crowds recede into the background and John centers attention on the impression Jesus made on a few individuals.

There was Nathaniel, who in a few minutes confessed, "You are the King of Israel." There was Nicodemus, who had to go home and think a while. There was the woman of Samaria, who accepted him as the Messiah; and the people of the village who said, "Now we believe, not because of your saying, for we have heard him ourselves and know that this is indeed the Christ, the Savior of the world." Then, to jump ahead, there were the officers who were sent to arrest him: They came back and reported, "Never man spoke like this man."

These officers, naturally, are not a lone individual. While the confrontations with lone individuals stand out vividly in *John*, there are some instances also where groups play an important role. The officers just mentioned, the five thousand who were fed, and the Pharisees are

*John, too, in certain places speaks about the crowds; but he chiefly describes lone individuals before Christ.*

such cases. In this last case, Jesus, as always, made a vivid impression, but it was not a favorable impression. In chapter 6 Jesus stirs up opposition. The teaching in the temple, given in the next two chapters, resulted in an attempt to kill Jesus. The man born blind, whose eyes were opened, frustrated and infuriated the Pharisees. The raising of Lazarus was intolerable; and the result was that they preferred Barabbas to Jesus.

These three differences between the Synoptics and *John*, namely, the difference in extent, in method, and in content, all depend on a fourth and basic difference, a difference in purpose.

Matthew's purpose, so it seems, was to convince the Jews that Jesus fulfilled Old Testament prophecies. To do this, he ignored the chronology of Christ's ministry (of course, he began with Jesus' birth and ended with the resurrection; but in between he pays little attention to time) by giving a sample of Jesus' preaching in chapters 5, 6, and 7; by then continuing with a series of miracles; and later by collecting a number of parables. Mark wrote a short account of Jesus' ministry, presumably for the Romans, chiefly. Luke was particularly interested in chronology. No doubt he (Matthew and Mark as well) hoped that people would come to believe on Christ because of his writing; but Luke had more of an historian's desire to set down the facts "in order," presumably chronological order. Luke's immediate purpose was to assure Theophilus of the certainty of his Christian instruction. Evangelism and the effect of the book on unbelievers is not mentioned.

> *John in his* Gospel *is the evangelist* par excellence.

But John in his *Gospel* is the evangelist *par excellence*. Stationed in the city of Ephesus, with its pagan worship of Diana, the scenes of his young manhood come back to the aged John, and before he departs this world he writes his final book, the *Gospel*, selecting the material so that its readers, including those of all future centuries, might believe that Jesus is the Christ, the Son of God, and that believing they might have life in his name.

## 2. The Prologue

To the ordinary devout Christian who simply wants to study through the *Gospel of John*, it must seem extremely unfortunate that the first five verses are so extremely difficult. One thus discouraged at the outset may well skip this passage and pass on to easier paragraphs; but let him not forget that he has skipped what John thought the best introduction to his message. There is no compelling reason why a person should not begin with chapter 3 or 4, or 5 or 6; but he must return, if he wishes to understand the *Gospel*, for the first five verses are as important as they are difficult.

Since verse 1 is both difficult and important, since indeed the *logos* is the subject of the present study, the general reader, though he has forgotten his high school Latin and has never had Greek, should patiently spend a few minutes on the mysteries of translation. The most pedestrian way to begin is to list the dictionary meanings of the Greek word *logos*: "In the beginning was the *logos*." What can *logos* mean?

Jerome, whose translation was superior to all previous Latin transla-
tions, translated it as *verbum*, and this became *word* in English. But *verbum* is not the cognate form of *logos*. *Verbum* is a digammated form of
the Greek *eiroo*, and *eiroo* is the root for *rheema*, not *logos*. Later in this
study *rheema* will be considered. But here we try to translate *logos*. Is
*word* a good translation?

*Liddell and Scott* (edition of 1940), the most thorough of all Greek
lexicons, has about five-and-a-half columns, ninety lines to the col-
umn, on *logos*. Some of the meanings listed are: *computation, reckoning,
account, measure, esteem, proportion, ratio, explanation, pretext, plea, argument, discourse, rule, principle, law, hypothesis, reason, formula, definition, debate, narrative, description, speech, oracle, phrase, wisdom, sentence,* and at the
very end, *word*.

*Because the usual
English translation
conveys no meaning
to the average mind,*
word *is a poor
translation in
verse 1.*

Because of this long list of possible choices, because also of the
etymological twist of Jerome's translation, and because the usual English translation conveys no meaning to the average mind, *word* is a
poor translation in verse 1. "In the beginning" will remind a Bible
student of creation in *Genesis*; but *word* suggests virtually nothing. There
is indeed an English word with the same root as *logos*. Though it would
make a somewhat inadequate translation, it would convey some meaning, a relatively accurate meaning; but for a peculiar reason, which this
study hopes to dispel, many people dislike it. But to begin in schoolboy fashion, let us try to pick a word from *Liddell and Scott's* list. Should
the inexperienced translator write, In the beginning was the *reckoning*?
Or, In the beginning was the *pretext*? The *hypothesis*, the *debate*? Clearly
the list of possible meanings, the list all by itself, is not of much help in
arriving at a good translation. One must know how the word *logos* was
used in Greek literature.

In addition to its use in ordinary language, *logos* in Greek became a
technical term of philosophy. Inasmuch as hostile critics have argued
that Christianity owes as much or more to pagan Greek philosophy
and religion than it owes to the Old Testament, that Paul was actually
an initiate of the mystery religions and from them derived the idea of
redemption, and that the Gospel was the result of a century of legend-
ary accretions, it is well to compare John's use of the term *logos* with its
use in pagan thought. This latter is part of the larger problem. It contributes to the decision as to whether the doctrine of the Trinity is a
pagan construction and whether the words *hypostases* and *ousia* in the
Nicene Creed come directly from Aristotle and the Neoplatonics. These
wider questions, however, must be laid aside now, for the immediate
problem has to do with the term *logos*.

*Logos* became a technical term in philosophy because of the work
of Heraclitus, a Greek scholar who lived in Ephesus about 500 B.C. He
thought that the universe was made of fire. The evidence is that everything is constantly changing, and fire is the fastest moving of the four
elements; therefore, all things must be made of fire. But throughout
the constant flux, there is a universal law that does not change. Heraclitus
called it the *Logos*. This law is indeed the original fire itself. It is a

wisdom that directs the course of nature. For which reason Heraclitus says, "It wills, and it wills not, to be called Zeus."

The Stoics, whose school was organized about 300 B.C., took over Heraclitus' doctrine and developed it. For them too the universe was made of fire, and the *cosmos* would end in a universal conflagration. At the present time this fire takes on the form of mountains, animals, men. That is to say, a spark of the divine *Logos* controls or even is each individual thing. These sparks, or *logoi*, *seminal logoi*, are thought of as seeds, from which grow all that we see. The Stoics may have emphasized, for religious purposes, that every man is a spark of divinity; but the theory requires that animals and mountains be sparks of divinity as well. Clearly Heraclitus and the Stoics were what we usually call pantheists. Certainly the Apostle John did not take over Greek pantheism when he used the word *logos*. Kittel in his immense *Theological Word-Book* rightly says that "There is a great difference between Hellenistic *Logos* speculation and the New Testament *Logos*" (90).

One of the most important differences is that the pagans did not say that their *Logos* was incarnate in one particular man at a given date in history. True, their *Logos* was, in a sense, incarnate in every man and animal. It manifests itself throughout the world. But for that very reason it has no unique manifestation, as John describes Jesus Christ. For the Stoics the activity of the *Logos* is entirely natural, repeated in every event; not something that occurred only once.

Philo, a Jewish philosopher in Alexandria at the time of Christ, made great use of the term *Logos*. He may have been influenced by Stoicism, but he was more influenced by Plato. Plato himself hardly had any *Logos* doctrine. For him a *logos* was a verbal expression of thought. Plato did assert the existence of supersensible Ideas in a world above this visible world. The world of Ideas was Plato's highest reality, even superior to the Demiurge (God?), who was the Maker of Heaven and Earth. Philo, with as much Jewish background as Platonic, represented the world of Ideas as ideas in the mind of God - something Plato explicitly denied. This world of Ideas he called the *Logos*, the Son of God. But his language was extremely figurative, and it is a reading back into him of Christian notions to think that he anticipated John or Athanasius. His language, however, was favorable to Christian (mis-)interpretation.

In addition to these reputable philosophers – the Stoics, Plato, Philo – there were about this time a number of popular religions, called mystery religions. They were mixtures of all sorts of notions. Among these, after the advent of Christianity, particularly in the second century, Gnosticism became a widespread religion. In contrast with the earlier mystery religions, Gnosticism made use of several Christian terms. Since Gnosticism was so widespread in the second century, it must have had its beginnings in the first century. Hostile critics have tried to explain Christianity as a form of Gnosticism, rather than Gnosticism as partly dependent on Christianity. This ties in with the attempt to date the *Gospel of John* in the late second century. But now

*Certainly the Apostle John did not take over Greek pantheism when he used the word logos.*

that the late date has been discredited, the fanciful reconstructions of the destructive critics are seen to have reversed the historical sequence.

For the explanation of John's Prologue, however, there remains the problem of why he used the word *logos*. If this term is to be understood as an element borrowed from Greek philosophy, if John's thought is construed as similar to that of the Gnostics and the Hermetic literature, it is strange that the further and frequent occurrences of the word in *John* are so totally devoid of such meaning. If, on the other hand, *logos* is simply an ordinary Greek word with all the meanings that *Liddell and Scott* list, and if John's thought and even the word itself have an Old Testament background, then a very different picture comes into focus.

Not that John was unaware of the philosophic use of the word. There remains one more thing to say about Gnosticism. Gnosticism flourished in the second century. By implication it must have appeared in some form in the first century. Evidence from the New Testament itself (*Ephesians, Colossians,* and the *Epistles of John*) corroborates this inference. This situation may help to explain why John wrote his Prologue. If we suppose that Gnostic ideas were growing in popularity before A.D. 90, it seems reasonable that a Christian author, not to say an apostle, might warn his readers against false views of the *Logos*. There were such false views. The so-called Hermetic literature, with *Poimander* as its first tractate, describes the *Logos* as emanating from a Light that is later identified as the Father-Intellect. The *Logos* is called the Son of God. *Poimander's* theology is extremely confused and contrasts with John's clarity. For example, some phrases in *Poimander* seem to teach that the *Logos* was not "in the beginning"; while others can be interpreted as implying that he was. One sentence says that the Intellect brought forth man co-equal with himself. This is obviously inconsistent with *John* and the New Testament. Even if one at first sight doubted that *Poimander* would have made man and God co-equal, and if therefore one wished to minimize the assertion, there can be no doubt that *Poimander's* salvation is a deification quite different from anything found in the New Testament. It requires egregious stupidity to suggest that the theology of *Poimander* had any influence on John's or Paul's theology. And although *Poimander* is usually dated about A.D. 125, there is as little reason to suppose that it derived any of its ideas from the New Testament.

Nevertheless, with such ideas in circulation, there is nothing absurd in supposing that John deliberately wrote his Prologue to warn Gentile Christians against false forms of the *Logos* doctrine.[7]

But there is some Old Testament background as well. When the Jewish scholars in Alexandria about 200 B.C. translated the Old Testament into Greek, they had to decide how to speak of the Word of God. The Hebrew root is *DBR*. What Greek word should be used for *word*? From *Genesis* to *Ruth* the Jewish translators preferred the Greek word *rheema*. This word and its relation to *logos* must be discussed later. In the prophets, however, the Alexandrian translators preferred *logos*, in fact, much preferred *logos*. Hence even from the standpoint of the Jew-

*A Christian author, not to say an apostle, might warn his readers against false views of the Logos.*

7. See Clark, *Selections from Hellenistic Philosophy*, 184-218.

ish background, John had reason to use this term; but the way he used it in the Prologue can, I believe, best be explained as a denial of pagan religions.

Now, in summary, the ordinary meaning of the Greek term, *i.e.*, the list in the lexicon, can fairly well be combined into the idea of thinking, or the expression of thought. The English cognate is *logic*, the science of valid reasoning. As a Greek philosophic term, *Logos* indicates a supreme intelligence controlling the universe. To be sure, this was pantheistically conceived by Heraclitus and the Stoics, but in more orthodox fashion by Philo. And, tautologically, the Old Testament gives the Biblical meaning. Therefore, if one hesitates to translate the first verse as, "In the beginning was the divine Logic," at least one can say, "In the beginning was Wisdom." This translation is accurate enough; it preserves the connotations; and it conveys a satisfactory meaning to the average mind.

There are modern themes also to which the idea of the *Logos* applies. Two such applications are the German Romanticism of the very early nineteenth-century and the twentieth-century Arianism of Jehovah's Witnesses. John said, with an evident reference to the first verse of *Genesis*, "In the beginning was the *Logos* (the Word, the Reason, the Wisdom)…and the Word was God." Jehovah's Witnesses refuse to say that the Word was God, and the German Romantics refused to say that God was Word or Reason. First, consider a very interesting passage from Goethe's *Faust*:

> 'Tis writ, "In the beginning was the Word!"
> I pause, perplexed! Who now will help afford?
> I cannot the mere Word so highly prize;[a]
> I must translate it otherwise,
> If by the spirit[b] guided as I read.
> "In the beginning was the Sense![c] Take heed,
> The import of this primal sentence weigh,
> Lest thy too hasty pen be led astray.
> Is *force* creative, then, of Sense the dower?[d]
> "In the beginning was the Power."
> Thus should it stand; yet, while the line I trace,
> A something warns me, once more to erase.
> The spirit aids! From anxious scruples freed,
> I write, "In the beginning was the Deed![e]

Certain explanatory notes are needed:

(a) Faust or Goethe is a Romantic. For him life is deeper than logic. Value consists in having the greatest possible number of experiences – except intellectual experiences. Life is "green" and all theory is "gray." Therefore, John is wrong in saying that Reason or Logic is the beginning of things.

(b) The spirit, the Earth-spirit, anything but the Holy Spirit, guides him to think that sensation is the source and explanation of all.

(c) As the Earth-spirit expresses Goethe's pantheism, so sensation is an expression of Romanticism. Yet *sensation* is not accurate enough.

*The English cognate is* logic, *the science of valid reasoning…. If one hesitates to translate the first verse as, "In the beginning was the divine Logic," at least one can say, "In the beginning was Wisdom."*

Faust, of course, seeks sense pleasures; but he also seeks other varieties of experiences. He wishes to dominate over other people and over all situations. Therefore

(d) the source of all had better be identified with power.

> *Ist es der Sinn, der alles wirkt und schafft?*
> *Es sollte stehen: im Anfang war die Kraft!*

Sense cannot produce and manage everything: It is power that sometimes works through sense.

(e) But Goethe still is not quite satisfied. The best way to translate *John* and explain the universe is to say, "In the beginning was the deed." This apparently is a reference to the philosophy of Fichte. Chronologically this seems possible, because Goethe took a long time to compose *Faust*. Fichte's philosophy was public knowledge before Goethe finally sent *Faust* to the printers. The two men surely agreed on some points. Fichte had difficulty in distinguishing himself from God; his *Ich* and his God were the same thing. This fits Goethe's pantheism. Then, too, Fichte stressed the freedom of man. Spinoza's intellectual determinism repelled him. It is not science, not intellect, that gives access to reality, but faith, a free choice. True, Fichte emphasized morality, and Goethe did anything but. Yet Fichte's emphasis is as much a free, subjective choice as Goethe's. Thus Goethe seems to be saying that the autonomous choice of man is the beginning of all things. Of course, one must not foolishly suppose that Goethe could not translate a line of Greek. It is not a matter of translation. It is a matter of opposing the Christian view of the universe.

*Fichte stressed the freedom of man.... It is not science, not intellect, that gives access to reality, but faith, a free choice.*

If such is the case with Romanticism, the second group of people mentioned above, Jehovah's Witnesses, are back on the level of schoolboy translation. The Romantics could not believe that God is *Logos*. The modern sect cannot believe that the *Logos* is God.

Jehovah's Witnesses have produced the *New World Translation of the Holy Scriptures*. In it *John* 1:1 reads, "Originally the Word was, and the Word was with God, and the Word was a god." An appendix supports this translation, first, by a reference to James Moffatt's *New Translation of the New Testament*, where he attacks the deity of Christ by translating the verse as "...and the Word was divine." Secondly, the Appendix explains the grammar behind the translation:

> The reason...is that it is the Greek noun *theos* without the definite article, hence an anarthrous *theos*. The God with whom the Word or Logos was originally is designated here by the Greek expression *ho Theos, theos* preceded by the definite article *ho*, hence an articular *theos*. Careful translators recognize that the articular construction points to an identity, a personality, whereas an anarthrous construction points to a quality about someone.

The zealous Jehovah's Witness who comes to your front door will repeat all this to you in the best pedagogical fashion approved for professors of Greek. Then if you have a copy of the Greek New Testament beside the door, you can hand it to him and ask for further explanation. A friend of mine did just this. I never quite had the opportunity. When a Witness caught me once with a Greek book in my hand, it was one of Plotinus' *Enneads*. The *Enneads* are very difficult Greek, and it was a dirty trick to ask a Witness to show his knowledge of Greek by translating Plotinus. But it is not reprehensible to offer a Greek Testament to one who presumes to teach you about anarthrous predicate nouns in John's *Gospel*. So my friend put a Greek New Testament into his hands. The man looked at it carefully. Then he turned it upside down and examined it again. Then, *mirabile dictu* (pardon me, that is Latin, not Greek), he turned the Testament on its side and looked at the lines now in vertical columns. Then he asked, What is this? My friend replied, That is a Greek New Testament, about which you have been talking.

Probably my friend did not quote *Goodwin's Greek Grammar*, which says, "A predicate noun seldom has the article." I am fairly sure he did not quote Aristotle 403b2, "The definition is the form." Here *form* is anarthrous. He might have quoted *1 John* 4:16, "God is love." Or, *John* 1:49, "You are the King of Israel," where, as in all these cases, the predicate noun is anarthrous (see *John* 8:39, *John* 17:17, *Romans* 14:17, *Galatians* 4:25, and *Revelation* 1:20).

Since the time of Goodwin, Ernest C. Colwell has done more work on predicate nouns; and he proposes the following rule for the New Testament — "A definite predicate nominative has the article when it follows the verb; it does not have the article when it precedes the verb."

Colwell's studies and their application to Jehovah's Witnesses have been well written up by Robert H. Countess in the *Bulletin of the Evangelical Theological Society* (now called the *Journal*).[8]

The deity of Christ is, as has been stated, the main message of the *Gospel of John*. To mistranslate the first verse is to misconstrue the whole book. Yet the first verse of *John* is not by any means the only passage where the deity of Christ is taught, either in *John* or in the New Testament as a whole. Since Jehovah's Witnesses make Christ a created angel, it is well also to show them *Hebrews* 1:5, "To which of the angels said he at any time, You are my Son, this day have I begotten you?" But as for *John* the theory of the *Logos* is not completed in verse 1. The great difference between the pagan theories of the *Logos* and the Christian *Logos* is that in the latter the *Logos* became flesh and dwelt among us. At this point the section on the *Logos* may end, and what remains can be placed under the exegesis of *John* 1:1-14.

John wanted to write of the ministry of Jesus Christ. The literary problem was to select a suitable introduction. The relationship between the Son and the Father that John will describe in many places in the *Gospel* naturally suggests a starting point in eternity. Therefore, John's first two words are *en archee, in the beginning*. These are also the first two words of the Old Testament in the *LXX* translation. This reference to the Old Testament is one of the many reasons for refusing

*To mistranslate the first verse is to misconstrue the whole book.*

8. *Bulletin of the Evangelical Theological Society*, X, 3, Summer 1967.

to accept the thesis that John's message is an adaptation from pagan Greek philosophy or religion. It is also an evidence that the subject of which John speaks is God: In the beginning God. Yet Jehovah's Witnesses are right to the extent of indicating that here in *John* there is a distinction to which *Genesis* does not allude. They say that the *Logos* cannot be the same as the God (with the article) with whom the *Logos* is. They conclude that the *Logos* therefore cannot be God.

The words *same* and *different*, however, are very flexible words. A cat is the same as a dog in the fact that they both have four feet. A square is the same as a circle in that they are both geometrical figures. When I was a boy there was a shoe polish called "Three in One." What precisely was the three and what the one, I do not remember; but there is no contradiction in saying that the same thing is three in one respect and one in another. Later on Jesus will say, I and my Father are one. When therefore John, or any author, makes a puzzling statement, perhaps to attract notice, it is not sound procedure to assume right off that he has contradicted himself. Some authors do indeed contradict themselves. Others think clearly; and if one grasps their thought, one will understand their logical consistency. Hence there just may be some sense in which the *Logos* can be *with* God and also be God.

Having now asserted the eternal identity of God and the *Logos*, John in verse 3 makes explicit the reference to creation. Here so soon is the second piece of evidence that the author did not get his ideas from pagan sources. They had no notion of a *fiat* creation, such as *Genesis* describes. For that matter, why should anyone search through the pagan religions to find the sources of John's thought? Some of these critics seem to forget completely that the first Christians were all Jews. Why should they not use the Old Testament?

Verse 4 says, "In him was life." The *was*, repeated from verses 1 and 2, is taken by one commentator to refer to the time of creation. In verse 5, however, the present tense occurs in the verb *shines*. Somewhere between verse 3 and verse 5 there must be a shift away from the time of creation to the present, even if it is a general present, rather than the particular time of John. Hence it is not clear that verse 4 must be restricted to a time before the fall of Adam.

With this understanding of the tenses, the verse says that the *Logos* was and still is the source of life. This life is hardly physical life: Mere physical life was taken care of under the previous reference to creation. Rather, under the figure of speech that "this life is the light of men," intellectual life must be meant. If anyone wishes to add moral life, well and good. Moral life is subordinate to intellectual life, for animals, who are below the level of reason, cannot be moral. That the life referred to is rational life is supported by both verse 5 and verse 9, as will become clear, as well as by the previous main thought that Reason, Wisdom, or Logic is God.

In anticipation, some emphasis should be put on the idea that intellectual life is life. Some people do not think so. Romanticism said, Life is green, all theory gray. Friedrich Schleiermacher and Søren

*Intellectual life is life.*

Kierkegaard introduced this notion into the stream of Christian theology. But it is not a Christian notion. John has something important to say about life; but one must not read Kierkegaard and Romanticism back into the *Gospel*.

The life that was in the *Logos*, the Creator, was the light of men; and the light shines in the darkness. Verse 5 surely cannot refer to physical darkness. The remainder of the *Gospel* squarely opposes any such literal view. The light is spiritual, and the darkness also is spiritual, rational, or intellectual. This understanding of the verse, along with the present tense *shines*, indicates that at this early stage the *Gospel* has advanced beyond the time of the creation of Heaven and Earth.

Again with this understanding, the moral or spiritual darkness did not comprehend, understand, or grasp it. The Greek word is *katelaben*. It means to grasp, to catch on. In colloquial English also the term *catch on* has an intellectual sense as often as or perhaps more often than its purely physical sense of holding something in one's hands.

Weymouth translates the verse, "The darkness has not overpowered it." Although this is grammatically possible, this particular meaning of the Greek verb does not occur in the New Testament; and such meaning conflicts with the parallel expressions in verses 10, 11, and 12.

With a look back to the German Romantics and a look forward to present-day mystics and dialectical theologians, this introductory paragraph is inimical to the theme that "life is deeper than logic." There is no hint, as yet at least, that the message of *John* will be self-contradictory, illogical, irrational. There is no such idea in the Old Testament. One may confidently expect the New Testament to continue the same way. Reason is the source of life; life is not the source of Reason. The evolutionary view of man, which makes rationality an accidental biological development, finds no support in the Bible.

The transition from verse 5 to verse 6 seems abrupt, but the connection is that John the Baptist came as a witness to the light. John was not himself the light, but a witness to the light – this is clear enough; but verse 9 is a little difficult. A very literal translation is, "It was the true light, which enlightens every man coming into the world." A new translation, called *A Contemporary Translation*, puts it, "The true light that gives light to every man was coming into the world." This is not a very good translation. Whether it is a good interpretation must be considered.

The point at issue is the identification of the noun which the phrase "coming into the world" modifies. Is it the light that is coming into the world, as *A Contemporary Translation* has it, or is it every man who comes into the world, as the *King James* says?

The simplest grammatical construction is to connect the phrase with the noun *man*. As the literal translation given above shows, the participle *coming* is the very next word after the word *man*. To make it refer to a word some distance before complicates the interpretation. Of course, this is possible, but it can be accepted only if there are very good non-grammatical reasons. One reason given is that the apostle

*Reason is the source of life; life is not the source of Reason. The evolutionary view of man, which makes rationality an accidental biological development, finds no support in the Bible.*

wished to emphasize Christ's coming and incarnation. This, of course, is true, especially if one suspects that John aimed to repudiate the pagan naturalistic theories of the *Logos*. But with respect to verse 9, the reason is inconclusive because, first, the incarnation is sufficiently emphasized in verse 11, and particularly in verse 14. Verse 14 does not need a weak anticipation in verse 9. Then, second, the light has always been in the world. The imperfect tenses of verse 4, and even of verses 1 and 2, and possibly verse 9, indicate a function that has been carried on since the creation of man. Therefore, it seems more likely that verse 9 refers to this function of long-standing as it has affected every man that comes into the world.

The sense of the verse, not too easily determined from the verse all by itself, seems to be that Christ enlightens every man ever born by having created him with an intellectual and moral endowment. Paul in *Romans* 1:32 says, "Who knowing the judgment of God...." The heathen of past ages all know that God punishes immorality. This knowledge is a part of the image of God in which God created Adam. Although this intellectual or spiritual endowment has been defaced and distorted by sin, yet it has not been annihilated: It remains as the basis of human responsibility and renders men inexcusable. Augustine in his *De Magistro* develops other phases of Christ's teaching function.

This *light* need not mean the light of salvation; in fact it cannot in the verses quoted. *Light* as a term is comprehensive. It can include actual salvation. But how much light a given passage refers to must be determined by the passage itself and the context.

The verses rush on. The *Gospel* begins in eternity. Then the creation. Then in verse 5 there is the fall, or at least the results of the fall. Then John the Baptist comes to witness to the Light that the darkness did not grasp; and the author proceeds quickly to the historical Jesus. Christ's coming and his rejection is a case of the darkness not receiving the Light. He came to his own inheritance, to his own possession, Israel, the chosen nation; but the people, his own people, did not receive him. And this results in the author's expounding some very important theology.

Verse 12 says that in contrast with the Jews who rejected him, Jesus gave to those who accepted him the right or power to become children of God. These people are identified by the fact that they believe in his name.

Some paragraphs above, care was taken to show that the apostle did not get his message from pagan sources. Greek philosophy and Greek religion did not produce the *Gospel*. But if it is necessary to distinguish the Christian message from ancient themes, it is also necessary, and more so for people today, to contrast Christianity with much modern religion. For nearly a century the universal Fatherhood of God and the universal brotherhood of man has been proclaimed as the essence of Christianity. In view of these immediate verses in *John*, it is surprising that such a notion ever should have risen. Of course, Jesus teaches the Fatherhood of God; but is not the universal kind of Fatherhood

> *If it is necessary to distinguish the Christian message from ancient themes, it is also necessary ...to contrast Christianity with much modern religion.*

that modern theology has in mind. Modern theology, like the Stoic theory, believes that God is the Father of all men, and that all men are his children. But if words are ever clear, verse 12 asserts that some men are not children of God and that God gives to some others the right to become children of God. They were not God's children before; but now they can become such.

There is a very curious twist in modern theology. Christianity with its doctrine of creation insists on the biological unity of the human race. All men are literal descendants of Adam and Eve. But as Augustine so well explained in the *City of God*, the human race is broken into a spiritual duality. There is the city of this world, and the City of God. Between Stalin and the Apostle John there is no spiritual unity. Yet the liberal evolutionism that characterizes much that passes for Christianity cannot assert the biological unity of the human race. According to the evolutionary theory, it is quite possible that human beings evolved from lower species at different times and at different places. Without such a biological unity how can the liberals assert the spiritual unity of the race and preach the universal brotherhood of man? How can they be sure that no higher species will arise with less spiritual unity than men now have?

In opposition to Modernism and Humanism, Christianity asserts that only those who believe in Jesus Christ have the power, the right, or the authority to become children of God. Later on it will be seen that Jesus says that those who do not believe on him are children of the devil. He minces no words: You are of your father the devil, and his works you do; since he is the father of lies, you are naturally liars! But rather than refer to a passage several chapters in advance, it is enough to proceed to the immediately following verse.

Verse 13, a most interesting verse, connects with the preceding "to those who believe on his name," and adds, "who were born, not of bloods, nor of the will of the flesh, nor of the will of man, but of God."

A few modern commentators have played with a Latin version plus half a dozen Latin authors who make the verse read, "who was born...." Thus they try to find a reference to the virgin birth in the singular verb and the singular relative pronoun. The argument is that the plural, "who were born," interrupts John's line of thought. The emphasis, so they say, is on Christ, not on believers; and to contrast the natural birth of men with their spiritual birth does not serve the main purpose of the paragraph. But, so they continue, a reference to the virgin birth in the phrase "not of bloods," a peculiar plural, makes the progress of the thought clear and plain.

One great objection destroys this argument: No Greek manuscript has the singular verb and relative pronoun; and conjecture does not outweigh evidence. The singular occurs only in a Latin version.

As for the progress of thought, it is undeniable in the first place that John is indeed interested in the spiritual birth of believers. Chapter 3 puts this beyond discussion. In the second place, the first chapter, in the preceding verse, has spoken of those who receive Christ, so that believ-

*Christianity asserts that only those who believe in Jesus Christ have the power, the right, or the authority to become children of God.*

ers have already been brought into the picture. Then, third, a reference to the virgin birth would put verse 14 out of joint. It is in 1:14 that we have the general statement of the incarnation: The Word became flesh; a particular account of how the Word became flesh might have followed the general statement, but could hardly have preceded it.

Geerhardus Vos, in his attempt to find the virgin birth in *John*, does not insist on the singular, though he strangely calls the argument for it "strong." He tries to compromise by suggesting that even the plural reading refers *implicitly* to the virgin birth because, if John had in mind *only* the spiritual birth of believers, he simply would have said, "Who were born not of flesh, but of God." The redundancies, "not of bloods, nor flesh, nor a man," indicate a comparison between the believers' new birth and another supernatural birth.

*Some people think that a man is regenerated because he wills to be.... Here it is stated that a man's will has nothing to do with regeneration.*

Here Vos, in spite of all his other excellencies, indulges in subjective speculation, and his conclusion could be rendered plausible only by showing that no other interpretation of the so-called redundant phrases is possible. But not only is there another interpretation: It is a much better one.

The primary meaning of the text is that the believer is born of God and is not born of something else. These believers were given the authority, or privilege, or power to become the children of God (compare 5:27 and 17:2). They did not previously have this power. It is a gift, a gift that God gave to some people and not to all people. This is the Calvinistic doctrine of unconditional election. Now, the so-called redundant phrases make this thought still clearer. If one asks, in view of verse 12, how Christ can be "received," the first part of the answer tells how Christ cannot be received. The first way not to receive or believe on Christ is the way of bloods. The plural doubtless refers to parents, and as such could have formed a contrast with the virgin birth, if the virgin birth had been there to form a contrast with. As it occurs, however, it directly denies the common Jewish conception that salvation depends on physical descent from Abraham. That this was a common opinion is seen from *Matthew* 3:9, where John the Baptist upbraids the Jews for thinking that they are safe because "we have Abraham as our father" (see also *Galatians* 3:7). Even today there are some people who rely on a godly heritage of one sort or another.

The second way not to become a child of God is "the will of the flesh." The term *flesh* is regularly used to designate sinful human nature. All men by birth are estranged from God. Hence there is no capability in generic human nature by which a person can become God's child. Then in the third place, this birth is not the result of "the will of a man." That is to say, no individual in the human race stands out so unusually gifted or meritorious or strong of will that he can become a believer in Christ. Some people think that a man is regenerated because he wills to be, and others are not regenerated because they do not will to be. Here it is stated that a man's will has nothing to do with regeneration. John says pointedly that the only way is to be born of God. Human initiative counts for nothing because there is no human initiative. A man believes because he first has been made alive. Just as in natural birth, it is the parents and not the baby who cause the birth, so too in the spiritual realm, it is God and not the man who causes spiritual life, belief, and the status of child. How fortunate! For otherwise the dry bones would not put on flesh, the dead would not rise to newness of life, and the carnal mind at enmity with God could never become his child.

These ideas are so important that the introduction of an obscure reference to the virgin birth spoils the sense.

Now comes the culmination of John's Prologue. Verse 14 has two parts. The first part is, "The Word became flesh and dwelt among us." This culminating idea, the great idea that differentiates the Christian *Logos* doctrine from every pagan philosophy and as well from the semi-Jewish Philonic doctrine, is the incarnation of the Word, the Reason, or the Wisdom of God. The *Logos* became flesh. So utterly contradictory and even repulsive to all pagan Greek speculation is this that one is astounded to read reputed scholars who characterize John as Hellenistic and dependent on Gnostic, Stoic, or Platonic sources.

*It is God and not the man who causes spiritual life, belief, and the status of child.*

For example, consider the views of Edgar J. Goodspeed. Giving the late date of A.D. 110 to the *Gospel*, Goodspeed asserts that various considerations "combine to show that its author was a Greek, not Jew." The chief part of this combination is represented in the following quotations:

> Greek genius...adopted the struggling Christian faith and became its standard bearer for a thousand years....To meet the needs of this Greek public...was there no way [to] be introduced to the values of the Christian salvation without being forever routed, we might even say detoured through Judaism? The old books of Christianity were unsuited to this new situation...Matthew...how unpromising!... The times demanded that Christianity be transplanted to Greek soil and translated into universal terms. The Gospel of John is the response to this demand.[9]

Before continuing with other quotations from Goodspeed, one will note that there is a certain amount of truth in what he says; but there is also a great deal that is erroneous. Of course, it is true that the membership of the church became predominantly Gentile, and that these Gentiles had been raised in a Greek or Hellenistic civilization. But can it be said that in the hundred years after A.D. 70, which marked the end of the early Jewish period, "Greek genius adopted the Christian faith"? Hardly. The Gentile Christians by and large were inferior intellectually even to the decadent Stoic, Aristotelian, and Platonic schools. Later on Origen, not one of the most stalwart defenders of the faith, might through courtesy be called a "Greek genius"; but Athanasius was not; and Augustine could not even read the Greek language. More important is the fact that the most orthodox theologians did not find their themes and concepts in pagan philosophy. Athanasius' *De Decretis*, his defense of the Nicene Creed, seems never to mention Plato or

9. *An Introduction to the New Testament.* University of Chicago Press, 1937, 315, 296-298.

Aristotle, and refers to the Stoics only three times, in a derogatory manner; while there are hundreds of references to the Old and New Testaments. Now, if some Neoplatonic influence is discerned in Augustine, who, remember, received his intellectual capital while he was yet a pagan, a careful reading will disclose that his writings progressively contain less and less of it.

In the next place Goodspeed petulantly asks, "Was there no way…[to] be introduced to the values of the Christian salvation without being…detoured [!] through Judaism?"

Contrast this with the much more honest appraisal by Karl Barth:

> Both in the early days and more recently there have been many proposals and attempts to shake off the so-called Old Testament altogether or to reduce it to the level of a deuterocanonical introduction to the "real" Bible (*i.e.*, the New Testament)…. Neither in the New Testament nor in the documents of the second century post-apostolic period do we find the slightest trace of anyone seriously and responsibly trying to replace the Holy Scriptures of Israel by traditions of other nations…. Even Marcion never plunged in this direction, although he was near enough to it. We cannot plunge in this direction…without substituting another foundation for the foundation on which the Christian church is built…as R. Wilhelm has suggested…and many recent fools in Germany[10]

and Chicago.

As for the *Gospel of John* itself, it does not present the Old Testament as a "detour." Consider the reference to *Isaiah* in *John* 1:23; and the great verse in 1:29, "Behold the Lamb of God that takes away the sin of the world." Then there is Jesus' statement, "For if you believed Moses, you would believe me; for he wrote of me. But if you believe not his writings, how shall you believe my words?" Of a book that so fully mirrors the Jewish, even the priestly, milieu, how can one say that "the Gospel of John is the response to this demand" to avoid the Old Testament detour?

The continued quotation comes from the same page: "Jesus is more than the Messiah of Jewish nationalistic expectation; he is the Logos – the Word of Revelation that came upon the prophets, and also that Reason by which the Stoic philosophy found its way to truth."

Now, it is perfectly correct to say that Jesus was more than the Messiah as conceived by "Jewish nationalistic expectation" at that time. For one thing, he was the Messiah as conceived by the Old Testament. It is also true, and the present writer wishes to emphasize it most particularly against its underemphasis in anti-intellectual theologies, that Jesus is the *Logos*, the Word of Revelation, that not only came upon the prophets but that created the universe. But one must deny that Jesus was the Reason by which the Stoic philosophy found its way to truth. As Athanasius indicated, Stoic philosophy found very little truth. Their materialism and their empiricism is not what the *Logos* taught them. This is not to deny that Jesus is the Reason that enlightens every man, Hindu as well as Stoic, who comes into the

*Jesus is the* Logos, *the Word of Revelation, that not only came upon the prophets but that created the universe.*

10. *Church Dogmatics*, I, 2, 488.

world. The point is that Stoic philosophy, and Platonic philosophy, in their integrity, are not the sources of Johannine theology written to satisfy the stated demand.

On the next page (299) Goodspeed says, "in the Gospel of John the function of Jesus is not so much sacrificial as to bring life and impart it.... Jesus' death has little of its old sacrificial meaning."

On the contrary, it is clear from the verses last quoted, *viz.*, *John* 1:29 and 5:46-47, that Jesus' death has all of the old sacrificial meaning. One should also reflect on 4:22, "Salvation is from the Jews," for this pointed answer to the Samaritan woman's question envisages the whole sacrificial system of *Leviticus*. But Goodspeed plasters over his antagonism to sacrifice by the vague comparison "not so much sacrificial as to bring life." This is the logical fallacy of false disjunction. Jesus brought and implanted life by his death on the cross. There is here no either-or, but a both-and. The sacrifice was essential to the new life.

Goodspeed also holds that John rejected the idea of a final judgment, so graphically portrayed in *Matthew*. His reason is the statement, "God did not send his Son into the world to pass judgment upon the world," and "the judgment of this world is now in progress" (*John* 12:31).

As before, Goodspeed's failure to think logically is evident. We could wish that the Logic that enlightens every man had been more effective in this case; but then we do not see the end from the beginning as God does. At any rate, the two verses Goodspeed quotes do not imply that John rejected the idea of a final judgment. At most the second verse implies that the final judgment is not exhaustive of God's judicial procedure: There is also a present judgment. Besides, Goodspeed's translation of the Greek is not very accurate. Had he paid attention, he might have recognized that the word *now* does not require the idea of some extended progress, as if this judgment extended throughout history. It is true that there is a divine judgment throughout history. *Romans* 1:26 reflects on such a judgment. But if one should pay attention to the context in *John*, one would see that the judgment referred to was the crucifixion of Christ. This assertion, the assertion that the world is judged by Christ's death, does not imply a rejection of a final judgment. The first verse Goodspeed quoted serves him no better. Once again, "God did not send his Son into the world to pass judgment upon the world," does not imply the rejection of a final judgment. It might seem more reasonable to infer that if God did not send his Son to judge, God thereby reserved the final judgment for himself. Hence the idea is not rejected by the text. So much for possible implications. The context, however, gives the reasons and indicates the correct implication: God's immediate purpose in the incarnation was to save the world; there was no need for Jesus to condemn the world, for it was condemned already.

Not only are logic and the immediate context ignored, what is worse, the actual teaching of John on the final judgment is suppressed. First of all there are the verses of 5:28-29, "Do not be amazed at this,

*Jesus brought and implanted life by his death on the cross.*

for a time is coming when all who are in their graves will hear his voice and come out — those who did good to the resurrection of life, and those who did evil to the resurrection of judgment (or, condemnation)." Then there are the several verses in chapter 6 that refer to the resurrection at the last day. Besides, Martha, whom Christ had taught, said, "I know he will rise again in the resurrection at the last day." True, in this last passage Jesus says, "I am the resurrection and the life," but Goodspeed's attempt to turn this into a denial of a final judgment is worthless. Can one imagine Jesus or the author John saying, "Martha, you are wrong. Lazarus will never rise again; he has had life in me already; nothing more follows."

*Goodspeed then argues that the* Gospel *is a product of Greek civilization…because the Jews never carried on conversations. Only Greeks did.*

As Goodspeed approaches the conclusion of his chapter, he summarizes: John "is in short one of those men who care more for truth than for fact" (306); "Topography and chronology were among the least of the author's concerns" (310).

Now, the distinction between "fact" and "truth" is a tenuous one, and in two other volumes I have discussed the philosophical problems involved.[11] Nothing here, on a colloquial level – and Goodspeed seems to speak colloquially – contradicts the other discussions. It is true then that John cares more for truth than for fact. The "truth" that Jesus is the Lamb sacrificed to God for sin is more important than the "fact" that Jesus one day sat on the edge of a well, thirsty. But in this sense Matthew, whom Goodspeed contrasts with John, also cares more for truth than for fact. The falsity of Goodspeed's paragraph, and the proof that his ambiguous words are not to be taken in their true sense, comes in the next sentence: "Topography and chronology were among the least of the author's concerns." Even this may be true literally; but the implication is clear that John paid no attention to topography and chronology and got his facts all mixed up. Had Goodspeed desired to improve his contrast between John and Matthew, he could easily have shown that Matthew did not intend to write a chronological account of Christ's ministry. John clearly did. Indeed, a conservative commentator, Plummer for instance, can well argue from John's meticulous attention to detail to the conclusion that the author must have been an eyewitness of the events. To be sure, the fact that the waterpots were stone and not clay is of less concern than the miracle, but still John wrote that they were stone. *Et cetera.*

Goodspeed then argues that the *Gospel* is a product of Greek civilization in its attempts to avoid the detour of Judaism because the Jews never carried on conversations. Only Greeks did. There are many conversations in John, and "this trait stamps the Gospel of John as distinctly Greek in feeling and method" (308). For support, Goodspeed appeals to Plato and Aristotle. He fails to note that there are no conversations in Aristotle, and that there are conversations in *Matthew* as well as in *John.*

11. See *The Philosophy of Science and Belief in God* and *Historiography: Secular and Religious.*

The main line of the present volume's discussion had come to the culmination of the Prologue; and this excursus on Goodspeed arose from the liberal inference that John based his views, not on the Old

Testament, but on Greek civilization. The greatest refutation of this claim is the culminating verse, "The Word became flesh."

Liberal interpretations of the verse itself and the complex of ideas therein reflected are also surprising. Bultmann writes,

> "The Word became flesh."… The Revealer appears…as a definite human being in history: Jesus of Nazareth. His humanity is genuine humanity: "the Word became flesh." Hence John has no theory about the preexistent one's miraculous manner of entry into the world, nor about the manner of his union with the man Jesus. He neither knows the legend of the virgin birth nor that of Jesus' birth in Bethlehem – or if he knows them, he will have nothing to do with them.[12]

Before the more important material on these pages from Bultmann is quoted, three remarks can be made on these preliminary lines. The first point is Bultmann's inference introduced by the word "Hence." Surely from the fact that Jesus' humanity was genuine and not docetic, it does not follow that John had no "theory" or notion about the preexistent one's miraculous entry into the world. Bultmann's inference is fallacious. Even the weakening qualification of the last phrase quoted, "or if he knows them…," does not remove the illogic of the passage. It is true, of course, that John's *Gospel* does not give an account of the virgin birth: It does not give any account of his birth. But this is not to say that he will have nothing to do with it, as if he repudiated *Matthew* and *Luke*. Even Bultmann cannot leave unqualified his suggestion that John, writing perhaps thirty years after Luke, "knows neither the legend of the virgin birth nor that of Jesus' birth in Bethlehem." Of course he knew them (though not as legend or myth).

The second point is whether Bultmann accepts even the statement, "the Word became flesh." He talks about a "preexistent one's…union with the man Jesus." This suggests that either there were two persons, the Word and Jesus, or that an impersonal Word, some divine principle or power, came to indwell the merely human Jesus. In either case Bultmann cannot work into his theory the teaching of John that the Word who created all things and is himself God became flesh.

The third point was somewhat covered under the first. In showing the illogicality of Bultmann's inference, it was also made clear that John cannot be accused of never having heard of *Matthew* and *Luke*. Now, to continue the quotation:

> Though Jesus says in departing from the earth, "I have manifested thy name to the men whom thou gavest me out of the world," still he has imparted no information about God at all, any more than he has brought instruction about the origin of the world or the fate of the self. He does not *communicate anything*, but *calls men to himself.*

The first chapter of the *Gospel* contains important information about the creation of the universe, the spiritual plight of man, the nature and mission of Christ, and something of Old Testament prophecy. The occurrence of this information does not contradict the quotation made just above because these verses are the words of John

*The first chapter of the* Gospel *contains important information about the creation of the universe, the spiritual plight of man, the nature and mission of Christ.*

12. *Theology of the New Testament,* II, 40-42.

and not of Jesus. Bultmann claims that Jesus offered no information. On this two things should be said. First, a Christian cannot permit himself to be restricted to the *ipsissima verba* of Jesus, as if the author's words were less true, less authoritative, less important. Redletter Bibles, if they do not strain the eyesight, have some small use; but only a small part of Christianity is found in the red sections. In the second place, there can be no objection to asking the question, Did Jesus himself impart any information about God? Did he only call men to himself without instructing them concerning their state and their fate? Did he *communicate* nothing at all?

Well, obviously he communicated several bits of information; and Bultmann himself quotes a part of it. Jesus, in the verse Bultmann cites, informs his disciples that God has given him a certain group of men chosen from out of the world's population. In fact, chapter 17 contains considerable information about God. It tells us that God gave author-ity to Jesus to give eternal life to those people God had chosen. Eter-nal life is defined as knowledge of God. God sent Christ into the world. All that belongs to God belongs to Christ. And a second time, God sent Christ into the world. God is in Christ and Christ is in God. Again, God gave Christ a certain people. God loved Christ before the creation of the world. These several items of information about God, to which no doubt a few implications could be added, are by them-selves enough to contradict Bultmann's rash assertion that "Jesus…has imparted no information about God at all."

*Eternal life is defined as knowledge of God.*

If one should summarize all the information about God that Jesus imparts in the *Gospel* as a whole, the account would be lengthy; yet it is of use to list some other items of information that Jesus communi-cated about God, the origin of the world, and the fate of the self – none of which occurs in the *Gospel*, according to Bultmann.

Though the first reference will be one of the poorer references, for the exact words are not given, Jesus convinced Andrew (*John* 1:41) and Nathaniel (1:49) that he was the promised Messiah, the Son of God, and the King of Israel. Let Bultmann refer to this as calling men to "himself"; it is also theological information.

The conversation with Nicodemus, more explicitly than the previ-ous verses, records a quantity of theological information. Jesus informs Nicodemus that God requires a man to be born again before he can enter God's kingdom. After continuing with this idea for ten verses, Jesus informs Nicodemus that he must be lifted up as Moses lifted up the brass serpent; that those who do not believe on the Messiah shall perish; and that he is the Savior. Jesus also informs Nicodemus of the evil of loving sin rather than righteousness. Granted, this is not ex-plained in full; granted also that Nicodemus did not understand the good news; granted even that it says nothing explicit about the origin of the world; but it is nevertheless news, information, and theology about God and the fate of the self.

Chapter 4 recounts the information Jesus gave to the woman at the well. No doubt he revealed *himself*; but he did so by giving information. This information included the fact that he was greater than Jacob; that he supplies "water" better than Jacob's; it also includes his supernatural knowledge of the woman's life with the implication that he is a prophet; he also very plainly informs her that salvation comes through the Jewish nation and that up to the present God requires his people to worship him in Jerusalem and not on Mount Gerizim; there follows the information that soon worship no longer will be restricted to Jerusalem. Then Jesus gives the woman the information that God is spirit and explicitly tells her that he is the Messiah. All this presupposes the truth of the Old Testament and therefore asserts divine providence through the course of history. How then can Bultmann write that Jesus imparted no information at all about God, about himself, and the fate of the self? He certainly cannot maintain his position on the basis of the text.

*Documentation against Bultmann is overwhelming.*

Chapter 5 gives information about the relationship of Jesus to the Father. Important as it is, need it be detailed here? It is strong trinitarian theology. The chapter also contains information about the Old Testament, much more explicitly than chapter 4. Next, chapter 6, among other things, gives information about the resurrection of believers: Surely this comes under the category of the "fate of the self." And as for solid, profound, and even disturbing theology, there is verse 44. It was disturbing information to the Jews because many of them who had followed Jesus to this point could not accept the theology here given and now deserted him because of it (6:65-66).

Without going tediously further into the later chapters, one can now conclude that the documentation against Bultmann is overwhelming. There is, however, a slightly amusing point. Though Bultmann distinguishes between what Jesus said and what John says, apparently preferring Jesus' own words, yet his favorite verse, "the Word became flesh," is one piece of information that Jesus did not communicate: These are the words of John. Is Bultmann then willing to accept all of John's statements as true, as "Gospel truth"; and if he is not, why should he so much prefer this one?

No further criticism is necessary; but two more paragraphs, twenty-some pages later, show the ingrained wrongheadedness and perversity of Bultmann's treatment of John.

> Jesus' words never convey anything specific or concrete that he has seen with the Father. Not once does he communicate matters or events to which he had been a witness by either eye or ear.... So it is clear that the mythological statements have lost their mythological meaning. Jesus is not presented in literal seriousness as a preexistent divine being who came in human form [*i.e.*, the Word did not become flesh; worse, John himself did not mean that the Word became flesh].... Practically all the words of Jesus in John are *assertions about himself* and no definite complex of ideas can be stated as their content and claimed to be the "teaching" of Jesus.... His words are assertions about himself. But this does not mean christological instruction or teaching about the metaphysical quality of his person.

That all this is wrong-headed is clear three times over. First, Bultmann's assertion that Jesus not even once relates what he has seen with the Father contradicts several passages. *John* 5:19 and 7:16, if they do not concretely mention the things Jesus saw with the Father, nonetheless state that everything that Jesus taught was seen by him with the Father. *John* 8:25-28 presumably refers to what Jesus has just said, but can imply all the rest of his teaching too. All this teaching is what Jesus saw with the Father. *John* 12:49 indicates that what Jesus said in the preceding verses, including the prediction of a final judgment, are parts of God's commandment to him. Similarly *John* 14:24 refers to the preceding context.

Second, Bultmann's statement that practically (?) all of Jesus' words are assertions about himself is partly false and totally irrelevant. It is partly false (depending on how one understands the *practically*) because Jesus asserted the Mosaic authorship of the Pentateuch, the need of a new birth, and something about the spiritual position of Abraham. It is also irrelevant because there is no reason why Christ should not have spoken about himself. Did he not have to explain who he was?

This leads to the third point. Christ spoke about himself, but, says Bultmann, this does not mean christological instruction or teaching about his person. But why does it not mean this? Jesus said, "I and my Father are one." Note again that Bultmann restricts his remarks to the reported sayings of Jesus. No attention is paid to the narrative or the interpretation of the author who reported them, except at the end of the paragraph where Bultmann concludes, "No wonder then that the evangelist can confer upon him for his preexistent period the mythological title Word (Logos)!" Indeed, with the exception of the one term, mythological, it is no wonder.

"The Word became flesh" is the culminating verse of the Prologue. If Bultmann had succeeded in eviscerating this verse of all its meaning, then Goodspeed would have an easier time in interpreting *John* as a device to avoid the "detour" through the Old Testament. He would still be defeated, however, by the powerful verses at the end of chapter 5. Since therefore the views of these critics cannot be maintained, there remains only the short task of completing the verse and concluding this account of the Prologue.

"The Word became flesh and dwelt among us, and we gazed at his glory, glory as of the only from the Father, full of grace and truth." That Jesus is the only one from the Father sets him and his ministry on a level that the prophets could not attain. The word *only* does not literally mean "only begotten." It means the only one of its kind. This little bit of Greek vocabulary, however, does not weaken the doctrine that Jesus is the only begotten Son. The word *beget* is found in *Hebrews* 1:5. Therefore, the fundamentalist theologian who argued against the eternal generation of the Son on the ground that the word in *John* did not mean generation was wrong because he forgot *Hebrews*.

Nor does the phrase "the only from God" injure the doctrine of the deity of Christ. If we should continue through the first chapter of *John*

*"The Word became flesh" is the culminating verse of the Prologue.*

to verse 18, we should find, not that Jesus was the only Son, but that Jesus is the only God. It might seem to make better sense to read verse 18 as "the only begotten Son who is in the bosom of the Father"; but the better text is, "the only God who is in the bosom of the Father." Whatever other difficulties this reading produces, at least it is a most emphatic statement of the deity of Jesus.

If the Prologue ends at verse 14, this verse is beyond its scope; but it enforces the culminating idea of the Prologue that the glory of the *Logos* is full of grace and truth.

## 3. *Logos* and *Rheemata*

The obvious importance of *logos* in chapter 1 demands an examination of its other instances in the remainder of the *Gospel*. At the same time there is another term to be compared with it. *Rheema* (singular, though it does not occur in the singular in *John*) and *rheemata* (plural) mean *word* and *words*, ordinarily spoken words. One therefore asks, Are these two terms, *logos* and *rheema*, identical in meaning, contrasted in meaning, or in any way related?

To begin with the etymology previously mentioned, *rheema* has the same root as the Latin *verbum* and the English *word*; *eiroo*, to *say*, *speak*, or *tell*. It occurs sixty times in the New Testament. *Logos* has the root *legoo*: to *say*, *speak*, or *tell*. It occurs over twelve hundred times. Though the two roots are almost identical in meaning, some modern theologians wish to contrast *rheemata* and *logos*. Investigation of this matter best begins with a list of the instances of each word in *John*. The *logos* list comes first.

One category of the instances of the term *logos* in *John*, a noticeable proportion of the total, defines it by giving examples. These make it indubitable that *logos* means a sentence, a proposition, a doctrine, an object of intellectual apprehension. They make it indubitable by quoting the proposition to which they refer.

The first such instance is *John* 2:22. After cleansing the temple at the beginning of his ministry, and being confronted by the Jewish authorities, Jesus says, "Destroy this temple, and in three days I shall raise it up." Naturally the Jews were nonplussed. But "when he was raised from the dead, the disciples remembered it, that he had said this, and they believed the Scripture and the word [*logos*] that Jesus had said." The word (*logos*) was, of course, the sentence, "Destroy this temple, and in three days I shall raise it up." This sentence is the "it" that the disciples remembered; it is the "this" that Jesus had said. Accordingly, the *logos* is this sentence.

The next such case is *John* 4:37. "For in this the saying (*logos*) is true, the one sows and another reaps." The adage or saying is the *logos*. It is stated to be true; and the only thing that can be true is a proposition or declarative sentence. Two verses below there is the next *logos*. "Many of the Samaritans from that city believed on him through the word of the woman who said that he told me everything I have ever done." The

> Logos *means a sentence, a proposition, a doctrine, an object of intellectual apprehension.*

*logos* is precisely the sentence, "He told me everything I have ever done." Another two verses down, "Many more believed because of his preaching." Here in *John* 4:41 *preaching* or *argument* is a good translation for *logos*. The actual words are not quoted, but the verse refers to two days of discussion and preaching that Jesus engaged in with the Samaritans. Still in the same chapter, but no longer concerning the Samaritans, *John* 4:50 tells us that the nobleman, who came to Jesus and requested him to heal his son, "believed the word Jesus said to him." The *logos* was, "Your son lives."

In the sixth chapter Jesus preaches about the bread from Heaven. He also refers to eating his flesh. Then in verse 60, "Many of his disciples, when they had heard, said, This doctrine [*logos*] is difficult; who can accept it?" *Logos*, here, although in the singular, must not be translated by "a word." Nor even by "a sentence." The reference is to the whole sermon. And if anyone dislikes the translation, "This doctrine is difficult," he may translate it, "This sermon is difficult." But the meaning is the same, for it was the intellectual content that caused the displeasure of the audience.

*John* 7:36, 40 are similar. In the first of these the *logos* is the assertion, "You will search for me, but you shall not find me." In the second, the plural occurs: "Some of the crowd, when they had heard these words, said, 'This man is indeed the prophet.'"

Restricting this section to instances where a definite sentence or sentences define the *logos*, we come next to *John* 10:19. Here Jesus had just said that he lays down his life voluntarily; no one can take it from him. "Then the Jews, because of these words [*logoi*], were again divided." The words referred to are roughly all of the first eighteen verses.

In several cases the *logos* is a verse in the Old Testament. *John* 12:38 quotes *Isaiah* 53:1. *John* 15:25 quotes a part of *Psalm* 35:19 and *Psalm* 69:4. *John* 18:9 refers to *John* 6:39 and 17:12. In this case the prophecy fulfilled was one that Jesus himself had made. The same essentially is true of *John* 18:32, where the words referred to are in *John* 3:14, 8:28, and 12:32-34. They are not actually quoted, but the *logos* is these assertions. The *word* is singular, and hence can be translated *thought, idea, doctrine,* or best, *the words* in the plural. Finally, there is a prophecy, a misunderstood prophecy, that spread among the disciples. Jesus had said, "If I want him to remain alive until I return, what is that to you?" This was the *logos*, the *rumor*, the *idea*, the *thought*. A further instance where *logos* refers to a definite sentence is *John* 15:20, "Remember the proverb [*logos*] I told you: The servant is not greater than his lord."

Two other instances where the *logos* is identified by an explicitly quoted sentence, though in these cases it is Pilate and the Pharisees who are involved, rather than Jesus, are *John* 19:8 and 13. In the first of these verses the *logos* that frightened Pilate was "He made himself the son of God." The second of these verses refers to several sentences. The *King James Version* is incorrect in using the singular. *Logos* here occurs in the plural: "When Pilate heard these words...." The words were the declaration by Jesus and the shoutings of the Jews.

*"Remember the proverb [logos] I told you: The servant is not greater than his lord."*

Here then is a long list of cases where the meaning of the term *logos* is determined by quoting it. It is always an intelligible proposition.

At this point, and before continuing with the list of instances of *logos*, the reader might want to know what the connection is between the sentences or propositions just given and the *Logos* of verse 1 who created the universe and enlightens every man who comes into the world. How did the argument get from Christ to sentences? The connection is this: The *Logos* of verse 1 is the Wisdom of God. To him his worshipers erected the architectural triumph Hagia Sophia, the church in Constantinople dedicated to the Holy Wisdom of God. To purloin Heraclitus' phrase, this is the Wisdom that steers the universe. But this steering, the plan on which the universe is constructed, the providential governing of all creatures and all their actions, is based on wise counsel. God does not work haphazardly. He acts rationally. Some of this wisdom is expressed in the propositions of the previous list. They are the mind of Christ: They are the very mind of Christ. In them we grasp the holy Wisdom of God. Accordingly, there is no great gap between the propositions alluded to and Christ himself. The Platonic Ideas, as interpreted by Philo, and by him called *Logos*, are the mind of God. Some of these Ideas are given to us in the words of *John*, or in the words of Christ recorded by John. This is how Christ communicates himself to us. Is it completely ridiculous to suggest that this is why John uses the term *logos* for these two superficially different purposes? But now to continue the list of instances.

Another category can be constructed of those instances where no definite sentence is quoted, but where the reference is clearly to previously spoken sentences. *John* 5:24 reports that Jesus said, "He who hears my word [*logos*] and believes him who sent me has eternal life." The phrase "He who hears my word," can equally well be translated, "He who hears my doctrine"; and it can be interpreted as, "He who accepts my doctrine or theology." Verse 38 of the same chapter says, "You do not have his word [*logos*] remaining in you because you do not believe the one he sent." This verse also refers generally to the doctrine or theology that Jesus had been preaching. *John* 8:31 and 37 are entirely similar. So is *John* 8:43, with the additional parallel between *logos* and *lalia*. This latter word means *speech* or *talk*. The translation can be, "Why do you not understand my talk? Because you cannot hear [accept or understand] my word." Verses 51 and 52 also use *logos* to refer generally to Jesus' preaching: "If anyone keeps my doctrine, he shall not see death ever." Three verses below Jesus contrasts himself with the Pharisees on the ground that he, Jesus, keeps God's *logos*.

Besides these verses in which the term *logos* refers generally to the preaching of Jesus, *John* 10:35 uses *logos* to designate the prophecies of the Old Testament. The prophets were men to whom the *Logos* of God came, and this *logos* as written in the Scripture cannot be broken. This is the first verse so far quoted that definitely links the *logos* to the *written* words of the Old Testament. The idea that the *logos* is some-

*There is no great gap between the propositions…and Christ himself…. This is why John uses the term* logos *for these two superficially different purposes….*

thing that can be written down on papyrus, parchment, or vellum is important, even if only because it is so distasteful to the dialectical theologians.

The paragraph before this last one compared *logos* with words, not as written, nor with words merely as such, but with spoken words. *John 12:48* identifies the *logos* with *rheemata* or words as such. The passage reads, "He who ignores me [or, sets me aside] and does not accept my words [*rheemata*], has a judge: The *logos* that I have spoken, that *logos* will judge him in the last day." Note that the *logos* is something spoken and naturally therefore consists of words.

If the listing of these verses seems tedious, it is at least overwhelming and leaves no defense for those who deprecate words and doctrine. *John 14:23-24* say, "If anyone love me, he will keep my *logos*.... He who does not love me, does not keep my *logous* [plural]; and the *logos* which you hear is not mine, but the Father's who sent me." The combination of singular and plural, of hearing and therefore of saying, enforces the point of the argument.

*Some fundamentalists also have accepted the anti-intellectualism of the liberals.*

Since some fundamentalists also have accepted the anti-intellectualism of the liberals, we must patiently plod through the list. *John 15:3* is, "You are already clean because of the theology [*logos*] I have spoken to you." *John 17:6* and *14* hardly need to be quoted. Verse *17* says that God's word (*logos*) is truth. And in verse *20* of the same chapter the *logos* referred to is the future preaching of the disciples.

To make this a complete list of all the occurrences of the term *logos* in the *Gospel of John*, we have only to add *John 1:1* and *14*. In the beginning was the *Logos*, the Logic, the Doctrine, the Mind, the Wisdom of God. The wisdom of God is God. This *Logos* became flesh and we saw the glory of his grace and truth.

Contemporary theology frequently distinguishes between the *Logos* and the *rheemata*: the Word and the words. The Word is in some sense divine. If it is contained in or somehow mediated by the Bible, the Bible is "authoritative," though not infallible. Just how false statements can be "authoritative," the liberals do not explain. Reception of the Word for them is a sort of mystic experience without intellectual content. The words, on the other hand, are human, fallible, and mythological. The supernatural truth of God is so different from human truth that they do not coincide at a single point and not even omnipotence has the power to express it in human language; therefore the words, the concepts, are mere pointers to an unknowable object.

A conservative theologian naturally wants to examine this view and compare it with the words of Scripture. A "Biblical" view could hardly be absent from the Bible.

After the meaning given in the lexicon is stated, the first step will be to list the occurrences of *rheema* in the *Gospel of John*.

*Souter's* Greek lexicon translates *rheema* as "a *spoken word, an utterance*, the concrete expression of *logos*: hence, perhaps Hebraistically, a subject of speech, a *matter*, a *thing*, a *fact*... in a solemn sense, of a divine word...the Christian *teaching*, the *gospel*..." *Liddell and Scott* do not add anything of great importance, except that in grammar *rheema* designates a verb (*verbum*) rather than a noun.

Jesus is never called the *Rheema*, as he is called the *Logos. Rheemata* in a very literal sense are the sounds that come out of one's mouth when one speaks. These are not thought; they are sounds in the air; they are the symbols of thoughts. When people belittle "mere words" they confuse the thought with the symbol. In the science of Logic there is a distinction made between sentences and propositions. A proposition is the thought symbolized; the sentence is the symbol. *Es regnet, il pleut,* and *it is raining* are three sentences; but they are one proposition. Any one of the three is a satisfactory symbol of the thought. In linguistics attention is paid to the symbols as such. Medieval philosophy had a theory of second intentions: To say that a cat is an animal is to use the word *cat* in its first intention; to say that a cat is a noun is to use the word in its second intention. But people other than philosophers and semanticists hardly think about these distinctions. Most of the time they keep in mind the thing symbolized, even though they may mention the symbol. But in an anti-theological epileptical seizure they will sometimes inveigh against mere words, forgetting the truths they stand for. In the present monograph we are not particularly interested in semantics; we are greatly interested in the truths conveyed by the symbols.

*Rheema* first occurs in *John* 3:34, "The man who accepts the testimony confirms the fact that God is true, for he whom God sent speaks the words of God, for God does not give the Spirit by measure." One notices here that the emphasis is on truth. God is truthful. Therefore, the words of God are true, and the Son, who speaks the words, does so because God has given him the Spirit without limit. Here *rheemata* cannot be put on any level lower than the divine *logoi*. The words are spoken under the limitless authority of the Holy Spirit.

The next reference, *John* 5:45-47, is one of the most important on the authority of words, both written and spoken. After healing the lame man at the pool of Bethesda, directing him to pick up his rug and walk, and at the climax of the ensuing confrontation with the Pharisees, Jesus (in a stern and awesome voice) exclaims, "Do not think that I will accuse you before the Father. Your accuser is Moses in whom you have put your hope. For if you believed Moses, you would believe me, for he wrote of me. But if you do not believe his writings, how can you believe my words!"

Here Moses appears as an accuser – naturally a legitimate accuser with a legitimate accusation – so much so that Christ himself need not accuse the unbelieving Pharisees. They had refused to believe what Moses had written. Of course, Moses had written words on parchment. These words receive the full approbation of Christ. Thus Christ attributes to Moses' written words the full divine authority of truth. Because the Pharisees do not believe Moses' written words, they cannot believe Christ's spoken words. These words, these *rheemata*, are (in part), "the Son makes those alive whom he wants to…the Father has

*"If you do not believe his writings, how can you believe my words!"*

121

given all judgment to the Son, that all may honor the Son, just as they honor the Father.... Indeed I tell you that whoever hears my *logos* and believes him who sent me has eternal life" (*John* 5:21-23). In these earlier verses the message of Christ is a *logos*; at the end of the chapter this same message is called *rheemata*. *Logos* and *rheema* designate the same thing.

Although the present study is confined to John's *Gospel*, Luke too uses *rheema* and *logos*; and in his *Gospel* as well can be seen the identity of the two terms. *Logos* occurs some thirty times in *Luke*, four times in chapter 1. *Rheema* also occurs in *Luke* 1:37, "No word of God shall be without power." The word immediately subsumed under this universal statement is the prophecy of the virgin birth. As a statement of intellectual content it differs in no wise from the four *logoi* of *Luke* 1:2, 4, 20, and 29. In fact, the *logos* of verse 29 is identical with the *rheema* of verse 37. That this proposition and all the other informative statements God makes are not without power means that they are all true. Nor can they be dismissed on the pretext that God's thoughts are not our thoughts and that therefore the omnipotent God has no ability to express information intelligible to man. The proposition, "You shall have a son," means precisely the same thing for both God and man. No doubt God knows other propositions he did not reveal to Mary; but this one *logos* and *rheema* God intended Mary to understand.

To return now to *John*, the next occurrences of *rheema* are found in 6:63 and 68. After giving his discourse on the bread of life, which if a man eat he will live forever, and when he perceived that his disciples whispered in discontent, Jesus said, "The Spirit is the one who gives life...the words that I have spoken to you are Spirit and life." Here the words Jesus speaks are identified as the spirit, or the Spirit, who gives life. Few people who center their thought on "mere words" are inclined to identify the words with the Spirit. But John says that the words are Spirit and life.

Since a list becomes tedious as it grows longer, and since the idea of life is most important, it is well at this point to emphasize that the words are eternal life. The emphasis will take the form of a contrast with an epileptic case of anti-intellectualism. An editorial in *Christian Heritage* (June 1971) states (and I shall quote the paragraph in its entirety to avoid the suspicion that I have somehow garbled it by omissions),

> It is a very strange paradox indeed: unbelievers cannot leave God alone, believers can and do. Unbelievers talk against God with zealous fanaticism, whereas believers hesitate to talk for him precisely because they do not want to appear to be fanatical. If ever the two confront one another both tend to recreate God in their own image, that is, they both underestimate the character of God. One attributes to him the cruelty and vindictiveness which they feel toward his disciples, the other reduces their Lord to loveless propositions and barren doctrinal definitions with which they would browbeat their faith-less opponents.

*The proposition, "You shall have a son," means precisely the same thing for both God and man.*

*John says that the words are Spirit and life.*

The exaggeration of the first part of this paragraph does not concern us. It describes neither all believers nor all unbelievers. But it makes clear that the subject of the latter part of the paragraph is believers and unbelievers. Therefore the last half of the last sentence, and this is the matter of concern, means that believers reduce the Lord to loveless propositions and barren doctrines with which they browbeat unbelievers. Since this is said to be true of all believers, and since the author does not brow-beat people, it would seem to follow that he is not a believer. But maybe he brow-beats believers, and so qualifies. The brow-beating comes in the words *loveless* and *barren*. The author wants us to believe that Christian doctrine is barren. It has no life, no spirit.

The Apostle John, however, and the words of Christ that he records, contradict the sentiment of the editorial. Christ said, "The words that I have spoken to you [the propositions] are Spirit and life." To have eternal life is to have these words; and such a life is not barren. The believer is justified by faith, by what he believes. This belief is not barren because justification inevitably and without exception produces sanctification.

In the verses that follow *John* 6:63, Jesus goes on to tell his disgruntled disciples that no one can believe his words or come to him unless the Father causes him to. This Calvinistic determinism offended the people and many of them deserted Jesus for that reason. But Simon Peter, answering for the twelve, said, "To whom shall we go? Words of eternal life you have! We have believed and we know that you are the Holy One of God." If Christ's discourse is *rheemata*, could *logoi* be any greater?

*Rheema* again occurs in *John* 8:20; aside from identifying the term with Jesus' claim to be the light of the world, the verse adds nothing further to the argument. More important is *John* 8:47. The tremendous discourse approaches its climax with the condemnation of the Jews as sons of the devil. He is their father – neither Abraham nor God. Because Jesus tells them the truth, these liars do not believe him. "He who belongs to God hears God's words: that is why you do not hear – because you do not belong to God." Here is the condemnation of our contemporary dialectical theologians: They disparage the words. They do not believe that Christ was virgin born; many of them, *e.g.*, Barth and Bultmann, do not believe in a resurrection at the end of history; they empty the words of their intellectual content and leave them bare symbols to be filled with foreign meaning. They do not hear the *rheemata* of Christ because they do not belong to God.

The next reference, *John* 10:21, "These are not the words of a demoniac," does not advance the argument. But *John* 12:47-48 combine *logos* and *rheema* in one passage. It must therefore be considered. "Jesus cried out and said…if anyone hear my *rheemata* and refuse to observe them, I do not judge him…. He who ignores and does not receive my *rheemata* has a judge: The *logos* that I have spoken will judge him on the final day." In the section on *logos* this passage has already been listed

*"The words that I have spoken to you [the propositions] are Spirit and life." To have eternal life is to have these words; and such a life is not barren.*

*Here is the condemnation of our contemporary dialectical theologians: They disparage the words.*

as showing the identity of *logos* and *rheemata* – explicitly the fact that *logos* can be a spoken as well as a written word or thought. It is further noteworthy that the *logos* judges the unbeliever on the last day, "the *logos* I have spoken." But the Judge on the last day is Christ himself because "the Father judges no one, but has given all judgment to the Son…he has given him authority to judge because he is the Son of Man" (the Messiah). It cannot be an inadvertence on John's part that he here identifies the spoken words with Christ himself. John was not a contemporary semanticist, nor a medieval philosopher distinguishing between first and second intentions. As a Jew he ignored the symbol as such – a symbol that differs from language to language. John was interested in the thought, the meaning, the truth. And as you and I are what we think, so the Divine Mind is the Truth.

Again, the next reference, *John* 15:7, "If you remain in me and my words remain in you…" adds nothing further to the argument. The final instance of *rheemata* in the *Gospel* is *John* 17:8, "I have given them the words you have given me."

These *rheemata* therefore are not just human words infected, as they may be, with sin and error; these *rheemata* are given by the Father to the Son. These same divine words, the Son gives to his disciples. They do not change in the two givings. They are transmitted *in toto* and without alteration from the Father to the Son to the disciple. Therefore the text of the *Gospel* diametrically contradicts the dialectical theology and all else that minimizes the grasp of intellectual, intelligible truth (there is no other kind) in favor of pictorial mythology and meaningless mysticism.

## 4. Truth

An earlier section, the exegesis of *John* 1:1-14, ended with the idea that the *Logos* was full of grace and truth. There are now two reasons why John's concept of truth should be studied. First, John emphasizes truth. This can be seen, in a preliminary way, in the fact that the term *truth* occurs twenty-four times in the *Gospel*; the adjective occurs thirteen times; and a less ordinary form of the same root occurs eight times; plus ten or eleven less important cases of the adverb. Numbers alone prove little. The verb *become* occurs at least forty-nine times, but nothing of theological value can be derived from a word-study of *ginomai*. The idea of truth, contrariwise, is of great philosophical and theological moment – as soon will be seen.

Aside from the sufficient fact that John emphasizes the notion of truth, there is a second reason for this study. Contemporary theologians these days often defend a type of "truth" quite different from the ordinary truth that past generations have acknowledged. Heretofore truth consisted of propositions. A truth was a sentence. An example would be, David was King of Israel. A falsehood was also a sentence, such as, David led the children of Israel out of Egypt. Now the twentieth century has invented a new kind of truth, and Emil Brunner, a convenient

*The text of the Gospel diametrically contradicts the dialectical theology and all else that minimizes the grasp of intellectual, intelligible truth (there is no other kind) in favor of pictorial mythology and meaningless mysticism.*

representative of this type of theology, wrote a book with the title, *Wahrheit als Begegnung – Truth as Encounter.* If I meet a person on the street, that is truth. Truth is not the sentences this person may say to me; it is simply the event of meeting him. The reason for this queer application of the word *truth* to something to which it was never before applied is that Brunner and the dialectical theologians wish to establish a theory of revelation devoid of information, that is, really devoid of truth. Revelation is an event: We meet God. He does not say anything to us; but the meeting itself is revelation and truth. God gives us no information; or if he should give us information, it could be false information because "God can, when he wants to, speak his word to a man even through false teaching."[13] Revelation itself has no intellectual content; there is nothing to be believed. From this it follows (does it not?) that we do not *know* even that it is God whom we meet. God and the medium of conceptuality, Brunner says, are mutually exclusive.

How untrue Brunner's theory is can be shown by listing and examining the occurrences of the word *truth* in the *Gospel of John*; and this will reinforce the truth of what has been said and what further will be said about the *Logos*.

The word *truth* (*aleetheia*), as indicated above, occurs twenty-four times in the *Gospel*. Not every instance is perfectly convincing for the purpose, but the entire list will be given to show that no instance contradicts the conclusion. For example, the first case is not so clear as some others. *John* 1:14 says, "The Word became flesh...and we beheld his glory...full of grace and truth." To say that Jesus was full of truth could mean that he was sincere. Even so, sincerity is a state of mind in which the speaker believes that what he is saying is true. But to be full of truth could also mean that Jesus had a great deal of information about God. When we speak of an enthusiastic teacher as being full of his subject, we mean that he knows a lot about the subject, and we use the expression because he is constantly communicating this information. There is no reason to deny that Jesus had a great amount of information to give. As a matter of fact Jesus later said, "I still have many things to tell you, but you cannot hold them now." Surely Jesus did not mean: I must encounter you many more times, but not today.

The second instance is *John* 1:17, "The Law was given by Moses, but grace and truth came into being by Jesus Christ." The dialectical theologians would doubtless writhe if the next verse were translated: "No one has ever seen God; the only begotten God, who is in the bosom of the Father, this very one has exegeted him." Nevertheless it is a good translation – however much the intellectual work of exegesis or interpretation fails to fit the dialectical notion of Jesus' mission. Verse 18 is surely in some way an explanation of verse 17. The truth that came into being by Jesus Christ is, at least partly, his explanation, interpretation, or exegesis of the unseen Father.

Next, *John* 3:21 is a verse that is sometimes used to argue that truth is not always intellectual, that there is another kind of truth, and that it is moral obedience. The verse says, "He who does the truth comes

*Brunner and the dialectical theologians wish to establish a theory of revelation devoid of information, that is, really devoid of truth.*

13. Brunner, German edition, 88; English edition, 117.

to the light in order that his works may be seen to have been done through [more literally, *in* or *by*] God." This phrase, "doing the truth," obviously signifies moral obedience. The context contrasts this man with those who do evil deeds and who try to hide them in darkness. The obedient man comes to the light so that all may see that his conduct is godly. This use of the word *truth*, however, gives no support to the dialectical notion of truth as encounter; nor is it so far removed from mind, knowledge, and intellect as the opponents of knowledge and intellect could wish.

Admittedly a moral command is not a proposition and cannot be either true or false. But the context not only refers to light and darkness as revealing or hiding men's deeds from observation; it also takes us back to the Light of chapter 1 that lights every man who comes into the world. This Light no doubt involves moral principles; but since it is the Word or Wisdom of God, rational and theological material is also included. One cannot separate moral principles from logical principles on the ground that the latter are intellectual or rational and the former are not. Moral principles, to be followed, must be known. While then a command as such cannot be true, it is a proposition and a truth that God commands men (for example) not to steal. Therefore there are no anti-intellectual overtones in speaking about *doing* the truth.

The next reference, containing both the noun and an adjective, may seem even more remote from the truth of a proposition. If all the verses were like these, someone might doubt that John's concept of truth had much to do with the cognitive meaning here maintained. But, for one thing, the later references are abundant and clear; and for another thing, *John* 4:23 requires the intellectual meaning as its background. Jesus was talking with the Samaritan woman. She wanted to know whether people should worship God on Mt. Gerizim or in Jerusalem. Jesus plainly tells her that the Samaritans were wrong: Up to the present Jerusalem has been the place that God had appointed for worship. Then Jesus adds, "But a time is coming, and has now arrived, when the true worshipers will worship the Father in spirit and in truth." The same thought and the same words are repeated in the following verse.

Since clearly Jesus is announcing something that goes beyond the Old Testament, and since the Old Testament condemns hypocrisy, these words are not a simple call to sincerity. They indicate a new administration of divine grace in which Jerusalem as a locality is of no importance. This is a truth. To worship God, therefore, now necessitates a recognition of this truth or proposition. No doubt it goes still further than a mere rejection of Jerusalem; nonetheless, such is contained in the meaning. What is further must be the whole New Testament revelation. Since Jesus here announces a new form of worship, his intent, though the particulars remain unexpressed, must envisage the new worship in its entirety. The conclusion is that Jesus explicitly presented the woman with at least two propositions: The sacrifices at Jerusalem have come to an end, and I am the Messiah; and implicitly he had in mind his atonement and all the rest.

*One cannot separate moral principles from logical principles on the ground that the latter are intellectual or rational and the former are not. Moral principles, to be followed, must be known.*

This verse also contains the adjective *true* (*aleethinos*); and rather than repeat the verse under the list of adjectives it is better to finish it here and indeed add several other verses where this adjective occurs. Earlier there was *John* 1:9 in which the phrase is, "the true light." Here, of course, it is "the true worshipers." In *John* 6:32 we have, "the true bread." *John* 15:1, "the true vine." *John* 17:3, "the only true God." This adjectival use is a derivative from the basic meaning of the noun. The phrase, it or he was the true light, simply means that the proposition, the *Logos* is the light, is a true statement. Therefore, we must not see in this adjectival use some unusual type of truth by which to disparage the ordinary variety. Augustine pleasantly explains this literary form. Phrases such as *the true bread, the true light*, and so on, picture the object as saying to the beholder, I am bread, I am light; and this claim is true.

The next instance of the word *truth* is flanked by another adjective *true* (*aleethees*). *John* 5:31-33 read, "If I testify concerning myself, my testimony is not true. There is another who testifies about me, and I know that the testimony that he testifies about me is true. You sent off to John, and he has testified to the truth." If the previous references needed a little bit of explanation to show that they referred to propositional truth and not to some other kind, the meaning here and in most of the following references lies on the surface. The situation described here resembles a law court. The witness of one man is not accepted as true; but if two witnesses concur, their witness is acceptable. Jesus has several witnesses, mentioned in various places in *John*. There is his own witness, the witness of John the Baptist, the witness of Jesus' works, the Father himself, the Scriptures, and in the Scriptures especially Moses. In this section the other witness is not John the Baptist, but the Father, as the following verses show. But the Baptist is referred to in the verses quoted.

The presence of witnesses and the picture of the law court show the meaning of *true* and *truth*. A witness makes a statement. It is either true or false. Such testimony in a colloquial manner may be called personal truth. It may be based on a face-to-face encounter between two men; and it may state something about the character of the person to whom the testimony refers. But it is still a proposition. There is no personal truth that is not propositional. Statements such as, Judas was a thief, and, Jesus was the Messiah, are as personal as anyone can rightly demand; but beyond these statements of intellectual or cognitive content, there is no meaning to the word *truth*.

In chapter 8 the idea of true witness in a court of law recurs; and although the word *truth* does not occur in verses 12 to 30, this is the best place to take account of these instances of the adjective. The phrases are: "Thy witness is not true," "my witness is true," "my judgment is true," "the witness of two men is true," and one other of the sort Augustine discussed – "he that sent me is true." These verses (13, 14, 16, 17, and 26) with the exception of the last, have the same meaning as those in chapter 5. Nothing further needs to be said, for the thing that is true is the statement made on the witness stand.

> *There is no personal truth that is not propositional…. [B]eyond these statements of intellectual or cognitive content, there is no meaning to the word* truth.

The noun *truth* occurs several times in the following section. It will be best to exegete verses 31 to 47.

After discussing the truth of Jesus' witness and his relation to the Father, we read in verse 31, "Accordingly, Jesus said to the Jews who believed him, If you remain in my doctrine [*logos*], you are really [truly] my disciples; and you will know the truth, and the truth will liberate you." Although the preceding section ends with the information that many of the Jews believed on him, and although this section begins by referring to the Jews who believed, the present verses indicate either that there were Jews in the crowd who did not believe, or that some of them believed only a few detached propositions. Whichever group it was that replied to Jesus, they paid no attention to the truths believed, but stumbled at the idea of becoming free:

> They answered him, "We are the descendants of Abraham and have never been servants of anyone. How can you say, 'You shall become free?'"
> Jesus replied to them, "Most assuredly I tell you that everyone who commits sin is the servant of sin. Now, the servant does not remain permanently in the home: The son remains permanently. If, therefore, the son liberates you, you will really be free. I know that you are descendants of Abraham; but you seek to kill me because my theology [*logos*] makes no progress in you. I speak what I have seen with my Father; and you do what you have heard with your father."

Note that *truth* and *word* or *doctrine* refer to the information that Jesus had presented in verses 12-30, and possibly to other sermons that he had preached still earlier. It is truth and knowledge that liberate; Jesus does not ask them to have some emotional experience; he requires that they believe.

The conversation continues. "They answered and said to him, 'Our father is Abraham.'" Jesus had just said that they did what their father told them to do. As in the earlier verses the Jews can think of only Abraham as their father. But Jesus says to them, "If you are sons of Abraham, you were doing the works of Abraham."

This over-literal translation obscures the sense. One is tempted to use a variant reading, not very well attested, and translate, "If you are sons of Abraham, do the works of Abraham." The best sense appears in a better, but not the best, attested reading: "If you are [or, were] the sons of Abraham, you would be doing the works of Abraham."

"But now you seek to kill me, a man who has told you the truth which I have heard from God. Abraham did not do this."

This is the only place where Jesus refers to himself as a man. The reason is doubtless that they want to kill him, and will eventually do so. Hence it is proper to refer to his human nature, since the divine nature cannot be killed. What is important for the present purpose is that Jesus is a man who has told the truth. It was the truth that angered them; and this truth is the message that Jesus had been preaching. The message, at least the immediate message of the chapter, was a matter of

*Jesus does not ask them to have some emotional experience; he requires that they believe.*

propositions such as: I know where I came from, but you do not know where you came from; and, You judge according to the flesh; you shall die in your sin; you are from below, I am from above. These are simple, ordinary sentences. They are expressions of intellectual content; and that is why Jesus said, I am a man who has told you the truth. Truth consists of propositions.

One of the implied truths is that Abraham is not the father of these Jews. They were not doing the works of Abraham. Instead, they were doing the works of their father. These assertions were not so easy for those Jews to understand, but nonetheless they are intellectual expressions. Since the Jews perceive the inference and understand that Jesus is denying that Abraham is their father, could it be that Jesus is accusing Sarah of adultery? Hardly, for Jesus, a few verses back, had admitted, "I know that you are descendants of Abraham." Then it dawns on these Jews that Jesus is talking about spiritual descent, so they say to him, "We were not born of fornication; we have one father, God." Jesus replied to them, "If God were your father, you would love me, for I came from God and here I am; nor have I come on my own initiative, but he sent me. Why do you not understand my language? Because you cannot hear my argument [*logos*]."

Note again that Jesus appeals to understanding a rational argument. It is not an emotional experience or dialectical encounter that he has in mind, but a simple grasping of logical content. Although this is a study of the *Gospel of John*, it may not be objectionable to quote *2 Corinthians* 4:3-4 because there too is a mention of the inability of people to understand intellectual propositions. Paul writes, "But if our Gospel is hidden, it is hidden in them who are perishing, in whom the god of this world has blinded the thoughts of the unbelievers in order that [*eis* with the infinitive is generally purposive; it can indicate result and be translated *so that*] the light of the Gospel might not dawn [on them]." Aside from the interesting fact that ancient Greek used the same idiom as modern English and made *dawn* a picture of the beginning of intellectual apprehension, one must note that the hidden thing is the good news, information, cognitive sentences; and that the work of Satan is not to give these people bad emotions but to prevent them from thinking the right thoughts. The antithesis is entirely intellectual.

Jesus now tells the Jews plainly who their father is. As in *2 Corinthians* it is the devil who blinded the thoughts of unbelievers, so here "You are of your father the devil, and you want to fulfil the desires of your father; he was a murderer from the beginning," so naturally you want to kill me; "and the platform on which he stands is not truth [or, a little more literally, he has not taken his stand in the truth] because truth is not in him. When he lies, he speaks out of his own resources, because he is a liar and the father of lies. [Since you are his children] you do not believe me for the simple reason that I speak the truth. Who among you convicts me of sin [the sin of lying]? If I speak the truth, why do you not believe me? He who is [the descendant] of God

*The work of Satan is not to give these people bad emotions but to prevent them from thinking the right thoughts.*

hears the words [*rheemata*] of God. That is why you do not hear: You are not [the children] of God."

In these last few verses the emphasis falls on the antithesis of truth, namely, lies. A falsehood is the contradictory of a truth. If it is true that Alexander the Great died young, it is false that he lived to an old age. If Abraham did not pursue the five kings and recover Lot's goods, it is false to say that he did. If it was a sin to kill Christ, then Caiaphas made a false statement when he said it was better for the Pharisees that Christ should be killed. There is no such antithesis between intellectual truth and morality as some superficial minds imagine. A lie, the denial of a truth, is immoral. It is a sin to think incorrectly. When a person thinks that it is profitable to steal, or when some of the ancients thought they could ward off illness by sacrificing to an idol, their false opinion was sin. There can be no such thing as morality unless there are true moral principles. Morality depends on truth.

> *There is no such antithesis between intellectual truth and morality as some superficial minds imagine. A lie, the denial of a truth, is immoral. It is a sin to think incorrectly.*

Note also in this section that truth is expressed, not only in arguments (*logoi*) but in words (*rheemata*). There is no such antithesis between truth and words as some modern theologians imagine. Jesus said, The child of God hears God's words. Now, very literally, it is the case that words are symbols. The word c-a-t does not look like a thing that meows, nor can it scratch. And *Katze*, though cognate, is not the same symbol. In this sense the word is not "the real thing." But in colloquial speech we usually make no distinction between the word and the concept. The reason is that we are not discussing linguistics; we are merely thinking about a cat. For this reason, Brunner is perhaps half right when he says, "All words have only an instrumental value." But he is all wrong when he adds, "Neither the spoken words nor their conceptual content are the Word itself, but only its frame."[14] According to the Apostle John and according to Jesus, the Word of God, the *Logos*, and the words, the propositions, the cognitive content, are identical; and this conceptual content is "the real thing."

The next references to truth are *John* 14:6 and 17. Here Jesus tells Thomas, "I am the way, the truth, and the life." Then, after several verses in which knowledge is emphasized, Jesus promises to send the Spirit of truth, whom the world cannot grasp because it does not know him.

The first of these verses can easily be understood to mean that Jesus is (to use ancient terminology) the World of Ideas, the Mind of God. This accords with the Prologue and there is no reason why it should not. However, while the verse must include this meaning, the context suggests a more immediate application to the difficulties of Thomas. The puzzled disciple does not know where Jesus is going and therefore cannot know the way. Under the circumstances it is not strange that Thomas and Philip were puzzled. It may seem strange that Jesus did not answer them in terms that they could understand. His answer goes far beyond the range of their thought. Nevertheless it includes their problem. I am the way, he says, the way of life; in fact, I am the life; and the reason I am the life is that I am the truth, the World of

14. *Divine Human Encounter*, 110.

Ideas, the plan of the universe, and therefore also the norm by which a disciple should conduct himself. The way to know the Father is to know me. And this knowledge is life. Then Jesus promises them another Advocate, the Spirit of truth, whom the world neither contemplates nor knows. Here the idea of knowledge determines the meaning of the word *truth*. It is the object of knowledge. To know the Spirit is to know the truth. Trinitarianism ascribes to each of the Persons all the attributes any of them has. The functions of the three Persons are somewhat differentiated, in that certain functions are more usually ascribed to one Person rather than to the other two, but in truth all three do everything together (excluding the human functions that are the God-man's alone). Therefore, one can say that the Spirit is the Truth and that the Son is the Truth. And surely the Father is not ignorant. Here the relation of truth to the Spirit is probably the fact that teaching is one of the functions regularly assigned to the Spirit. Verse 26 specifies the action of the Spirit in causing the apostles to remember correctly what Jesus had said and done in order that they might write it down without error.

John 16:7 says, "I tell you the truth." The truth that Jesus here tells his disciples is that he is going away. A few verses before, he told them that they would suffer persecution. Several times he emphasizes the fact that he is telling them something. What he tells them is so indisputably information, plain ordinary intellectual content, that to suppose truth to be some mystic encounter is wilful blindness. In verse 12 Jesus says that he has more to tell them: more information, what else? But since the disciples cannot carry it away at the moment, the Spirit of truth, when he comes, will direct them in all the truth. This truth, which the Spirit takes from Christ, the Spirit will announce or report to the disciples. Note that announcing or reporting has to do with propositions. If it be said that one announces people or reports people, a quick glance at the morning's newspaper will show that the announcement consists of propositions.

John 17:17 says, "Sanctify them by the truth; your word, doctrine, argument, theory is truth." Just a page or two back the *logos*-word and the *rheema*-word were seen to be identical. Thus the truth here that sanctifies is the message of the Scripture. Sanctification is basically an intellectual process. No doubt it eventuates in external conduct; but before one can act rightly, one must think rightly; and so we are sanctified by truth. The idea is repeated in verse 19: "I sanctify myself for them, in order that they may sanctify themselves by truth."

It is hard to see how anyone can be sanctified by encounter. Improvement in conduct, in holy living, in moral action, requires instruction and information. If children have not been brought up in the nurture and admonition of the Lord, if they have not been given normative principles of Scriptural content, an emotional evangelistic appeal or experience can have no Christian meaning. As someone has well said: Christianity is taught, not caught. The Christian message, the truth, comes to a man through his mind or intellect. To believe it, it

*What he tells them is so indisputably information, plain ordinary intellectual content, that to suppose truth to be some mystic encounter is wilful blindness.*

must be understood. An encounter without propositional content is an hallucination. Or, better, it is not even an hallucination, for an hallucination has content, though false. "That the soul be without knowledge [or, desire without knowledge] is not good" (*Proverbs* 19:2).

Emphasis on knowledge, understanding, and truth is found explicitly in many chapters of the Bible; but the *Gospel of John* with twenty-four instances of the word *truth* is the book in which the greatest emphasis is found. The remaining three instances now conclude this section.

*John* 18:37 contains two of these three and the next verse has the final instance. Pilate asks Jesus, Are you a king? Pilate is asking for information; and Jesus' answer is affirmative. The form of speech is somewhat unfamiliar to English-speaking people. It can be translated, "You speak [well] because I am [indeed] a king." The remainder of the verse leaves no doubt that Jesus claims to be a king. Even the form of speech is not totally foreign to English, if we use slang. Then the translation is: "You said it! I am a king." Then Jesus continues, "I was born for this purpose, and for this purpose I have come into the world. The purpose is to witness to the truth." What truth? No doubt many other propositions also, but at least to this piece of information, that I am a king. Then, next, "Everyone who depends on the truth hears my voice."

At this Pilate asks, and it is the last instance in the *Gospel*, "What is truth?" This question is a little hard to interpret with certainty. Had Pilate been a philosopher, he might have asked, What is the nature of truth – What is the correct theory of epistemology? This would have required the definite article before the noun *truth*, and the article is not in the text. Did Pilate mean, What is the truth in this case before me? Yet, though he may not have believed that Jesus was a king, he was convinced of the truth of Jesus' innocence with reference to the accusations. It seems best to me to suppose that Pilate, though he was not a philosopher, asked about the abstract nature of truth. Jesus had said, not only that he was a king, but that he had come into the world to bear witness to the truth. Here the definite article appears. Pilate seems to have spoken with this in mind, even if he did not use the article. After all, professional philosophers are not the only persons who sometimes think about the nature of truth.

Along with the twenty-four instances of *truth*, seven cases of the adjective (*aleethees*) were discussed. The remaining six are *John* 3:33, 4:18, 7:18, 10:41, 19:35, and 21:24. They all reinforce what has already been said. Five instances of the other adjective (*aleethinos*) have been mentioned. Three others are *John* 4:37, 7:28, and 19:35. The adverb occurs ten times. They add nothing further. Truth therefore is propositional, and these propositions we are called upon to believe.

The concept of truth, immutable truth, is of first importance to Christianity, for without it the Gospel would not be true. It could not even be pragmatically useful; for if it were, then it would have to be true that it is useful. Nor could morality exist without truth because, if it is not true that God imposes obligations and punishes disobedience,

*The concept of truth, immutable truth, is of first importance to Christianity, for without it the Gospel would not be true. It could not even be pragmatically useful.*

it would not be true that man is obliged to do anything, nor could any motive for virtue and sanctification exist.

The twentieth century in large measure has rejected truth and has accepted relativism. Joseph Fletcher exhibits the immoral consequences of relativism in his situational ethics. He insists that one ought – and saying *ought* he contradicts himself, for he cannot justify any *ought* – to disobey every one of the Ten Commandments. It is John Dewey, however, who goes to the root of the matter and provides situational ethics with its philosophical foundation. Dewey insists not only that the "truths" of science and history change, but that the very forms of logic change. Aristotelian logic used to be true. In the past one could validly argue: All Americans are human beings; therefore, some human beings are Americans.[15] But now, Dewey asserts, this is no longer valid. If some other elements of Aristotelian logic still remain true, obversion perhaps, they too will sooner or later change. What has been valid will become invalid, and what has been invalid will, at least eventually, become valid. If Dewey does not say in so many words that "All Americans are human beings implies that no Americans are human beings" will become valid, at least he repeatedly denies all limits to change in logic. Since there are no eternal truths in Dewey's philosophy, the absurd inference cannot forever be invalid.[16]

Dewey is a twentieth-century example of the reaction against Hegel that set in with Karl Marx and Søren Kierkegaard. The German philosopher G. W. F. Hegel, early in the nineteenth century, exploded Immanuel Kant's assertion of an unknowable Thing-in-Itself. But in correcting Kant he gave the unfortunate impression that he thought he had discovered just about all the truth there is. His enemies took advantage of this (not altogether justifiable) impression. But in rejecting many propositions that Hegel claimed to have established, a twentieth-century movement, including Instrumentalists, the dialectical theologians, and the Existentialists, rejects the possibility of any fixed, immutable, eternal truth. Not only is this the case with liberals and left-wingers, but some people who consider themselves evangelicals also have tendencies to disparage truth. These men have adopted relativism, not by studying the history of philosophy, for they have not done much studying; but rather, being ignorant of the source, they unwittingly accept ideas that have become popular and fail to perceive how the new views are inimical to Christian truth. So as to avoid generalities, to be concrete, and to rebut in advance the charge of knocking down a straw man, the specific case of A. W. Tozer will be examined.

Although Dr. Tozer, in the sermon to be quoted, disparages Fundamentalism, most people who knew him and his denomination, the Christian and Missionary Alliance, would probably classify him as a Fundamentalist. Surely he considered himself a conservative evangelical. Furthermore, the sermon from *Tozer Pulpit*, Volume 3, was reprinted by *The Presbyterian Journal*, February 11, 1970 – a journal that claims to defend orthodox Presbyterianism from the onslaughts of the dialectical theologians. When thus the ostensible defenders of the faith accept

*Dewey insists not only that the "truths" of science and history change, but that the very forms of logic change.*

15. Or any example with universal premises and a particular conclusion.

16. See my monograph, *Dewey*, and *Thales to Dewey*, chapter 11.

the position of the enemy, unwittingly of course, one can measure the strength of the contemporary rebellion against the truth. What is worse, Dr. Tozer appeals to the *Gospel of John*. The following criticism aims to show that Dr. Tozer and *The Presbyterian Journal* completely misunderstand the *Gospel* and make it say precisely what it denies.

First of all, Dr. Tozer distinguishes between two kinds of truth, though as in Kierkegaard the second kind is not precisely distinguished. The first kind of truth is the kind the unbelieving Jews had. It is "intellectual merely.... I gather this not only from verse 17 [*John* 7:17, "If a man chooses to do God's will, he will find out whether my teaching comes from God or whether I speak on my own"] but from the whole *Gospel of John*. To these people truth was an intellectual thing, just as we know two times two is four." Apparently Dr. Tozer thinks that if doctrine and teaching come from God, instead of from the rabbis, it cannot be intellectual.[17]

For Dr. Tozer intellectual truth is somehow inferior. "Two times two is four: that is truth, but it is an intellectual truth only....They [the Jews] believed that if you had the words of truth, if you could repeat the code of truth, you had the Truth. That if you lived by the word of truth, you lived in the Truth." There is some confusion here. The Pharisees and all the unbelieving Jews had many sins to account for, but respect for the truth was not one of them. One of the Pharisees' sins was hypocrisy: They did not believe what they said they believed. This makes it hard to know exactly what they believed. But it is not likely that many of them believed that "if you had the words of truth, if you could repeat the code of truth," you had the Truth in any saving sense. They insisted on circumcision; and a Gentile who merely repeated aloud the Mosaic code was not thereby saved. Dr. Tozer is more accurate when he adds, "If you lived by the word of truth, you lived in the Truth." This they believed (let us say); but this is no sin. *Romans* 2:6-7, 10, 13 definitely assert the principle that Dr. Tozer opposes. Jesus himself, in the *Gospel of John*, insists on obedience to the truth. The fault of the Jews was not their honoring of the truth as such; if they believed that the truth saves, they were right. Their sin was that what they honored and believed was not the truth. They did not believe Moses and the prophets. It was for this that Jesus condemned them. He did not condemn their alleged rationalism, intellectualism, or respect for the truth. The difference between the Jews and Jesus lay in the propositions to be believed.

Dr. Tozer seems little interested in what a person believes. He is little interested because he has a low opinion of intellectual truth. He wishes to substitute a different kind of "truth." Exactly what it is, he does not make clear; but whatever it is, it is incompatible with evangelical theology and contradictory of John's *Gospel*. Read the quotation carefully:

> The battle line, the warfare today, is not necessarily between the fundamentalist and the liberal. There is a difference between them, of course. The fundamentalist says God made the heaven and the earth.

17. When the feast was half over, Jesus went into the temple and taught. The Jews were astonished because Jesus had never "learned" in a rabbinical school. If now Jesus had said he needed no schooling, but spoke on his own authority, the Jews would have called him an impostor. To get their attention Jesus claims to have had a teacher: Someone sent him and his doctrine is that taught by the "someone." Note that the word here is *didachee*, a rather technical term emphasizing a "school of thought," a professional view, a claim to authority. If *didachee* is not intellectual, one would have difficulty in saying what it is. The "someone" who taught and sent Jesus is, of course, God; and Jesus then tells his enemies how they may learn whether his *didachee*, his theological teaching, comes from God or not. Thus we come to the seventeenth verse from which Dr. Tozer claims to deduce the theory of two kinds of truth. The verse is, "If anyone resolutely wills to obey his commandments, he will know concerning the *didachee*, whether it comes from

The liberal says, Well, that's a poetic way of stating it; actually it came up by evolution. The fundamentalist says Jesus Christ was the very Son of God. The liberal says, Well, he certainly was a wonderful man and he is the Master, but I don't quite know about his deity. So there is a division, but I don't think the warfare is over these matters any more. The battle has shifted to another more important field. The warfare and dividing line today is between evangelical rationalists and evangelical mystics.

Note how Dr. Tozer disparages the difference between believing that God is creator, that Jesus is the Son of God, and presumably other fundamental doctrines, and believing that God did not create the world, that Jesus is no more than human, and that a good part of the Bible is untrue. He admits that there is a difference between the liberal and the fundamentalist, but he seems little interested in that difference. This warfare is over – says Dr. Tozer. But for a true Christian, if he has average common sense, this warfare is not over. A true Christian cannot treat the deity of Christ so lightly, nor the doctrine of creation, either. There may be a sense in which the battle line of the twenties has shifted in the seventies; but it is not such a new field as that between "evangelical rationalists and evangelical mystics." In one sense, a very fundamental sense, the battle line has not shifted at all. The old battle line that centered on Harry Emerson Fosdick's denial of the virgin birth and his warning against worshiping Jesus was itself a question of the truth of the Bible. Some people may have seen only that the deity of Christ and the atonement were involved. But scholars like J. Gresham Machen saw clearly that the whole Bible and all of Christianity were involved. This is still the battlefield. What may be new, since the middle of the nineteenth century, is a view that Truth is not true, and that the Bible instead of being honestly false, as Wellhausen asserted, is dishonestly "true" like Aesop's fables. For the new "Truth" is simply the old falsehood.

The attempt to belittle intellectualism and the old truth by reducing belief to a mere memorization of words is a misrepresentation that occurs in several places in the sermon. The two are not the same. One can memorize a passage in Baruch Spinoza or Karl Marx without believing it, in fact, for the purpose of arguing against them. But Dr. Tozer says, the Jews thought that "if you want to know the truth, go to the rabbi and learn the Word. If you get the Word [by memory, not by belief] you have got the truth. There is today an evangelical rationalism which is the same as that of the Jews" which tells us "If you learn the text, you have got the truth." Now it may be that fundamentalists, not being very well educated and often misunderstanding what the Bible teaches, say some peculiar things; but do any of them mean that memorization apart from belief gives salvation? The trouble here is that Dr. Tozer holds belief in low esteem and therefore tries to belittle it by talking about "getting" the words.

Naturally, once or twice Dr. Tozer uses the word *belief*, for it is belief that he is belittling by reducing it to repetition and memorization.

God or whether I speak on my own." What does this verse mean? Does it mean, as Pascal said: Go through the motions, say the rosary, attend mass, *s'abêtir* – stupefy yourself, and you will come to believe? Surely this cannot be the meaning. The text does not say, "he who does God's will, will know." Rather, the text speaks of one who is willing to do God's will after he learns what it is. This is not what Pascal had in mind. Pascal's stupefaction consists in going through the motions before knowing that they are God's commands. It seems, rather, that Jesus is directly addressing his Jewish audience in their own situation. They were not willing to obey the Mosaic law. This Old Testament background is explicit in verse 19. Jesus charges them with plotting to kill him. If they had been willing to put away their murderous plot and obey the Ten Commandments, they would have recognized that Jesus' teaching came from God. Or, in other words, taken from *John* 8:37-41, if these Jews had the faith of Abraham, they would have believed what Jesus said.

Hence he says, "Your evangelical rationalist…says what the Pharisees, the worst enemies Jesus had while on earth, said: Well, truth is truth and if you believe the truth you've got it." What Dr. Tozer fails to notice is that the so-called evangelical rationalist believes that Jesus is the Son of God who gave his life a ransom for many, and the Pharisees believed that Jesus was an impostor and blasphemer. Dr. Tozer fails correctly to evaluate belief because he believes that belief, no matter in what, has little value.

Therefore Dr. Tozer claims that the new and more important battle line is between evangelical rationalists and evangelical mystics. Does Dr. Tozer know what the term *evangelical* means? The Protestant Reformation, *i.e.*, the evangelical movement, has, in Aristotelian language, a formal principle and a material principle. The material principle is the doctrine of justification by faith. The formal principle is *sola Scriptura*, the Bible alone.[18] But a mystic is precisely one who rejects the principle of the Bible alone. He has a source of revelation outside the Bible. Hence there cannot be an evangelical mystic.

Dr. Tozer's unevangelical views and un-Johannine religion are unmistakable in the following quotation:

> There is something behind the text that you've got to get through to…. Is the body of Christian truth enough? Or does truth have a soul as well as a body? The evangelical rationalist says that all talk about the soul of truth is poetic nonsense. The body of truth is all you need; if you believe the body of truth you are on your way to heaven and you can't backslide and everything will be all right and you will get a crown in the last day…. Just as *Colossians* argues against Manichaeism and *Galatians* argues against Jewish legalism, so the book of *John* is a long, inspired, passionately outpoured book trying to save us from evangelical rationalism, the doctrine that says the text is enough. Textualism is as deadly as liberalism.

If now the reader will kindly note the points quoted and compare with the criticisms below, he will see the significance of the debate. First of all one must ask whether a man who insists on the truth of God's Word, and in fact understands the Bible as well as or even better than most evangelicals, is a greater enemy than, as Dr. Tozer says he is, or even as great an enemy as, a man who denies that God created the world and denies the deity of Christ – the two items by which the quoted author distinguishes between fundamentalists and liberals.

In the second place, does a distinction between the body and the soul of truth have a meaning or is it poetic nonsense? A century or two ago some Puritans wrote books on theology and used the title, *The Body of Divinity*. This title is a figure of speech, yet it has an intelligible meaning. It means the several theological doctrines that the author thinks most important. But when a contrast is made between the truths themselves and something different from them called their soul, intelligible meaning is surely replaced by poetic nonsense. The best evidence of its poetic nonsense is that its meaning cannot be stated in literal language. The meaning of the title *Body of Divinity* can be so

*"The book of John is a long, inspired, passionately outpoured book trying to save us from evangelical rationalism, the doctrine that says the text is enough. Textualism is as deadly as liberalism."*
*– A. W. Tozer*

18. See "The Presidential Address to the Evangelical Theological Society," December 29, 1965, in the *Bulletin of the Evangelical Theological Society*, IX, 1, Winter 1966.

stated: It is the several important truths themselves. But neither the author quoted nor others explain what this "soul" is. The author contents himself with disparaging the truth, or the body of truth, without giving any indication of what this other thing is.

Then, third, it is amazing that the author describes the *Gospel of John* as a passionate attack on "evangelical rationalism." John's *Gospel* contains at least twenty-four instances of the word *truth*, none of which disparages the truth; it also contains thirteen instances of the adjective *true*, and eight instances of another adjective of substantially the same meaning; in addition to which there are about ten instances of the adverb, some of which, however, contribute little to the present subject. John also lays stress on the *Word* and the *words*, beginning in his very first verse and working up to a tremendous condemnation of the Jews, in chapter 5, for their refusal to believe the words of Moses.

This passage and others similar show the inaccuracy of classifying "evangelical rationalists" with the Pharisees. The author had said, "Your evangelical rationalist...says what the Pharisees, the worst enemies Jesus had while on earth, said: 'Well, truth is truth and if you believe the truth you've got it.'" This attempt to picture the "evangelical rationalists" as the worst enemies Jesus has had since he was on Earth fails because the Pharisees did not believe the truth. If they had believed the writings of Moses, they would have believed the words of Christ.

The sermon's appeal to the *Gospel of John* is so incredible that it is worthwhile to examine again at least one paragraph of that *Gospel*. Consider *John* 8:48ff.

The Jews had just accused Jesus of being a devil-possessed Samaritan. In rejecting their accusation Jesus says, "If anyone keep my word, he shall never never see death ever." It is to be admitted and insisted upon that this verse requires more than simply *understanding* Jesus' word or words. In fact, Jesus' enemies often understood him fairly well. They understood on a previous occasion that he made himself equal with God. At the end of the present passage they apparently understand his claim to Deity, for they attempted to stone him. Had he merely claimed to be the Messiah, they would not have stoned him. They might have rejected and ridiculed him, but they did not equate a messianic claim with a claim to Deity. Others had made messianic claims without incurring such hatred. Later on the young man who was to become the Apostle Paul understood perfectly what the Christians were preaching: That is why he persecuted them. Clearly then Jesus in *John* 8:51 demands more than a simple understanding of his claim.

The "more" that goes beyond simple understanding is "keeping" his word. The verb "to keep" means: *watch over, take care of, guard; give heed to, observe, notice, test by observation or trial; preserve, retain.* From these connotations it follows that if some of the words or doctrines are commands, *keeping* means obedience. Other words, not commands, but doctrines such as the claims to be the Messiah, to be one with the Father, to be the Bread of Life and the Light of the world, are "kept" simply by believing them. Of course, no one can believe what he does

*"If anyone keep my word, he shall never never see death ever."*

not understand. Understanding is a prerequisite to belief, otherwise a missionary would not need to learn the native language.

Nevertheless, the sole object Jesus refers to is his Word, his words, his doctrine, dogma, or teaching. It is this that must be kept. Jesus does not speak of anything in addition to, hidden behind, or exalted above his doctrine. There is nothing irrational, mystical, illogical, or inexpressible to which he directs attention. The promise of escaping death is based completely and solely on Jesus' word: "If anyone keep my word, he shall never never see death ever."

Repetition may be tedious, but nevertheless kindly note again what John had said in a previous verse: "You seek to kill me because my doctrine makes no progress in you" (8:37). With this insistence on doctrine and word, it is positively amazing that even an Arminian can so misconstrue the *Gospel of John* and so attack those who believe John's words.

The sermon does not restrict itself to the *Gospel of John* and to complete the argument we may follow it into *1 Corinthians.* Dr. Tozer writes, "The theological rationalists say your faith should stand not in the wisdom of man but in the Word of God. Paul didn't say that at all. He said your faith should stand in the power of God. That's quite a different thing."

Is it? I do not think it can be quite a different thing. The antithesis between word and power is strained, for Dr. Tozer seems to have forgotten *Luke* 1:37, "No word from God is without power."[19] Remember also that the words are Spirit and life (*John* 6:68). And though Dr. Tozer uses the epistle, he makes no mention of *1 Corinthians* 1:24, where Christ, the *Logos*, is called the power of God as well as the wisdom of God. Power, wisdom, and word are identical, for in the simplicity of the divine essence all attributes merge. But let us see what Dr. Tozer says about *1 Corinthians* 2:9-14.

It is the familiar passage: "Eye has not seen, nor ear heard...the things of God knows no man, but the Spirit of God." To the end of verse 11, the author quotes in full, even the verse that says, "Unto us God revealed them through the Spirit." But verses 12 and 13 are omitted: "We received not the spirit of the world but the Spirit which is from God that we might know the things that were freely given to us of God. Which things also we speak, not in words which man's wisdom teaches, but which the Spirit teaches, combining spiritual things with spiritual [words]." Then the author continues with verse 14. The impression that Dr. Tozer apparently wants to make, although he does not expressly draw the implication, is that knowledge of the truth is unimportant or even impossible. If this is not what he means, his quotation hangs in mid-air: It does not connect with his immediately preceding antithesis between the power of God and the Word [capital W] of God. But when the passage is read in its entirety, one sees that this knowledge, unobtainable by scientific, or empirical methods, is possible by revelation and was understood and believed by "us." The apostle certainly distinguishes between two proposed methods

---

*There is nothing irrational, mystical, illogical, or inexpressible to which he directs attention.*

19. Any person who wants to empty the word of power must also have forgotten *Hebrews* 4:12, "The Word of God is living and active, sharper than any two-edged sword." Some but not all ancient commentaries took *Hebrews* to refer to Christ; but Protestants usually refer it to the Bible (see Calvin and Owen, *in loc.*). Reformed theologians sometimes accuse Lutherans of so emphasizing the Word of God that they render the Spirit superfluous. The Lutherans, of course, deny the charge; but true or not, the Lutherans could hardly have produced a doctrine subject to such a misunderstanding unless the Scripture itself had assigned great power to the word.

of learning; but there is no disparagement of the truth nor any appeal to a "soul" that is different from the body of truths.

Tozer's sermon does indeed contain several true and important statements. One is the author's insistence on the need of illumination. He says, "Revelation is not enough. There must be illumination before revelation can get into your soul." This is true. But the antithesis that the author draws between revelation and illumination is false. Illumination is not the "soul" of the truth. There is no implication that "the truth is *more* than the text." It is false to say that "there is something behind the text that you've got to get through to." Rather, illumination is what enables you to "get through" to the text. Illumination is a figure of speech, but it is not poetic nonsense. The figure compares light shining on a physical object with God's causing us to accept the truth. Note that it is the truth that God illumines. He does not substitute some other object beside, behind, or above the truth. Illumination does not alter, add to, or subtract from the truth. It causes us to focus on the truth just as it is. Thus, although the antithesis between experience and revelation is sound, the idea that illumination adds something to the truth and "gets us through to" some different object is unsound and false. If we want some poetry that is not nonsense, let us sing with Cowper, "The Spirit breathes upon the Word and brings the truth to sight."

*Illumination does not alter, add to, or subtract from the truth. It causes us to focus on the truth just as it is.*

The whole plan of salvation, so far as it is represented in this sermon, is unscriptural. It is substantially correct to say that "Conversion is a miraculous act of God by the Holy Ghost"; though it would be more accurately phrased as, Regeneration is a supernatural act of God, the Holy Spirit, for the Reformation, in opposition to Romish superstition, insisted that the age of miracles is past. Faith too is a supernatural gift of God. But the life which the new birth initiates and the faith that is its exercise is informed by the truth. It is not true to say, "God taught him in secret that truth had a soul as well as a body [this is poetic nonsense], and he dared to get through and pursue by penitence and obedience until God honored his faith and flashed the light on." Note how unbiblical this is. The human being "dares," "to get through" – whatever that means – and because of repentance and obedience, which are indubitably Scriptural requirements, God honors his faith and gives him illumination. This attributes merit to a man's daring. It obscures, really it denies that faith is a gift of God. Then because of this daring and faith, God rewards the man by giving him illumination. Preposterous! It is hard to get the plan of salvation more backwards than this. The Scripture nowhere teaches that faith is a reward of repentance and obedience. It is the free gift of God. One must first believe that what Christ says is true before he can repent and obey. Unless "the light is flashed on" at the beginning, a man will not accept the Scripture as truth.

Then, too, salvation includes sanctification as well as repentance, many other things, and finally glorification. Through the course of this life salvation is mostly the process of sanctification. Now, how is sanctification to be advanced? A few pages back, in the section on Truth, the verse was quoted, "Sanctify them by the truth: Your Word is truth." Dr. Tozer's disparagement of truth and his substitution for it of something the Gospel never mentions would make sanctification, *i.e.*, the whole Christian life, impossible. It is the truth, the word, that sanctifies. Therefore the most important battle line is that between the acceptance and the rejection of God's truth. Everything else is subsidiary. Or better, there is nothing else, for God's truth includes the doctrine of creation, the doctrine of the atonement, and everything else. The Jews did not accept, they did not assent, to the truth of God. To them Jesus said, "If anyone retains my *doctrine*, he shall never never see death ever."

*It is the truth, the word, that sanctifies. Therefore the most important battle line is that between the acceptance and the rejection of God's truth.*

Disparagement of doctrine, in our age, derives mainly from Søren Kierkegaard. Schleiermacher, the father of Modernism, may have lent some indirect help. When he replaced the word of revelation with religious experience, he undermined all Christian doctrine. But he did not mean to repudiate all doctrine. By a psychological analysis of religious experience he aimed to establish some principles of religion. He even thought that these principles would be Christian. But the history of the movement has demonstrated, as Ludwig Feuerbach early saw, that the result is atheistic humanism. Yet humanism has dogmas too, not so eternally fixed and true as Christian doctrine, but, tentative though they may be, intellectual propositions concerning the values of life. It may possibly be that they think their empirical method eternally fixed and true and not merely tentative. But the values change. Some of Schleiermacher's disciples also, toward the end of the nineteenth century, especially in stressing Schleiermacher's Kantianism, decided that life's values could not be intellectually supported and therefore made religion a matter of the emotions. In this way they contributed to anti-intellectualism. But the most powerful and responsible source of anti-intellectualism, the one whose influence is so widespread today, is Søren Kierkegaard.

Many religious people who have never studied the history of philosophy, among them a number of devout but uninstructed Christians, are impressed with Kierkegaard's earnestness and zeal. When he speaks of passionate inwardness, he strikes in them a responsive chord. They echo Goethe's dictum that life is green and theory gray. They want excitement, not understanding. They want even less understanding than Kierkegaard required.

20. Or at least Johannes Climacus, in the *Concluding Unscientific Postscript*; for this is not the place to discuss the relationship between Kierkegaard and his pseudonyms.

21. Translated by Swenson and Lowries, Princeton University Press, 1941.

Kierkegaard[20] required and insisted that a Christian must understand that orthodox theology is absurd. The incarnation and the doctrine of the God-man, and by implication everything else, are not merely "above reason," they are precisely *against* reason – a phrase found at least a dozen times in the *Postscript*. Further reading will discover that Kierkegaard considers Christian doctrine as a violation of the laws of logic - identity, contradiction, and excluded middle. On pages 238-239 of the *Postscript*[21] he repeats the problem of Abraham as an example, and on page 518 he says, "Sin is not a dogma or a doctrine for

140

thinkers…it is an existence-determinant, and precisely one which cannot be thought." Three lines below he says that the paradox of Christianity "requires faith against the understanding." A few pages earlier (513) he speaks of a contradiction that cannot be resolved and finds that the incarnation is "contradictory to all thinking." Kierkegaard does indeed insist on understanding, for a Christian must understand that doctrine is irrational "in order to believe against understanding" (503). "Faith requires a man to give up his reason…here again it appears how improper it is to transform Christianity into a doctrine to be understood" (337). "Christianity is not a doctrine but an existential communication expressing an existential contradiction" (339).

In opposition to Kierkegaard two things may be said. The first is a speculative remark, philosophical, theoretical, altogether intellectual, and absolutely conclusive. It is this: A writer who allows himself one contradiction cannot deny himself or anyone else another contradiction. Hence when Kierkegaard asserts that Christianity is not a doctrine, but an existential contradiction, one may reply: Yes, you are right, but since absurdity is permissible, Christianity is also a doctrine and not an existential contradiction. More generally expressed: The assertion of a contradiction is absurd, nonsense, meaningless, and needs no other refutation.

*A writer who allows himself one contradiction cannot deny himself or anyone else another contradiction.*

The second thing to be said in opposition to Kierkegaard is that his views are completely opposite to the *Gospel of John*, and are therefore Antichristian. The evidence for this assertion is all the exposition found in the present study of the *Gospel*. But one point will make the matter utterly clear. Kierkegaard repeatedly says that it makes no difference what one believes: The important thing is how one believes it (compare page 540). The crucial case is that of a Hindu idolater:

> If one who lives in the midst of Christendom goes up to the house of God, the house of the true God, with a true conception of God in his knowledge, and prays, but prays in a false spirit;[22] and one who lives in an idolatrous community prays with the entire passion of the infinite, although his eyes rest upon the image of an idol: where is the most truth? The one prays in truth to God, though he worships an idol…[179-180].

We object. If the Hindu worships in truth, then it is useless to command Christians to "Make disciples of all nations, teaching them to observe all things whatsoever I commanded you." And Jesus must have taught falsehood when he said, "No one comes to the Father but by me."

## 5. Saving Faith

In view of the clear and repeated assertions of the *Gospel* it is strange that anyone who considers himself conservative or even orthodox should minimize faith or belief and try to substitute for it some emotional or mystic experience. Two possible explanations may be sug-

22. Question: Is it possible to hold a true conception of God and pray in a false spirit? At any rate, the present writer's argument contains no defense of hypocrisy.

gested. The first is that these people are so impressed by the spectacular conversion of the Apostle Paul that they think all conversions should conform to this type. Such a view cannot be rationally justified. In the first place the persecutor on his way to Damascus was not merely converted: Christ appeared unto him (making him a witness of the Resurrection) "to appoint you a minister and a witness both of the things wherein you have seen me, and of the things wherein I will appear unto you; delivering you from the people, and from the Gentiles, unto whom I send you, to open their eyes…" (*Acts* 26:15-18). Such an appointment to apostleship should not be made the required type for every conversion. Indeed, it is not the type even for every apostle. There were eleven others. Who appeals to their conversion experiences? Their conversion experiences are not recorded; and the various other conversions that are recorded differ from Paul's and from each other. It is therefore wrong to elevate anyone's experience to the level of a norm for everyone.

*People who do not suffer ecstasies of joy or depths of despair are said to be devoid of Christian experience. But such a view has more in common with the pagan Goethe than with the Apostle John.*

The second possible explanation of the strange disparagement of faith or belief is the Romantic notion that sensory titillation is "experience." Hence people who do not suffer ecstasies of joy or depths of despair are said to be devoid of Christian experience. But such a view has more in common with the pagan Goethe than with the Apostle John. It is likely that Romanticism thrives on inborn tendencies plus an inability to think clearly, especially to think clearly about one's own (I shall not say experience) mental life. These people do indeed have beliefs. Many of them believe that the Bible is the Word of God and that Christ's death was a substitutionary sacrifice. But because they have studied so little, because their theology is limited to a few fundamentals, and because they assume the detailed and onerous duties of pastors and evangelists where their limited theology is inadequate, they conclude from the meagerness of their thinking that thinking and believing are inadequate. Combined with this is their failure to notice the effect of their few beliefs on their own conduct.

*Because their theology is limited to a few fundamentals,…they conclude from the meagerness of their thinking that thinking and believing are inadequate.*

As a man thinks, so is he. Out of the heart — and as we shall see some pages further on, *heart* means mind or intellect — are the issues of life. If a man says he has faith, but does not have works, we tend to conclude that he has no faith. Conduct, particularly habitual conduct, is the best criterion fallible men have for judging hypocrisy. What a man believes, really believes, even if he says the contrary, will show in his living. Therefore these popular evangelists show by their conduct that they believe in some things. Their intellectual capital controls their actions so far as their capital reaches. But because they are undercapitalized, and because they have too little intellectual endowment to recognize how intellectual beliefs control them, they minimize theology and take refuge in Romanticism.

In these introductory remarks in this chapter the meaning of the Scriptural term *heart* has been anticipated. Faith and belief have been emphasized. Even apart from these introductory inducements the nature of saving faith is an important division of theology. Therefore one should pay strict attention to what John's *Gospel* says on the subject.

Although John never uses the noun *faith* (*pistis*) in his *Gospel*, and only once in his epistles, he scatters its verb (*pisteuoo*) about in abundance – just about one hundred times. The main uses can be divided into two categories, depending on its object. The first object is a noun or pronoun governed by the preposition *in* (*eis* with the accusative or *en* with the dative). The second object is a clause. Sometimes also a noun occurs without a preposition, and there are instances when the object is unexpressed.

The usage with the noun-object seems to lend support to the liberal contention that Christians must believe in a person, not a doctrine. God, they say, never reveals any thing, information, or doctrine: He reveals himself. Of course, modern theologians care little for the words of Scripture, and why they should accept the use of *pisteuoo* with a noun while rejecting many other things in Scripture is what they cannot explain. Nevertheless a conservative, an evangelical, one whose principle is *sola Scriptura*, must examine these words and this usage regardless of liberal oscillations.

From among the many instances of the noun-object the following are typical.

*John* 1:12, 2:23, 3:18 have the phrases "believed in his name" (*eis to onoma*). Comments on the usage will be postponed until the list is ended; but one may note how Hebraic and non-Hellenistic the reference to the name is. The phrase, "believed in him" is found in *John* 2:11; 3:15 (*en autooi*); 3:18; 4:39; 6:29 (*eis on*); 6:35 (*eis eme*); 6:40, on to 16:9 (*eis eme*). To "believe on the Son" occurs in *John* 3:36; 9:35; 12:11 (on Jesus). There are also instances where the noun or pronoun is a simple dative without a preposition. The pronoun is *me* in *John* 4:21, 5:46; 8:45-46; and 10:37. The pronoun *him* is in *John* 5:38 and 8:31. These listings are not complete or exhaustive, but they are typical and will serve the present purpose.

The present purpose is to show that these noun or pronoun objects are linguistic forms that simplify the text by implying without expressing the propositions to be believed. One of the clearest is *John* 4:21, "Woman, believe me." In this case the proposition to be believed follows explicitly: "Woman, believe me, that a time is coming when...." There is no antithesis between believing Jesus as a person and believing what he says. Similarly *John* 5:46 compares believing Moses (dative without a preposition) and believing me. In both cases the object of belief is not a person without words, but definitely the words of the person. The *me* of *John* 8:45-46 again refers to the truth I am saying. The "Do not believe me" of *John* 10:37 means, "Do not believe what I say." The same explanation holds for 5:38 and 8:31. In both cases the reference is to an explicit *logos*.

The instances with the preposition *eis* are not always so obvious; but obviously they do not contradict what has just been said. For example, "to those who believe on his name" (1:12); "many believed on

*The object of belief is not a person without words, but definitely the words of the person.*

his name" (2:23); and "he has not believed on the name of the only Son of God" (3:18); all these with their Old Testament background imply that what is believed or not believed is the claim Jesus makes. If 2:23 can be closely connected with 2:22 (it is clearly the same place, the temple; and the time cannot be much later), the background is *Psalm* 69:9 and the words of Jesus himself. His act of cleansing the temple caused many to believe these propositions.

The second category of the uses of the verb *believe* has the propositional object explicit in the text. Without counting the cases where the object is clearly a proposition, although not explicitly given, a full 25 percent of the instances of *believe* have the proposition written out in full.

*The immediate and proper object of belief or faith is a truth (or falsehood), a meaning, the intellectual content of some words; and this intellectual content is in logic called a proposition.*

The first verse, already cited (2:22), does not itself contain the propositions believed: They are in the preceding context. The disciples believed *Psalm* 69:9 and the words Jesus had addressed to the Jews.

The second verse (3:12) also finds the explicit proposition in the context. Jesus said to Nicodemus, "If I have spoken to you of earthly matters [such as the new birth and the Spirit's effect on men] and you do not believe, how will you believe [my propositions] if I speak of heavenly matters [such as the doctrine of the eternal generation of the Son and the intertrinitarian relationships]?" The second set of propositions is of course not given; the first set constitutes the previous conversation explicitly reported.

The third verse (4:21), also previously cited, itself contains the proposition. *John* 4:41, 50 both have the noun-object *words* or *word*; but the propositions are explicit in the context. Similar are the two instances in 5:47, *viz.*, Moses' writings, not quoted, and Jesus' words contained in the preceding verses.

*John* 6:69 says, "We believe and know that you are the Holy One of God." *John* 8:24 says, "You do not believe that I am [Jehovah, or, the one I claim to be]." *John* 9:18, "the Jews did not believe that he had been blind." *John* 10:25-26, "I told you [that I am the Christ] and you do not believe [that proposition]; the works I do…testify of me [that I am the Messiah], but you do not believe [the propositions they assert]." *John* 11:26-27, "Everyone who is alive and believes in me will never die. Do you believe this [proposition]? Yes, Lord, she said, I have believed that you are the Messiah, the Son of God, who comes into the world." In *John* 11:42 Jesus spoke out loud "so that the crowd would believe that you did send me." But why tediously quote in addition 12:38, 47; 13:19; 14:10-11, 29; 16:27, 30; 17:8, 21; 19:35 and 20:31?

The conclusion is, not only that the verb *believe* (*pisteuoo*) may have a clause or proposition for an object, but that this is the fundamental meaning of the verb *believe*. In literary usage one may say that one believes a person; but this means that one believes what the person says. The immediate and proper object of belief or faith is a truth (or falsehood), a meaning, the intellectual content of some words; and this intellectual content is in logic called a proposition.

It may possibly be the case that the *King James Version* has been a small factor contributing to anti-intellectualism. In German the Greek verb *pisteuoo* is translated *glauben*, and the noun is *der Glaube, belief.* Therefore *Matthew* 9:22 in German is, "*Tochter, dein Glaube hat dir geholfen.*" And *Matthew* 6:30 is, "*O ihr Kleingläubigen.*" But in English the connection between the Greek verb *believe* and its Latin noun is obscured by translating the noun as *faith* instead of *belief.* The Latin language has not been an unexceptional advantage to theology. *Dikaioo* was translated *justus-facere*; and thus the New Testament word for *acquit* or *pronounce righteous* was taken to mean *make righteous.* The result was a theory of infused grace that obscured the method of salvation until the time of Luther and the Reformation. So too it would have been better if the *King James Version* had omitted the word *faith* and emphasized the root meaning of *belief.*

Because *fides* or faith permits, though it does not necessitate, a non-intellectual interpretation, the liberals today want us to have "faith" in a god who is unknowable and silent because he is impotent to give us any information to believe. This Latin anti-intellectualism, permitted by the noun *fides*, undermines all good news and makes Gospel information useless. Although the theologians of the sixteenth and seventeenth centuries would have repudiated twentieth century anti-intellectualism, their Latin heritage adversely affected some of their views. Before this earlier material is discussed, however, we must turn once again to the text in order to see precisely what is the effect of believing certain propositions.

This part of the study pays no attention to the grammatical object of the verb. Reliance is now placed on the conclusion already drawn that noun and pronoun objects are linguistic simplifications of the intended propositional object. To believe a person means precisely to believe what he says.

The first case, *John* 1:12, asserts that those who believe in his name have the right, graciously given by God, to be the children of God. The phrase "in his name," I take it, means his character as Messiah and Lord. Those who believe that Jesus is the Messiah prophesied in the Old Testament have the authority to be God's children.

The same idea occurs in *John* 3:15, 36. Everyone who believes in Jesus, believes that he is the Messiah, has eternal life. The converse is stated in verse 18. That the noun-object, or phrase *in his name*, bears this meaning is a little clearer in 5:24, where the person who hears Jesus' discourse (*logos*), and believes the Father who sent him with the message, has eternal life and has (already) crossed over from death to life. To be sure, a random intellectual belief of an unregenerate man will not save him. The difficulty lies, not in belief as such, but in the fact that an unregenerate man is incapable of believing the necessary propositions. As *John* 12:30-40 says, "They could not believe because ...he has blinded their eyes and hardened their hearts." If God had opened their eyes and had exchanged their heart of stone for a heart of flesh, they would have believed the Gospel message and so would already have passed from death to life. It is regeneration to eternal life

*This Latin anti-intellectualism, permitted by the noun* fides, *undermines all good news and makes Gospel information useless.*

that causes the intellectual belief. Thus acceptance of the propositions is a mark of having been regenerated and of having eternal life.

Again, *John* 6:40, 47, "Everyone who contemplates the Son and believes on him has life eternal.... Most assuredly I tell you, the man who believes has eternal life." Similar phrases are found in 7:38; 8:31; and 11:25.

More explicit verses are the following. *John* 8:24 puts the matter negatively: "if you do not believe that I am [Jehovah, or, the Messiah] you will die in your sins." The force of this negative is important. The proposition "all believers have eternal life" does not imply that all non-believers lack eternal life. Such an implication would be invalid, as may be seen in an example from daily affairs: The proposition "all voters are residents" does not imply "all non-voters are non-residents." Therefore the simple statement "all believers are saved" allows the possibility that some unbelievers are saved as well. Belief may well guarantee eternal life; but without further information to the contrary something else may also guarantee eternal life. This elementary lesson in logic points up the importance of the explicit negative statement: If you do not believe, you will die in your sins. All believers are saved, and all the saved are believers.[23]

*John* 10:25-28 say, "You do not believe because you do not belong to my flock. My sheep listen to my voice.... I give them eternal life." This states what is essentially both the negative and the positive proposition; and the negative is clearly implied in 16:9, "He will convict the world of sin...because they do not believe on me." Then if one supposes that God granted the petitions of the high-priestly prayer, the positive statement is implied in 17:8-10, 16-17, 20-22, and 26.

Be sure to note that the Apostle John never mentions a mystic experience. He never says that one must get behind the text to something other than the words or doctrine. He repeatedly says, if you believe, you are saved. Belief is the whole thing. Indeed *John* 20:31 asserts this very thing in stating the purpose for writing the *Gospel*: that you may believe the proposition that Jesus is the Messiah and that believing this proposition (and not in some other way) you may have life by his name.

The next question is, What does it mean to believe? This question is usually asked in Latin rather than in Greek, and so phrased the question becomes, What is faith? Various theologians have offered psychological analyses of faith. The most common Protestant analysis is that *fides* is a combination of *notitia, assensus*, and *fiducia*. If these last three Latin words can be explained, then one may compare *fides* and *pistis* or *pisteuoo* to see if they are synonymous. If these Latin terms cannot be clearly defined, then they do not constitute an analysis of faith.

*Notitia* is not hard to define. The word refers to the intellectual content known. According to one large Latin lexicon, *notitia* means *a being known, acquaintance with a person (also sexual intercourse), knowledge, conception, notion*. Examples would be the proposition that two and two are four, the realization that I must get my work done, the concept of

---

*The Apostle John never mentions a mystic experience. He never says that one must get behind the text to something other than the words or doctrine. He repeatedly says, if you believe, you are saved. Belief is the whole thing.*

---

23. Jesus was speaking to adult Pharisees. The question of the salvation of infants is not here envisaged. Will not the mystics argue that since Jesus was speaking to Pharisees, his words do not apply to Gentiles today, who must do something other than believe?

*Liliaceae* in botany, and the doctrine of justification by faith. In specifying *notitia* as the first element in faith, the traditional Protestant analysis, whatever incipient anti-intellectualism may be buried in it, clearly intends to affirm that faith has an intellectual content.

Since some people understand the Gospel propositions – the Pharisees understood Jesus' claim better than the disciples did – but do not accept or believe them, *fides* must also contain acceptance or assent. Indeed, *assensus*, one's voluntary acceptance of a proposition, seems to be more the essence of faith than anything else is. If we think of belief as believing, *i.e.*, the subjective psychological activity, belief may be equated with assent. Objectively, belief, one's belief, is the *notitia*, the proposition believed. In the morning worship service, we recite our creed, our belief, our faith. Samuel Butler in *The Way of All Flesh* reports that the Anglican congregations in the eighteenth century recited The Belief, not The Creed. This belief is what the worshiper assents to. When the minister preaches the Gospel, a person may understand what the speaker means; he may then assent to it; *i.e.*, he believes. Instead of enumerating three elements in faith, one could better say that subjective belief and assent are synonymous.

But then, apparently in opposition to Romanism, the Reformers wanted to say something else. In addition to believing, *i.e.*, understanding and accepting, *fides* was said to include and require *fiducia*. What now is *fiducia*, this third element in saving faith?

The nature of saving faith and the difficulties of defining *fiducia* can be better appreciated by recalling some largely forgotten history. Luther and Calvin were not so clear on the matter as might be wished. Both of them in several places made assurance of salvation essential to faith. The implication is that unless one is certainly assured that God has saved him, he is not regenerate. Now, Luther's impetuosity led him many times to exaggerate his expressions: for example, his statement, Sin boldly! Luther also corrected his words, and there are passages in which he seems, at least seems, to deny that assurance is essential to saving faith. Calvin was much more cautious and careful than Luther. But Calvin too seems, at least seems, to say that assurance is essential. But elsewhere he indicates that this is not really his opinion. It is possible that his unfortunate expressions came to mean something that he did not intend; for as time went on the later Lutheran and Reformed theologians gave more attention to assurance and developed distinctions that Calvin did not make. These developments took place after the first great controversies with the Roman Church. Calvin's and Luther's chief attacks on Romanism centered on justification by faith. The nature of faith was indeed involved, but assurance was a minor issue; and the result was that they paid it insufficient attention. Nor is it the chief interest here. The subject is faith and *fiducia*. But if we examine the Reformers, earlier and later, the subject of assurance somewhat distorts the discussion.

Since the matter is of interest and importance, Calvin's own account will be given first. Calvin, *Institutes of the Christian Religion*, Book

*Assensus, one's voluntary acceptance of a proposition, seems to be more the essence of faith than anything else is. If we think of belief as believing, i.e., the subjective psychological activity, belief may be equated with assent.*

III, chapter 2, has as its title "Faith Defined." The first paragraph is a transition from the preceding material and introduces the attempt to define faith by a reference to "the pernicious tendency of the mistakes of multitudes in the present age on this subject." Thus Calvin approaches his analysis with the contemporary situation in mind. Since he wrote before the Council of Trent, there is reasonable likelihood that the position he opposes is that of widespread common opinion rather than official Roman Catholic dogma. In view of this, and in view of Turretin, LeBlanc (who enumerates, as we shall see further on, several differences among the Reformers), and the *Westminster Confession*, one may today wish to amend Calvin's remarks without any desire to detract from his great and amply deserved fame.

"A great part of the world," he continues, "when they hear the word *faith*, conceive it to be nothing more than a common assent to the evangelical history." He then distinguishes the "schools" from "a great part of the world." The schools (apparently) do a little better and identify God as the object of faith; but this too is inadequate. They should have specified Christ, for no man comes to God except by Christ. The schools also (in paragraph 2)

> have fabricated the notion of implicit faith, a term with which they have honored the grossest ignorance.... Is this faith – to understand nothing? ...Faith consists not in ignorance, but in knowledge.... By this knowledge, I say, not by renouncing our understanding, we obtain entrance into the kingdom of heaven.

The intellectualism of this opening statement, so opposite to the worse than Romish ignorance of twentieth-century liberalism, must be taken to govern the following exposition. If Calvin denies that faith is one kind of knowledge, he must not be twisted to mean that faith is not knowledge.

Paragraph 3 continues, "Faith consists in a knowledge of God and Christ...[the opponents, on the contrary] pretend that truth is held in error, light in darkness, and true knowledge in ignorance." In the following three paragraphs Calvin acknowledges that all Christians, even the apostles, are ignorant of some things, and that Christians normally and eventually learn more. Faith is indeed knowledge, but it is not omniscience.

In paragraph 7 Calvin explains why faith cannot simply be defined as a knowledge of God. Adam and Cain both knew God, but their knowledge terrified them. Hence faith requires a knowledge of God's mercy, not merely of God's law. Even so, if we know God's promises, yet if our knowledge is mixed with doubts, it is not faith. Faith is "uniform and steady," not "wavering and undecided." "Now, we shall have a complete definition of faith, if we say, that it is a steady and certain knowledge of the Divine benevolence toward us, which, being founded on the truth of the gratuitous promise in Christ, is both revealed to our minds and confirmed in our hearts by the Holy Spirit."

This definition and its preceding discussion are, in the main, excel-

*"By this knowledge, I say, not by renouncing our understanding, we obtain entrance into the kingdom of heaven."*
*— John Calvin*

lent. They not only exploded the Romanism of their time, but they remain today superior to much of popular fundamentalism. There is, however, one point that needs criticism. Calvin seems to say that faith cannot be mixed with doubts; faith must be uniform and steady, not wavering and undecided. But this does not seem to square with John the Baptist's doubts when he was in prison. Nor do these phrases accord very well with the idea of faith as a grain of mustard seed; with the cry, "Lord, I believe, help my unbelief"; and with Christ's refusal to quench smoking flax. Calvin's definition seems to equate faith with assurance – something the later Calvinists did not do. However this may be, one thing is clear: Calvin's definition is not complete. The relationships between knowledge, which he stresses, and assent, which he will discuss a little later, and *fiducia*, if it be a third element, are not mentioned. This is not said to belittle Calvin, but to justify the researches of the later Calvinists.

In paragraph 8 Calvin attacks those who "maintain faith to be a mere assent, with which every despiser of God may receive as true whatever is contained in the Scripture." This statement is puzzling. It seems strange that a person who has received as true whatever is contained in Scripture could despise God. Does the Bible give any example of such a man? Did Simon Magus despise God? He placed a high value on the ability to confer the Holy Ghost by the laying on of hands. No doubt selfish from one point of view, he nonetheless wanted this power, not for his own profit, but in order to give the Spirit to other people and so bless them. After being rebuked by Peter, he asked Peter to pray for him. Was this request insincere? At any rate, he could not have believed everything the Bible contains because he believed that apostolic gifts could be bought with silver. Nor does Calvin's next sentence provide him help for this puzzling statement. "But first," he continues, "it should be examined whether every man acquires faith for himself by his own power, or whether it is by faith that the Holy Spirit becomes the witness of adoption." The reference to adoption seems again to identify faith with assurance, and this is not the subject of discussion. Insofar as it implies that faith is a gift of God and is produced, not by the will of man, but by the Spirit's regenerating activity, well and good. But neither does this explain the nature and place of assent.

Embarrassing as it may be to the present writer in his aim of commending Calvin, the great Reformer actually says a few lines below (III, ii, 8), "The assent which we give to the Divine word . . . is from the heart rather than from the head, and from the affections rather than the understanding." But even here, it is still assent. When Calvin in his next phrase calls it "the obedience of faith," the word *obedience* warns us that assent is voluntary: It is an act of will, not of the affections. The will is active (activated by the Spirit, of course); affections, as the name indicates, are passive.

Even if in this section Calvin seems to disparage understanding, previous quotations show (I hope) his basic intellectualism. Here too

*It seems strange that a person who has received as true whatever is contained in Scripture could despise God. Does the Bible give any example of such a man?*

he says, "Nothing is more precious to him [the Lord] than his own truth." Then he appends a remark that establishes assent: "As this is by no means a dubious point [the point that truth is precious to the Lord], we conclude at once, that it is an absurdity to say that faith is formed by the addition of a pious affection to an assent of the mind; whereas even this assent consists in a pious affection." Though the present writer is not enamored of the word *affection*, for it denotes nothing voluntary, yet the result clearly makes faith an act of assent. That this act of assent is pious and caused by the Spirit is an emphasis with which the present writer agrees in Calvin's attack on any other view. The conclusion is that Calvin, perhaps not with perfect clarity, held that faith is assent.

*The term* fiducia, *which today is often confidently joined with knowledge and assent to make the definition of faith, has never been unambiguously explained.*

Two nineteenth-century theologians have written on this history. Robert L. Dabney, *Discussions: Evangelical and Theological*, Volume 1, in an examination of the aberrations of the Plymouth Brethren, goes over some of this Reformation history. His work should be consulted. But since his main subject is the Plymouth Brethren, it is better to spend a little space on the more directly pertinent article of William Cunningham, "The Reformers and the Doctrine of Assurance," in his *The Reformers and the Theology of the Reformation*. This thirty-eight page chapter is a gem. The present interest, however, is only to show that the term *fiducia*, which today is often confidently joined with knowledge and assent to make the definition of faith, has never been unambiguously explained.

On page 122 Cunningham writes, "With respect to the nature of saving faith, the principal ground of controversy was this, that the Romanists held that it had its seat in the intellect, and was properly and fundamentally assent (*assensus*), while the Reformers in general maintained that it had its seat in the will, and was properly and essentially trust (*fiducia*). The great majority of eminent Protestant divines have adhered to the views of the Reformers upon this point, though some have taken the opposite side, and have held faith, properly so called, to be the mere assent of the understanding to truth propounded by God in his word...."

Before another quotation is given, a small comment on the above should be made. The distinction between *assensus* and *fiducia* is here connected with a psychology that separates the intellect from the will. Probably a third faculty, either emotion (rarely considered by the Reformers) or sensibility, is joined to these to constitute the person. If this type of psychology is rejected, and if more stress is put on the unitary person and his acts, it is at least possible that the analysis of faith will have to be altered. In the second place, in the history of theology, and even as far back as Stoic epistemology, assent was an act of will, not an act of intellect. Hence Cunningham has incorrectly reported Romanism and also makes a mistake in the psychological analysis.

More to the present point is the list of different meanings attached to the term *fiducia*. On page 130 Cunningham quotes LeBlanc, professor of theology at Sedan, as saying, "*fiduciam apud doctores Reformatos pluribus modis sumi…*" (trust is taken in several ways by the Reformed theologians). On the next page LeBlanc's words mean, "the Reformed theologians speak in various ways concerning *fiducia*; some say it is the primary part of faith; others deny this and hold that it is an effect of faith, but not properly essential to it; and others understand it one way and others another." LeBlanc then specifies four different meanings, of which Cunningham gives two. To these he adds three meanings specified by Turretin. A loose and incomplete translation is: *Fiducia* is the assent or persuasion that arises from the practical judgment of the intellect concerning the truth and goodness of the Gospel promises and concerning the power, will, and fidelity of the promising God. Second, *fiducia* is the act of receiving Christ, by which the faithful Christian, when he has come to know the truth and goodness of the promises, flees to Christ, and embracing him, depends on his merit alone. Third, *fiducia* is the confidence or acquiescence and tranquility which arises from the soul's taking refuge in Christ. Then Turretin adds, the first and second meanings are of the essence and definition of faith; but the third is only an effect and not part of the definition.

Cunningham concludes,

> as these distinctions were not present to the minds of the Reformers, but were the growth of later speculations, we should not attribute to them any one of these distinct and definite opinions, without specific evidence bearing on the precise point to be proved, and should not allow ourselves to be carried away by the mere words, *trust* and *confidence, certainty* and *assurance*, without a full and deliberate consideration of the whole evidence bearing upon the meaning of the statements.

Before the Roman Catholic position is more definitely stated, a worse mistake than Cunningham's confusion will be given as an example of a common opinion. The Rev. Albert N. Martin, pastor of Trinity Church, North Caldwell, New Jersey, one of the best Puritan preachers of our day – and that means one of the best preachers of our day – in a pamphlet titled, "What's Wrong with Preaching Today," after making many wise and sobering remarks, says,

> We must never forget…that faith was something more than an "assensus," a mere nodding of the head to the body of truth presented by the church as "the faith."…a mere nodding assent to the doctrines they are exposed to is not the essence of saving faith [18].

Mr. Martin is indubitably correct when he insists that "saving faith involved…a trust and commitment involving the whole man…." But he seems to have misunderstood the nature of *assensus*. Assent is by no means "a mere nodding of the head." The Roman Church may be a synagogue of Satan; the pope may be the Antichrist; but Roman Catholicism, which Mr. Martin contrasts with the Reformers on the point in question, never held what he says it held.

The *New Catholic Encyclopedia*, in the article "Faith," says:

*Assent is by no means "a mere nodding of the head."*

[The etymology of the word *faith*] points to an act of the intellect assenting at the command of the will for moral rather than severely intellectual reasons....Divine faith is fiducial assent to revealed truth... faith as such is an assent to truth.... Faith is the firm assent at the command of the will and under the inward motion of God's grace to the saving truths and supernatural mysteries God has revealed.... St. Thomas...argued that in the act of divine faith there is a case of the will moving the mind to assent...that excludes all deliberate fear of being in error.[24]

Although faith is so certain and is moreover "a gratuitous gift of God" ("Loss of Faith," 804), a man may lose his faith because he can lose sanctifying grace. "Grace requires a man's free cooperation. This free cooperation can be withheld."

The second paragraph from the *New Catholic Encyclopedia* denies the Reformation doctrine of the perseverance of the saints. It reduces the power of God to a dependence on man's cooperation. This is, of course, utterly unscriptural. But the first paragraph in analyzing faith even used the word *fiducia* in the phrase "fiducial assent to revealed truth." Apparently Romanism holds that *fiducia*, instead of being a third independent element in faith, is a characteristic of assent. But it shows how wrong certain Protestants are when they identify assent with a mere nodding of the head. Since such mistakes are made in reporting Romanism – which ought to be a reasonably easy matter – it is possible that the more difficult psychological analysis may also be imperfect.

It has already been established that Protestant theologians have proposed several different analyses. LeBlanc noted the fact and specified four possibilities. Then he added three others from Turretin, one of which identifies *fiducia* and *assensus*; and this definition Turretin considers the essence of faith, while the third is not part of the definition.

The question now is, Can *fiducia* be so defined as to make it an independent third element in faith, or is faith essentially assent to a known proposition?

The Puritan writer Thomas Manton in his excellent commentary on the *Epistle of James* gives a characteristic and significant answer. The paragraph in question discusses *James* 2:19, "The devils also believe, and tremble." "This instance showeth," says Manton, "what faith he disputeth against, namely, such as consisteth in bare speculation and knowledge.... *Thou believest*; that is, assentest to this truth; the lowest act of faith is invested with the name of believing."

Manton's argument here is that since the devils assent and true believers also assent, something other than assent is needed for saving faith. This is a logical blunder. The text says the devils believe in monotheism. Why cannot the difference between the devils and Christians be the different propositions believed, rather than a psychological element in belief? Manton assumes a different psychology is needed. It is better to say a different object of belief is needed.

According to Manton, the devils' psychology is one of bare specu-

*Manton's argument here is that since the devils assent and true believers also assent, something other than assent is needed for saving faith. This is a logical blunder.*

24. *The New Catholic Encyclopedia*, 1967.V, 798–800.

lation. However, he does not explain what this is. If it is the so-called faith, discussed on his preceding pages, that produces no works, one cannot object. This so-called faith Manton calls a "dead faith," or better a "false faith," and therefore not a saving faith at all. Faith without works is dead. Agreed. But if this is not saving faith at all, and is yet called faith and belief, the difference will be found in the object, not in the psychological analysis. The analysis is the same whether a person believes a saving truth, a non-saving truth, or even a falsehood.

Manton makes an attempt to avoid the force of this consideration. "There is one God," he continues. "He instanceth in this proposition, though he doth limit the matter only to this: partly because this was the first article of the creed…by it intending also assent to other articles of religion…."

Now, just what devils believe and do not believe, the Bible does not fully explain. The psychology of Satan is something of a puzzle. Apparently Satan really believed that Job would curse God. Like the Arminians he did not believe in the perseverance of the saints. One cannot be certain, but possibly Satan believed the promise he himself made to Eve. Did he not also believe that he might possibly tempt Christ to sin? If he had believed it impossible, why should he have tried three times? There must therefore be a good bit of the Bible that the devils do not believe.

In this difficulty it is best to stay close to the text, and James says only that the devils believe there is one God. The text nowhere says that this proposition stands for all the articles of the creed. It has just now been proved that it does not. If human beings can be monotheists without believing in the atonement, or even in Christ, one might suppose the devils could too. Because Manton adds to the creed of the devils propositions James does not specify, his argument becomes confused. Depending on an hypothesis that has no textual foundation, he fails to escape the objection above: It is illogical to conclude that belief is not assent just because belief in monotheism does not save. The clearer inference is that if belief in monotheism does not save, then one ought to believe something else in addition. Not assent, but monotheism is inadequate.

Manton definitely asserts, "*The devils also believe*; that is, assent to this truth, and other truths revealed in the word." Of course they do: They believe that Eve yielded to their temptation; no doubt they believe that Moses led the Israelites out of Egypt. But to suggest that they believe all other truths revealed in the Word goes beyond James' text, and contradicts other parts of Scripture.

Manton continues. "Bare assent to the articles of religion doth not infer true faith." Here the weasel word is "bare." Does he mean a mere nodding of the head? Probably not, for the devils' belief or assent is more than that. It is difficult to guess what Manton's psychology of "bare" assent is. The truth that saving faith produces works does not advance the argument. To say that true or saving faith (since belief in a falsehood is true or genuine belief) produces works does not imply

*If belief in monotheism does not save, then one ought to believe something else in addition. Not assent, but monotheism is inadequate.*

153

that faith is other than assent. Why should not assent produce works? It produced trembling. But if "bare" assent is not identified with assent minus works, then Manton assigns no meaning to the word on which he so much depends.

We agree that "True faith uniteth to Christ, it is conversant about his person." But we question "It is not only *assensus axiomati*, an assent to a gospel-maxim or proposition; you are not justified by that, but by being one with Christ." But is it not assent to the Gospel that makes a man one with Christ? What is meant by "being one with Christ"? Manton operates on the mistaken philosophical view, prevalent among contemporary dialectical theologians, that there are two kinds of knowledge. He admits that the Reformers did not accept this philosophy: "It was the mistake of the former age to make the promise rather than the person of Christ to be the formal object of faith." But this was not a mistake. The earlier Reformers and the later Scottish Presbyterians had the right idea. There is no divorce between Christ's words and himself. Christ's *logoi* and *rheemata* are Christ's mind, and Christ's mind is himself. The detailed study of John's *Gospel*, traced carefully in the previous chapters, shows the apostolic emphasis on words and argument. There is no theory of two kinds of knowledge.

But if assent is not enough, as Manton argues, what else is needed? Do these people who disparage belief in opposition to John have anything definite to add? If they cannot specify and identify the addition they have in mind, they have no addition in their minds, and their contention falls. Here now is the explanation Manton offers.

> In short, there is not only *assent* in faith, but *consent*; not only an assent to the truth of the word, but a consent to take Christ;[a] there must be an act that is directly and formally conversant about the person of Christ. Well, then, do not mistake a naked illumination[b] or some general acknowledgment of the articles of religion for faith. A man may be right in opinion and judgment, but of vile affections; and a carnal Christian is in as great danger as a pagan, or idolater, or heretic;[c] for though his judgment be sound, yet his manners are heterodox and heretical. True believing is not an act of the understanding only, but a work of "all the heart" Acts viii.37).[d] I confess some expressions of scripture seem to lay much upon assent, as 1 John iv.2, and v.1; 1 Corinthians xii.3; Matt. xvi.17; but these places do either show that assents, where they are serious, and upon full conviction, come from some special revelation;[e] or else, if they propound them as evidences of grace, we must distinguish times: the greatest difficulty lay then upon assent, rather than affiance. The truths of God suffering under so many prejudices, the Gospel was a novel doctrine, contrary to the ordinary and received principles of reason, persecuted in the world, no friend to natural and carnal affections, and therefore apt to be suspected. The wind that bloweth on our backs, blew in their faces; and that which draweth on many to assent to the gospel was their discouragement. Consent and long prescription of time, the countenance and favour of the world, do beget a veneration and reverence to religion; and therefore assent now is nothing so much as it was then, especially when it is trivial and arreptitious

*Manton operates on the mistaken philosophical view, prevalent among contemporary dialectical theologians, that there are two kinds of knowledge.*

[demonic or raving], rather than deliberate; for this is only the fruit of human testimony, and needeth not supernatural grace.[f] Therefore do not please yourselves in naked assents; these cost nothing, and are worth nothing. There is "a form of knowledge" (Rom. ii.20), as well as "a form of godliness" (2 Tim. iii.5). "A form of knowledge" is nothing but an idea or module of truth in the brains, when there is no power or virtue to change and transform the heart.

Manton's argument is typical of and fuller than most of those that aim to add a third element to *notitia* and *assensus*. In spite of its length, it has been given in full to assure the reader that nothing of importance has been omitted. Criticism will show that certain of its propositions are indubitably true, but that a few unscriptural assertions and considerable confusion make the whole a logical fallacy. Since the points are numerous, it seems best to frame the criticism after the manner of footnotes, numbering each in sequence so as to make it easy to follow.

a. The psychological element that Manton wishes to add to knowledge and assent in order to constitute faith is *consent*. This is his conclusion, stated first; and the remainder of the quotation is his argument to support the conclusion. If the word *consent* has a definite meaning different from knowledge and assent, and if his argument is valid, Manton will have proved his point. But if he fails in either of these two requirements, he fails *in toto*.

b. It is interesting to note that Manton minimizes illumination, while this was what Dr. Tozer considered to be the all-important element. Of course, Dr. Tozer misunderstood the Reformed meaning of illumination, and what Manton thinks "naked" illumination is, is not clear. One of Manton's unpleasant habits is that of attaching obfuscating adjectives to important nouns. When the Bible talks about illumination, even if the word itself is not used, it refers to the power of the Holy Ghost as he causes a man to understand and accept the truth. If the adjective "naked" is attached, it probably means, since neither Manton nor Dr. Tozer want to deny that man himself is present, that truth and revelation are not present. But with this understanding of Manton's word "naked," his argument applies to nothing at all. Scriptural illumination always focuses the mind on the message.

c. That a carnal Christian is in as great danger as a pagan is unscriptural. No one is to be commended for his carnality. Paul berated the carnal Christians in Corinth. But though their works shall be burned up, yet they themselves shall be saved. The carnal Christian is even somewhat better off than this. Since justification inevitably produces sanctification, the most depraved sinner who is born again must improve, perhaps slowly and with much difficulty, or sometimes with the success of John Newton. The pagan is in danger of Hell fire; the carnal Christian is not. To the extent that Manton depends on this false premise, to that extent his argument is vitiated.

d. Here Manton falls into a great, though common, confusion. The trouble is not that *Acts* 8:37 is spurious. None of the earliest and best

> *That a carnal Christian is in as great danger as a pagan is unscriptural.... Since justification inevitably produces sanctification, the most depraved sinner who is born again must improve.... The pagan is in danger of Hell fire; the carnal Christian is not.*

manuscripts have it, but there are many other verses that insist one must believe with the heart: *e.g.,* "If you shall confess with your mouth…and believe in your heart…" [*Romans* 10:9-10]. Rather the trouble is that Manton has failed to understand what the Bible means by the term *heart*. He wrote, "True believing is not an act of the understanding only [and he really means, not of the understanding and of the will together], but a work of the heart." For him, therefore, the *heart* is something other than the understanding. But in the Bible the *heart*, in about 70 or 75 percent of the instances, means the understanding, without affirming or denying the presence of a volition. In another 20 percent, approximately, the term *heart* means the will, with or without an explicit reference to the understanding. Accordingly, less than 10 percent of the instances refer to anything other than intellect and will. Manton's spurious verse itself says that the heart believes. Now, belief is definitely intellectual and volitional. The good news, *i.e.,* information, must be understood and assented to. This is belief; and it is the *heart* that believes. Therefore the heart is the intellect.

*The heart is the organ of understanding and knowledge. It is the heart that thinks.*

Some other verses that show the intellectual nature of the heart now follow, but the reader is urged to check through a concordance and examine all the occurrences of the term.

*Genesis* 6:5: "Every imagination of the thoughts of his heart was only evil continually."

*Genesis* 8:21: "Jehovah said in his heart, I will not again…."

*Genesis* 17:17: "Then Abraham…said in his heart, shall a child be born…."

*Genesis* 20:6: "In the integrity of your heart you have done this."

*1 Samuel* 2:35: "A faithful priest that shall do according to that which is in my heart and in my mind."

*Psalm* 4:4: "Commune with your own heart."

*Psalm* 12:2: "They speak falsehood…and with a double heart do they speak."

*Psalm* 14:1: "The fool has said in his heart, There is no God."

*Psalm* 15:2: "He…speaks truth in his heart."

*Isaiah* 6:10: "Lest they…understand with their heart."

*Isaiah* 10:7: "Neither does his heart think so."

*Isaiah* 44:18, 19: "He has shut…their hearts that they cannot understand. And none calls to mind [the same word, heart]; neither is there knowledge nor understanding."

A moderately careful study of these verses will show that the heart is the organ of understanding and knowledge. It is the heart that thinks. When any popular preacher contrasts the head and the heart, meaning that the heart is something other than the intellect, he is distorting Scripture and thinks falsehoods in his heart. Since this particular misunderstanding of Scripture is uniformly a part of the argument against identifying faith or belief with assent, these verses and many others constitute a complete refutation.

e. The Scripture is so clear that believing is volitional assent to an understood proposition that Manton cannot avoid paying some attention to a few such references. He lists *1 John* 4:2 and 5:1, also *1 Corinthians* 12:3, and *Matthew* 16:17. He could have added *Romans* 10:9-10 and many other verses in the *Gospel of John*. Manton tries to escape the plain force of these verses by arguing that "assents, where they are serious and upon full conviction, come from some special revelation." This quotation contains both error and confusion. It is confused because it seems to presuppose that some acts of assent are not "serious." Every act of assent is serious or honest, since assent is never a mere nodding of the head. But though honest, it does not have to be with "full conviction." According to Manton's words, the only person who could assent with full conviction would be a recipient of a special revelation, *i.e.*, a prophet or an apostle. Now, some people may assent with full conviction or assurance of salvation. *1 John* 5:1, which Manton cites, speaks of "Whosoever believes…" not just an apostle. Of course the apostles, who received the message directly from God, assented upon full conviction. Others do too. But still others do not. There are people with little faith, like a grain of mustard seed. Thus Manton's argument is both confused and contains error. It therefore breaks in pieces on the rock of Scripture.

*Astonishing as it may seem, Manton never even tried to define "consent."*

f. He has, however, given himself another hatch of escape: If assent is taken as evidence of grace, and not of a prerogative of an apostle only, then "we must distinguish the times." Now, at the beginning, it would seem that if assent was saving faith in the first century, the plan of salvation has not so changed that assent is no longer saving faith in the seventeenth and twentieth centuries. One cannot accept the proposition that what saved then no longer saves now. Of course, it is true that the Gospel was a strange, novel, and alien message in pagan Rome. It was a well-known and favorably regarded message in seventeenth-century England. Therefore one may agree that there were fewer hypocrites in Rome than in England. But then Manton tries to denigrate full conviction by joining to it what is "trivial and arreptitious." Obviously, therefore, his argument is a fallacy. Assent still needs "supernatural grace." And as the work of the Holy Spirit's irresistible grace, it is saving faith. Manton then reasserts "naked assents" (which are not assents), and compares them with "a form of knowledge" (that is not knowledge). All this is irrelevant.

What is relevant and what was necessary he has omitted: a precise definition of "consent" that would clearly distinguish it from both *notitia* and *assensus*. Astonishing as it may seem, Manton never even tried to define "consent." Without its being arreptitious, consent remains a naked and trivial word without meaning. Saving faith remains an intellectual assent – not to any random proposition, such as "there is one God," but to the doctrine of the atonement.

The desire to find a third element in faith, in addition to understanding and assent, seems, if we may judge by popular preaching, to be aided by a psychological illusion. Preachers often use an illustration such as this: You may believe that a bank is sound by having read its financial statement, but you do not and cannot trust it until you deposit your money there. Making the deposit is faith. So, these preachers conclude, belief in Christ is not enough, no matter how much you read the Bible and believe that it is true. In addition to believing you must also trust Christ. That is faith.

The psychological illusion arises from the fact that the two cases are not parallel. In the case of the bank, there is the factor of depositing money. I have some dollar bills to be deposited; I go and deposit them in Bank X and not in Bank Y. Therefore I trust Bank X and do not trust Bank Y. But such is not the case. The reason I deposit money in this bank and not another is simply that my financial condition is far from warranting two bank accounts. I believe that Bank Y is quite as sound as Bank X. Both have competent administrators. Then, too, they both insure all depositors up to $10,000 and my account is less then one-tenth of this. I choose Bank X, not because I trust it more, but simply because it is nearer my home. This is a matter of convenience – not of faith. What is more, in the bank illustration there is a physical factor – depositing bills or checks; whereas in saving faith there is no such factor. Thus arises the illusion. Those who use such illustrations import into a spiritual situation something, a physical motion, that cannot be imported into it. There is nothing in the spiritual situation analogous to depositing the currency. There is believing only: nothing but the internal mental act itself. To suppose that there is, is both a materialistic confusion and an inadmissible alteration of the Scriptural requirement.

What better conclusion can there be other than the express statements of the Bible? Permit just one outside of *John*. *Romans* 10:9-10 says, "If you confess with your mouth that Jesus is Lord and believe in your mind that God raised him from the dead, you shall be saved." There is no mystical getting behind, under, or above the text; the only consent there is, is belief in the propositions. Believe these, with understanding, and you shall be saved. Anyone who says otherwise contradicts the repeated *rheemata* of Scripture.

Certainly John agrees with Paul and repeats Paul's idea: "Whoever believes in the Son has eternal life" (3:15, 36). "The believer has eternal life" (6:40, 47). "If anyone keeps my doctrine, he shall not see death ever" (8:51), and conversely, "He who does not receive [or grasp; compare *John* 1:5] my words [*rheemata*]…that word [*logos*] which I have spoken will judge him in the last day" (*John* 12:48).

> *"If you confess with your mouth that Jesus is Lord and believe in your mind that God raised him from the dead, you shall be saved."*

## 6. Conclusion

One reason, in my opinion, why popular evangelicalism, even though it professes the formal principle of *sola Scriptura* (and no one can call himself an evangelical in the traditional sense of the word unless he believes that Scripture is inerrant), stumbles at the view here derived from John's *Gospel* is its ignorance of the history of Christian doctrine. When a young person is brought up under a certain type of instruction, as for example Darby's dispensationalism, the person so brought up, even though the doctrine is only one generation old and had never before appeared in Protestantism, tends to think that it is standard orthodoxy. Conversely an old doctrine, forgotten, or better, never learned by contemporaries, is looked upon as a new heresy. To combat this condition, Calvin was quoted; and Cunningham gave some account of several Reformed analyses of faith. But the doctrine of assent is far older than Calvin. Augustine in his *De Praedestinatione Sanctorum* (2, 5) says, "To believe is to think with assent." The present monograph therefore proposes no new heresy, but defends an old established orthodoxy.

Another reason for contemporary reluctance to accept the Scriptural view of the "heart" or mind, and the role of faith or belief in salvation is the influence of Romanticism and the anti-intellectualism of the reaction against Hegel. This is aided by the post-Kantian emphasis on experience and the substitution of psychological analyses of feeling in place of revealed truth.

Those who have never studied philosophy and know nothing about the history of ideas absorb many of their opinions, unconsciously and at random, from the environing social climate. Unaware that their minds are being formed by the philosophic debris of a previous century, they unthinkingly consider their own views as Christian. One trained in philosophy knows the sources of his ideas. If he adopts some, he recognizes what he is doing. For example, Thomas Aquinas rejected Augustinianism and adopted Aristotelianism. He did so consciously, in opposition to the prevailing philosophy, because he thought that Aristotle could provide a better philosophic basis for Christianity than Augustine could. Since his procedure was deliberate and not at random, his results were fairly consistent. The mind of the uneducated man is full of contradictions. Thus it is that popular evangelicalism can profess *sola Scriptura* and have a doctrine of truth that borrows too much from Schleiermacher and Goethe.

The argument or *logos* of the present book, however, has paid only minimum attention to philosophy and the history of doctrine. It appeals directly to Scripture. And although the material comes almost exclusively from the *Gospel of John*, with only a few references from other books of the Bible, every objection to the doctrine of *logos*, or truth, or saving faith has been met or at least touched upon. Misunderstandings arise only because minds saturated with opposing views fail to give proper weight to what they read.

Understanding and assent are particularly objectionable to those who have romantic ideas of life. One devout and zealous Christian friend wrote that God is Will as well as Mind. Presumably his thought was that if man is made in God's image and man is mind only, God can have no will. Since, however, the view here defended has repeatedly stressed assent as an act of intelligent will, it seems strange that any reader would conclude that Mind and Will are two separate things.

*Unaware that their minds are being formed by the philosophic debris of a previous century, they unthinkingly consider their own views as Christian.*

This person also insisted that life, Christian life, is not assent only, but also a life of hope, "new hope for the present and expectation for the future." But what is hope other than assent to and belief in certain propositions? Hope is the belief that God will receive me on the judgment day through the merits of Christ. Hope therefore is assent.

It has also been objected that assent does not produce life and that we trust a person with the heart rather than believe the truth with the head; and that experience should be decisive.

These matters have all been covered. Perhaps one point should be repeated. Assent is not the cause of eternal life. Nothing in this monograph says that it is. Assent, instead of being the cause, is the result of the Spirit's regenerating activity. The unregenerate mind is enmity against God. People do not believe because they are not part of the chosen flock; they cannot believe because God has blinded their eyes. Therefore regeneration must, absolutely, must precede assent. For this reason assent or belief is the life that the Spirit gives. "He who hears my word and believes him who sent me...has passed from death to life" (5:24). The verb is in the perfect tense. A dead man can neither will nor believe; therefore God must first regenerate a man and give him the life that is necessary to voluntary assent.

> "You are already clean because of the theology I have spoken to you."

This life of faith is a life of sanctification. Sanctification is a work of God's grace by which he renews his image in the regenerated subject. This process of sanctification takes place basically through an increase of knowledge (see 2 Peter 1:3ff.). Jesus very pointedly said, "The words I have spoken to you are Spirit and life" (6:68); and "You are already clean because of the theology I have spoken to you" (15:3); and "Sanctify them by your truth; your word is truth" (17:17). Hence it is knowledge of and assent to the Bible that advances the Christian life.

This last verse points to the reason for it all and indicates the necessary connection between the *Logos*-doctrine and the doctrine of saving faith. *John* 17:17 shows that the Bible is truth. Because Jesus is the *Logos*, he was full of truth; truth arose or came into being through Jesus Christ. In fact, Jesus is the truth – the truth that is the way and the life as well. Behind all this stands the principle that God is Truth, and they that worship him must worship him in spirit and in truth.

Men are rational or intellectual beings because God created them in his image. To contemn truth and to embrace the irrationalities of mystic theology – which cannot in truth be *theo-logia* at all – is to contemn God. Conversely, if anyone guards my doctrine,

θάνατον οὐ μή θεωρήσῃ εἰς τὸν αἰῶνα!

# Scripture Index

12:47 *144*
12:47-48 *123*
12:48 *120, 158*
12:49 *116*
13:19 *74, 144*
14:1 *76*
14:6 *130*
14:10-11 *144*
14:17 *130*
14:23-24 *120*
14:29 *74, 144*
15:1 *127*
15:3 *120, 160*
15:7 *124*
15:20 *118*
15:25 *118*
16:7 *131*
16:9 *143, 146*
16:12 *131*
16:27 *74, 144*
16:30 *74, 144*
17:2 *108*
17:3 *127*
17:6 *120*
17:8 *74, 84, 124, 144*
17:8-10 *146*
17:12 *118*
17:14 *120*
17:16-17 *146*
17:17 *103, 120, 131, 160*
17:19 *131*
17:20 *120*
17:20-22 *146*
17:21 *75, 144*
17:26 *146*
18:9 *118*
18:32 *118*
18:37 *132*
19:8 *118*
19:13 *118*
19:35 *132, 144*
20:31 *75, 144, 146*
21:24 *132*

**1 John** *83*
4:2 *46, 154, 157*
4:16 *103*

5:1 *154, 157*
5:10 *54*

**2 John** *100*

**3 John** *100*

**Jude**
20 *35*

**Leviticus** *111*
1:4 *12*

**Luke** *95, 113, 122*
1 *122*
1:2 *122*
1:4 *122*
1:20 *77, 122*
1:29 *122*
1:37 *122, 138*
1:45 *77*
24:25 *77*

**Malachi** *33*

**Mark** *92, 95*
1:15 *64*
9:42 *75*
11:22 *34*
16:16 *73*

**Matthew** *61, 95, 111-113*
3:9 *108*
5-7 *97*
5:8 *59*
5:28 *59*
6:21 *59*
6:30 *145*
9:4 *60*
9:22 *145*
11:29 *60*
12:34, 40 *60*
13 *35*
13:15, 19 *60*
15:8 *60*
15:18-19 *60*
16:17 *46, 154, 157*

18:6 *75*
18:35 *60*
22:37 *61*
24:48 *61*
28:19-20 *82*
28:20 *28*

**1 Peter**
1:21 *76*

**2 Peter**
1:3 *36, 160*

**Philippians**
1:27 *78*

**Proverbs**
19:2 *132*

**Psalms**
4:4 *57, 156*
7:10 *58*
12:2 *58, 156*
14:1 *58, 156*
15:2 *58, 156*
35:19 *118*
69:4 *118*
69:9 *144*
78:21-22, 32 *33*
78:22 *74*

**Revelation** *33, 93*
1:20 *103*
2:13,19 *35*
13:10 *35*
14:12 *35*

**Romans** *61, 79*
1 *85*
1:21 *61*
1:26 *111*
1:32 *106*
2:5 *61*
2:6-7 *134*
2:10 *134*
2:13 *134*
2:15 *61, 85*

# Index

# The Crisis of Our Time

Historians have christened the thirteenth century the Age of Faith and termed the eighteenth century the Age of Reason. The present age has been called many things: the Atomic Age, the Age of Inflation, the Age of the Tyrant, the Age of Aquarius; but it deserves one name more than the others: the Age of Irrationalism. Contemporary secular intellectuals are anti-intellectual. Contemporary philosophers are anti-philosophy. Contemporary theologians are anti-theology.

In past centuries, secular philosophers have generally believed that knowledge is possible to man. Consequently they expended a great deal of thought and effort trying to justify knowledge. In the twentieth century, however, the optimism of the secular philosophers all but disappeared. They despaired of knowledge.

Like their secular counterparts, the great theologians and doctors of the church taught that knowledge is possible to man. Yet the theologians of the present age also repudiated that belief. They too despaired of knowledge. This radical skepticism has penetrated our entire culture, from television to music to literature. *The Christian at the beginning of the twenty-first century is confronted with an overwhelming cultural consensus – sometimes stated explicitly but most often implicitly: Man does not and cannot know anything truly.*

What does this have to do with Christianity? Simply this: If man can know nothing truly, man can truly know nothing. We cannot know that the Bible is the Word of God, that Christ died for his people, or that Christ is alive today at the right hand of the Father. Unless knowledge is possible, Christianity is nonsensical, for it claims to be knowledge. What is at stake at the beginning of the twenty-first century is not simply a single doctrine, such as the virgin birth, or the existence of Hell, as important as those doctrines may be, but the whole of Christianity itself. If knowledge is not possible to man, it is worse than silly to argue points of doctrine – it is insane.

The irrationalism of the present age is so thoroughgoing and pervasive that even the Remnant – the segment of the professing church that remains faithful – has accepted much of it, frequently without even being aware of what it is accepting. In some religious circles this irrationalism has become synonymous with piety and humility, and those who oppose it are denounced as rationalists, as though to be logical were a sin. Our contemporary anti-theologians make a contradiction and call it a Mystery. The faithful ask for truth and are given Paradox and Antinomy. If any balk at swallowing the absurdities of the anti-theologians who teach in the seminaries or have graduated from the seminaries, they are frequently marked as heretics or schismatics who seek to act independently of God.

There is no greater threat facing the church of Christ at this moment than the irrationalism that now controls our entire culture. Totalitarianism, guilty of tens of millions of murders – including those of millions of Christians – is to be feared, but not nearly so much as the idea that we do not and cannot know the literal truth. Hedonism, the popular philosophy of America, is not to be feared so much as the belief that logic – that "mere human logic," to use the religious irrationalists' own phrase – is futile. The attacks on truth, on knowledge, on propositional revelation, on the intellect, on words, and on logic are renewed daily. But note well: The misologists – the haters of logic – use logic to demonstrate the futility of using logic. The anti-intellectuals construct intricate intellectual arguments to prove the insufficiency of the intellect. Those who deny the competence of words to express thought use words to express their thoughts. The proponents of poetry, myth, metaphor, and analogy argue for their theories by using literal prose, whose competence – even whose possibility – they deny. The anti-theologians use the revealed Word of God to show that there can be no revealed Word of God – or that if there could, it would remain impenetrable darkness and Mystery to our finite minds.

## Nonsense Has Come

Is it any wonder that the world is grasping at straws – the straws of experientialism, mysticism, and drugs? After all, if people are told that the Bible contains insoluble mysteries, then is not a flight into mysticism to be expected? On what grounds can it be condemned? Certainly not on logical grounds or Biblical grounds, if logic is futile and the Bible unknowable. Moreover, if it cannot be condemned on logical or Biblical grounds, it cannot be condemned at all. If people are going to have a religion of the mysterious, they will not adopt Christianity: They will have a genuine mystery religion. The popularity of mysticism, drugs, and religious experience is the logical consequence of the irrationalism of the present age. There can and will be no Christian reformation – and no restoration of a free society – unless and until the irrationalism of the age is totally repudiated by Christians.

## The Church Defenseless

Yet how shall they do it? The official spokesmen for Christianity have been fatally infected with irrationalism. The seminaries, which annually train thousands of men to teach millions of Christians, are the finishing schools of irrationalism, completing the job begun by the government schools and colleges. Most of the pulpits of the conservative churches (we are not speaking of the obviously apostate churches) are occupied by graduates of the anti-theological schools. These products of modern anti-theological education, when asked to give a reason for the hope that is in them, can generally respond with only the intellectual analogue of a shrug – a mumble about Mystery. They have not grasped – and therefore cannot teach those for whom they are responsible – the first truth: "And you shall know the truth." Many, in fact, explicitly contradict Christ, saying that, at best, we possess only "pointers" to the truth, or something "similar" to the truth, a mere analogy. Is the impotence of the Christian church a puzzle? Is the fascination with Pentecostalism, faith healing, Eastern Orthodoxy, and Roman Catholicism – all sensate and anti-intellectual religions – among members of Christian churches an enigma? Not when one understands the pious nonsense that is purveyed in the name of God in the religious colleges and seminaries.

## The Trinity Foundation

The creators of The Trinity Foundation firmly believe that theology is too important to be left to the licensed theologians – the graduates of the schools of theology. They have created The Trinity Foundation for the express purpose of teaching believers all that the Scriptures contain –

not warmed over, baptized, Antichristian philosophies. Each member of the board of directors of The Trinity Foundation has signed this oath: "I believe that the Bible alone and the Bible in its entirety is the Word of God and, therefore, inerrant in the autographs. I believe that the system of truth presented in the Bible is best summarized in the *Westminster Confession of Faith*. So help me God."

The ministry of The Trinity Foundation is the presentation of the system of truth taught in Scripture as clearly and as completely as possible. We do not regard obscurity as a virtue, nor confusion as a sign of spirituality. Confusion, like all error, is sin, and teaching that confusion is all that Christians can hope for is doubly sin.

The presentation of the truth of Scripture necessarily involves the rejection of error. The Foundation has exposed and will continue to expose the irrationalism of the present age, whether its current spokesman be an existentialist philosopher or a professed Reformed theologian. We oppose anti-intellectualism, whether it be espoused by a Neo-orthodox theologian or a funda-mentalist evangelist. We reject misology, whether it be on the lips of a Neo-evangelical or those of a Roman Catholic Charismatic. We repudiate agnosticism, whether it be secular or religious. To each error we bring the brilliant light of Scripture, proving all things, and holding fast to that which is true.

## The Primacy of Theory

The ministry of The Trinity Foundation is not a "practical" ministry. If you are a pastor, we will not enlighten you on how to organize an ecumenical prayer meeting in your community or how to double church attendance in a year. If you are a homemaker, you will have to read elsewhere to find out how to become a total woman. If you are a businessman, we will not tell you how to develop a social conscience. The professing church is drowning in such "practical" advice.

The Trinity Foundation is unapologetically theoretical in its outlook, believing that theory without practice is dead, and that practice without theory is blind. The trouble with the profess-ing church is not primarily in its practice, but in its theory. Churchgoers and teachers do not know, and many do not even care to know, the doctrines of Scripture. Doctrine is intellectual, and churchgoers and teachers are generally anti-intellectual. Doctrine is ivory tower philosophy, and they scorn ivory towers. The ivory tower, however, is the control tower of a civilization. It is a fundamental, theoretical mistake of the "practical" men to think that they can be merely practical, for practice is always the practice of some theory. The relationship between theory and practice is the relationship between cause and effect. If a person believes correct theory, his practice will tend to be correct. The practice of contemporary Christians is immoral because it is the practice of false theories. It is a major theoretical mistake of the "practical" men to think that they can ignore the ivory towers of the philosophers and theologians as irrelevant to their lives. Every action that "practical" men take is governed by the thinking that has occurred in some ivory tower – whether that tower be the British Museum; the Academy; a home in Basel, Switzerland; or a tent in Israel.

## In Understanding Be Men

It is the first duty of the Christian to understand correct theory – correct doctrine – and thereby implement correct practice. This order – first theory, then practice – is both logical and Biblical. It is, for example, exhibited in Paul's *Epistle to the Romans,* in which he spends the first eleven chapters expounding theory and the last five discussing practice. The contemporary teach-ers of Christians have not only reversed the Biblical order, they have inverted the Pauline empha-sis on theory and practice. The virtually complete failure of the teachers of the professing church to instruct believers in correct doctrine is the cause of the misconduct and spiritual and cultural impotence of Christians. The church's lack of power is the result of its lack of truth. The *Gospel* is the power of God, not religious experiences or personal relationships. The church has no power because it has abandoned the Gospel, the good news, for a religion of experientialism. Twentieth-first-century American churchgoers are children carried about by every wind of doctrine, not knowing what they believe, or even if they believe anything for certain.

The chief purpose of The Trinity Foundation is to counteract the irrationalism of the age and to expose the errors of the teachers of the church. Our emphasis – on the Bible as the sole source of knowledge, on the primacy of truth, on the supreme importance of correct doctrine, and on the necessity for systematic and logical thinking – is almost unique in Christendom. To the extent that the church survives – and she will survive and flourish – it will be because of her increasing acceptance of these basic ideas and their logical implications.

We believe that The Trinity Foundation is filling a vacuum in Christendom. We are saying that Christianity is intellectually defensible – that, in fact, it is the only intellectually defensible system of thought. We are saying that God has made the wisdom of this world – whether that wisdom be called science, religion, philosophy, or common sense – foolishness. We are appealing to all Christians who have not conceded defeat in the intellectual battle with the world to join us in our efforts to raise a standard to which all men of sound mind can repair.

The love of truth, of God's Word, has all but disappeared in our time. We are committed to and pray for a great instauration. But though we may not see this reformation in our lifetimes, we believe it is our duty to present the whole counsel of God, because Christ has commanded it. The results of our teaching are in God's hands, not ours. Whatever those results, his Word is never taught in vain, but always accomplishes the result that he intended it to accomplish. Professor Gordon H. Clark has stated our view well:

> There have been times in the history of God's people, for example, in the days of Jeremiah, when refreshing grace and widespread revival were not to be expected: The time was one of chastisement. If this twentieth century is of a similar nature, individual Christians here and there can find comfort and strength in a study of God's Word. But if God has decreed happier days for us, and if we may expect a world-shaking and genuine spiritual awakening, then it is the author's belief that a zeal for souls, however necessary, is not the sufficient condition. Have there not been devout saints in every age, numerous enough to carry on a revival? Twelve such persons are plenty. What distinguishes the arid ages from the period of the Reformation, when nations were moved as they had not been since Paul preached in Ephesus, Corinth, and Rome, is the latter's fullness of knowledge of God's Word. To echo an early Reformation thought, when the ploughman and the garage attendant know the Bible as well as the theologian does, and know it better than some contemporary theologians, then the desired awakening shall have already occurred.

In addition to publishing books, the Foundation publishes a monthly newsletter, *The Trinity Review.* Subscriptions to *The Review* are free to U.S. addresses; please write to the address on the order form to become a subscriber. If you would like further information or would like to join us in our work, please let us know.

The Trinity Foundation is a non-profit foundation, tax exempt under section 501 (c)(3) of the Internal Revenue Code of 1954. You can help us disseminate the Word of God through your tax-deductible contributions to the Foundation.

JOHN W. ROBBINS

# Intellectual Ammunition

The Trinity Foundation is committed to bringing every philosophical and theological thought captive to Christ. The books listed below are designed to accomplish that goal. They are written with two subordinate purposes: (1) to demolish all non-Christian claims to knowledge; and (2) to build a system of truth based upon the Bible alone.

## Philosophy

*Ancient Philosophy*
Gordon H. Clark                                      Trade paperback $24.95

This book covers the thousand years from the Pre-Socratics to Plotinus. It represents some of the early work of Dr. Clark – the work that made his academic reputation. It is an excellent college text.

*Behaviorism and Christianity*
Gordon H. Clark                                      Trade paperback $5.95

*Behaviorism* is a critique of both secular and religious behaviorists. It includes chapters on John Watson, Edgar S. Singer, Jr., Gilbert Ryle, B. F. Skinner, and Donald MacKay. Clark's refutation of behaviorism and his argument for a Christian doctrine of man are unanswerable.

*A Christian Philosophy of Education*                    Hardback $18.95
Gordon H. Clark                                      Trade paperback $12.95

The first edition of this book was published in 1946. It sparked the contemporary interest in Christian schools. In the 1970s, Dr. Clark thoroughly revised and updated it, and it is needed now more than ever. Its chapters include: The Need for a World-View; The Christian World-View; The Alternative to Christian Theism; Neutrality; Ethics; The Christian Philosophy of Education; Academic Matters; and Kindergarten to University. Three appendices are included: The Relationship of Public Education to Christianity; A Protestant World-View; and Art and the Gospel.

*A Christian View of Men and Things*                     Hardback $29.95
Gordon H. Clark                                      Trade paperback $14.95

No other book achieves what *A Christian View* does: the presentation of Christianity as it applies to history, politics, ethics, science, religion, and epistemology. Dr. Clark's command of both worldly philosophy and Scripture is evident on every page, and the result is a breathtaking and invigorating challenge to the wisdom of this world.

*Clark Speaks from the Grave*
Gordon H. Clark                                                                Trade paperback $3.95
   Dr. Clark chides some of his critics for their failure to defend Christianity competently. *Clark Speaks* is a stimulating and illuminating discussion of the errors of contemporary apologists.

*Ecclesiastical Megalomania: The Economic and Political Thought of the Roman Catholic Church*
John W. Robbins                                                                Hardback $21.95
   This detailed and thorough analysis and critique of the social teaching of the Roman Church-State is the only such book available by a Christian economist and political philosopher. The book's conclusions reveal the Roman Church-State to be an advocate of its own brand of faith-based fascism. *Ecclesiastical Megalomania* includes the complete text of the *Donation of Constantine* and Lorenzo Valla's exposé of the hoax.

*Education, Christianity, and the State*
J. Gresham Machen                                                              Trade paperback $10.95
   Machen was one of the foremost educators, theologians, and defenders of Christianity in the twentieth century. The author of several scholarly books, Machen saw clearly that if Christianity is to survive and flourish, a system of Christian schools must be established. This collection of essays and speeches captures his thoughts on education over nearly three decades.

*Essays on Ethics and Politics*
Gordon H. Clark                                                                Trade paperback $10.95
   Dr. Clark's essays, written over the course of five decades, are a major statement of Christian ethics.

*Gordon H. Clark: Personal Recollections*
John W. Robbins, editor                                                        Trade paperback $6.95
   Friends of Dr. Clark have written their recollections of the man. Contributors include family members, colleagues, students, and friends such as Harold Lindsell, Carl Henry, Ronald Nash, and Anna Marie Hager.

*Historiography: Secular and Religious*
Gordon H. Clark                                                                Trade paperback $13.95
   In this masterful work, Dr. Clark applies his philosophy to the writing of history, examining all the major schools of historiography.

*An Introduction to Christian Philosophy*
Gordon H. Clark                                                                Trade paperback $8.95
   In 1966 Dr. Clark delivered three lectures on philosophy at Wheaton College. In these lectures he criticizes secular philosophy and launches a philosophical revolution in the name of Christ.

*Language and Theology*
Gordon H. Clark                                                    Trade paperback $9.95
    There were two main currents in twentieth-century philosophy – language philosophy and existentialism. Both were hostile to Christianity. Dr. Clark disposes of language philosophy in this brilliant critique of Bertrand Russell, Ludwig Wittgenstein, Rudolf Carnap, A. J. Ayer, Langdon Gilkey, and many others.

*Logic*                                                                    Hardback $16.95
Gordon H. Clark                                                    Trade paperback $10.95
    Written as a textbook for Christian schools, *Logic* is another unique book from Dr. Clark's pen. His presentation of the laws of thought, which must be followed if Scripture is to be understood correctly, and which are found in Scripture itself, is both clear and thorough. *Logic* is an indispensable book for the thinking Christian.

*Lord God of Truth, Concerning the Teacher*
Gordon H. Clark and
Aurelius Augustine                                                Trade paperback $7.95
    This essay by Dr. Clark summarizes many of the most telling arguments against empiricism and defends the Biblical teaching that we know God and truth immediately. The dialogue by Augustine is a refutation of empirical language philosophy.

*The Philosophy of Science and Belief in God*
Gordon H. Clark                                                    Trade paperback $8.95
    In opposing the contemporary idolatry of science, Dr. Clark analyzes three major aspects of science: the problem of motion, Newtonian science, and modern theories of physics. His conclusion is that science, while it may be useful, is always false; and he demonstrates its falsity in numerous ways. Since science is always false, it can offer no alternative to the Bible and Christianity.

*Religion, Reason and Revelation*
Gordon H. Clark                                                    Trade paperback $10.95
    One of Dr. Clark's apologetical masterpieces, *Religion, Reason and Revelation* has been praised for the clarity of its thought and language. It includes these chapters: Is Christianity a Religion? Faith and Reason; Inspiration and Language; Revelation and Morality; and God and Evil. It is must reading for all serious Christians.

*The Scripturalism of Gordon H. Clark*
W. Gary Crampton                                                  Trade paperback $9.95
    Dr. Crampton has written an introduction to the philosophy of Gordon H. Clark that is helpful to both beginners and advanced students of theology. This book includes a bibliography of Dr. Clark's works.

*Thales to Dewey:*
*A History of Philosophy*                                          Hardback $29.95
Gordon H. Clark                                                    Trade paperback $21.95
    This is the best one-volume history of philosophy in print.

*Three Types of Religious Philosophy*
Gordon H. Clark                                        Trade paperback $6.95
    In this book on apologetics, Dr. Clark examines empiricism, rationalism, dogmatism, and contemporary irrationalism, which does not rise to the level of philosophy. He offers an answer to the question, "How can Christianity be defended before the world?"

*William James and John Dewey*
Gordon H. Clark                                        Trade paperback $8.95
    William James and John Dewey are two of the most influential philosophers America has produced. Their philosophies of instrumentalism and pragmatism are hostile to Christianity, and Dr. Clark demolishes their arguments.

*Without A Prayer: Ayn Rand and the Close of Her System*
John W. Robbins                                        Hardback $27.95
    Ayn Rand has been a best-selling author since 1957. *Without A Prayer* discusses Objectivism's epistemology, theology, ethics, and politics in detail. Appendices include analyses of books by Leonard Peikoff and David Kelley, as well as several essays on Christianity and philosophy.

# Theology

*Against the Churches: The Trinity Review 1989-1998*
John W. Robbins, editor                                Oversize hardback $39.95
    This is the second volume of essays from *The Trinity Review*, covering its second ten years, 1989-1998. This volume, like the first, is fully indexed and is very useful in research and in the classroom. Authors include: Gordon Clark, John Robbins, Charles Hodge, J. C. Ryle, Horatius Bonar, and Robert L. Dabney.

*Against the World: The Trinity Review 1978-1988*
John W. Robbins, editor                                Oversize hardback $34.95
    This is a clothbound collection of the essays published in *The Trinity Review* from 1978 to 1988, 70 in all. It is a valuable source of information and arguments explaining and defending Christianity.

*The Atonement*
Gordon H. Clark                                        Trade paperback $8.95
    In *The Atonement,* Dr. Clark discusses the covenants, the virgin birth and incarnation, federal headship and representation, the relationship between God's sovereignty and justice, and much more. He analyzes traditional views of the atonement and criticizes them in the light of Scripture alone.

*The Biblical Doctrine of Man*
Gordon H. Clark                                        Trade paperback $6.95
    Is man soul and body or soul, spirit, and body? What is the image of God? Is Adam's sin imputed to his children? Is evolution true? Are men totally depraved? What is the heart? These are some of the questions discussed and answered from Scripture in this book.

*By Scripture Alone*
W. Gary Crampton                                    Trade paperback $12.95
    This is a clear and thorough explanation of the Scriptural doctrine of Scripture and a refutation of the recent Romanist attack on Scripture as the Word of God.

*The Changing of the Guard*
Mark W. Karlberg                                    Trade paperback $3.95
    This essay is a critical discussion of Westminster Seminary's anti-Reformational and un-Biblical teaching on the doctrine of justification. Dr. Karlberg exposes the doctrine of justification by faith and works – not *sola fide* – taught at Westminster Seminary for the past 25 years, by Professors Norman Shepherd, Richard Gaffin, John Frame, and others.

*The Church Effeminate*
John W. Robbins, editor                             Hardback $29.95
    This is a collection of 39 essays by the best theologians of the church on the doctrine of the church: Martin Luther, John Calvin, Benjamin Warfield, Gordon Clark, J. C. Ryle, and many more. The essays cover the structure, function, and purpose of the church.

*The Clark-Van Til Controversy*
Herman Hoeksema                                     Trade paperback $7.95
    This collection of essays by the founder of the Protestant Reformed Churches – essays written at the time of the Clark-Van Til controversy in the 1940s – is one of the best commentaries on those events in print.

*A Companion to The Current Justification Controversy*
John W. Robbins                                     Trade paperback $9.95
    This book includes documentary source material not available in *The Current Justification Controversy*, an essay tracing the origins and continuation of this controversy throughout American Presbyterian churches, and an essay on the New Perspective on Paul by Robert L. Reymond.

*Cornelius Van Til: The Man and The Myth*
John W. Robbins                                     Trade paperback $2.45
    The actual teachings of this eminent Philadelphia theologian have been obscured by the myths that surround him. This book penetrates those myths and criticizes Van Til's surprisingly unorthodox views of God and the Bible.

*The Current Justification Controversy*
O. Palmer Robertson                                 Trade paperback $9.95
    From 1975 to 1982 a controversy over justification raged within Westminster Theological Seminary and the Philadelphia Presbytery of the Orthodox Presbyterian Church. As a member of the faculties of both Westminster and Covenant Seminaries during this period, O. Palmer Robertson was an important participant in this controversy. This is his account of the controversy, vital background for understanding the defection from the Gospel that is now widespread in Presbyterian churches.

*The Everlasting Righteousness*
Horatius Bonar                                                    Trade paperback $8.95
   Originally published in 1874, the language of Bonar's masterpiece on justification by
faith alone has been updated and Americanized for easy reading and clear understanding.
This is one of the best books ever written on justification.

*God and Evil: The Problem Solved*
Gordon H. Clark                                                  Trade paperback $5.95
   This volume is Chapter 5 of *Religion, Reason and Revelation,* in which Dr. Clark presents
his solution to the problem of evil.

*God-Breathed: The Divine Inspiration of the Bible*
Louis Gaussen                                                   Trade paperback $16.95
   Gaussen, a nineteenth-century Swiss Reformed pastor, comments on hundreds of passages in which the Bible claims to be the Word of God. This is a massive defense of the
doctrine of the plenary and verbal inspiration of Scripture.

*God's Hammer: The Bible and Its Critics*
Gordon H. Clark                                                 Trade paperback $10.95
   The starting point of Christianity, the doctrine on which all other doctrines depend, is
"The Bible alone, and the Bible in its entirety, is the Word of God written, and, therefore,
inerrant in the autographs." Over the centuries the opponents of Christianity, with Satanic
shrewdness, have concentrated their attacks on the truthfulness and completeness of the
Bible. In the twentieth century the attack was not so much in the fields of history and
archaeology as in philosophy. Dr. Clark's brilliant defense of the complete truthfulness of
the Bible is captured in this collection of eleven major essays.

*The Holy Spirit*
Gordon H. Clark                                                  Trade paperback $8.95
   This discussion of the third person of the Trinity is both concise and exact. Dr. Clark
includes chapters on the work of the Spirit, sanctification, and Pentecostalism. This book is
part of his multi-volume systematic theology that began appearing in print in 1985.

*The Incarnation*
Gordon H. Clark                                                  Trade paperback $8.95
   Who is Christ? The attack on the doctrine of the Incarnation in the nineteenth and
twentieth centuries was vigorous, but the orthodox response was lame. Dr. Clark recon-
structs the doctrine of the Incarnation, building and improving upon the Chalcedonian
definition.

*The Johannine Logos*
Gordon H. Clark                                                  Trade paperback $5.95
   Dr. Clark analyzes the relationship between Christ, who is the truth, and the Bible. He
explains why John used the same word to refer to both Christ and his teaching. Chapters
deal with the Prologue to John's Gospel; *Logos* and *Rheemata*; Truth; and Saving Faith.

*Justification by Faith Alone*
Charles Hodge                                          Trade paperback $10.95
    Charles Hodge of Princeton Seminary was the best American theologian of the nine-
teenth century. Here, for the first time, are his two major essays on justification in one
volume. This book is essential in defending the faith.

*Karl Barth's Theological Method*
Gordon H. Clark                                          Trade paperback $18.95
    *Karl Barth's Theological Method* is perhaps the best critique of the Neo-orthodox theolo-
gian Karl Barth ever written. Dr. Clark discusses Barth's view of revelation, language, and
Scripture, focusing on his method of writing theology, rather than presenting a comprehensive analysis of the details of Barth's theology.

*Logical Criticisms of Textual Criticism*
Gordon H. Clark                                          Trade paperback $3.25
    Dr. Clark's acute mind enables him to demonstrate the inconsistencies, assumptions, and
flights of fancy that characterize the science of New Testament criticism.

*Predestination*
Gordon H. Clark                                          Trade paperback $10.95
    Dr. Clark thoroughly discusses one of the most controversial and pervasive doctrines of
the Bible: that God is, quite literally, Almighty. Free will, the origin of evil, God's omniscience, creation, and the new birth are all presented within a Scriptural framework. The
objections of those who do not believe in Almighty God are considered and refuted. This
edition also contains the text of the booklet, *Predestination in the Old Testament.*

*Sanctification*
Gordon H. Clark                                          Trade paperback $8.95
    In this book, which is part of Dr. Clark's multi-volume systematic theology, he discusses
historical theories of sanctification, the sacraments, and the Biblical doctrine of sanctification.

*Study Guide to the Westminster Confession*
W. Gary Crampton                                          Oversize paperback $10.95
    This *Study Guide* can be used by individuals or classes. It contains a paragraph-by-para-
graph summary of the *Westminster Confession,* and questions for the student to answer. Space
for answers is provided. The *Guide* will be most beneficial when used in conjunction with
Dr. Clark's *What Do Presbyterians Believe?*

*A Theology of the Holy Spirit*
Frederick Dale Bruner                                          Trade paperback $16.95
    First published in 1970, this book has been hailed by reviewers as "thorough," "fair,"
"comprehensive," "devastating," "the most significant book on the Holy Spirit," and "scholarly." Gordon Clark described this book in his own book *The Holy Spirit* as "a masterly and
exceedingly well researched exposition of Pentecostalism. The documentation is superb, as
is also his penetrating analysis of their non-scriptural and sometimes contradictory conclusions." Unfortunately, the book is marred by the author's sacramentarianism.

*The Trinity*
Gordon H. Clark                                              Trade paperback $8.95
    Apart from the doctrine of Scripture, no teaching of the Bible is more fundamental than the doctrine of God. Dr. Clark's defense of the orthodox doctrine of the Trinity is a principal portion of his systematic theology. There are chapters on the Deity of Christ; Augustine; the Incomprehensibility of God; Bavinck and Van Til; and the Holy Spirit; among others.

*What Calvin Says*
W. Gary Crampton                                            Trade paperback $10.95
    This is a clear, readable, and thorough introduction to the theology of John Calvin.

*What Do Presbyterians Believe?*
Gordon H. Clark                                             Trade paperback $10.95
    This classic is the best commentary on the *Westminster Confession of Faith* ever written.

*What Is Saving Faith?*
Gordon H. Clark                                             Trade paperback $12.95
    This is the combined edition of *Faith and Saving Faith* and *The Johannine Logos*. The views of the Roman Catholic Church, John Calvin, Thomas Manton, John Owen, Charles Hodge, and B. B. Warfield are discussed in this book. Is the object of faith a person or a proposition? Is faith more than belief? Is belief thinking with assent, as Augustine said? In a world chaotic with differing views of faith, Dr. Clark clearly explains the Biblical view of faith and saving faith.
    In *The Johannine Logos*, Dr. Clark analyzes the relationship between Christ, who is the truth, and the Bible. He explains why John used the same word to refer to both Christ and his teaching. Chapters deal with the Prologue to John's Gospel; *Logos* and *Rheemata;* Truth; and Saving Faith.

## Clark's Commentaries
## on the New Testament

| | | |
|---|---|---|
| *Colossians* | Trade paperback | $6.95 |
| *Ephesians* | Trade paperback | $8.95 |
| *First Corinthians* | Trade paperback | $10.95 |
| *First John* | Trade paperback | $10.95 |
| *First and Second Thessalonians* | Trade paperback | $5.95 |
| *New Heavens, New Earth* | | |
| (*First* and *Second Peter*) | Trade paperback | $10.95 |
| *The Pastoral Epistles* | Hardback | $29.95 |
| (*1* and *2 Timothy* and *Titus*) | Trade paperback | $14.95 |
| *Philippians* | Trade paperback | $9.95 |

All of Clark's commentaries are expository, not technical, and are written for the Christian layman. His purpose is to explain the text clearly and accurately so that the Word of God will be thoroughly known by every Christian.

## The Trinity Library

We will send you one copy of each of the 58 books listed above for $500 (retail value $800), postpaid to any address in the U.S. You may also order the books you want individually on the order form on the next page. Because some of the books are in short supply, we must reserve the right to substitute others of equal or greater value in The Trinity Library. This special offer expires October 31, 2006.

# Order Form

NAME _____

ADDRESS _____

_____

TELEPHONE _____

E-MAIL _____

Please:

❏ add my name to the mailing list for *The Trinity Review*. I understand that there is no charge for single copies of *The Review* sent
to U. S. addresses.

❏ accept my tax deductible contribution of $ _____ .

❏ send me _____ copies of *What Is Saving Faith?* I enclose as
payment U.S. $ _____.

❏ send me The Trinity Foundation Library of 58 books. I enclose
U.S. $500 as full payment.

❏ send me the following books. I enclose full payment in the
amount of U.S. $ _____ for them.

_____

_____

_____

_____

The Trinity Foundation
Post Office Box 68
Unicoi, Tennessee 37692
Website: http://www.trinityfoundation.org/
United States of America

Shipping: Please add $6.00 for the first book, and 50 cents for
each additional book. For foreign orders, please add $1.00 for each
additional book.